CHILDREN'S
BOOK OF THE
BIBLE

CONTRIBUTING WRITERS:
WALLIS C. METTS, JR., PH.D.
LINDA KERR CAUSEY

CONSULTANT:
GARY BURGE, PH.D.

PUBLICATIONS INTERNATIONAL, LTD.

Wallis C. Metts, Jr., Ph.D., chairs the department of communication at Spring Arbor College in Spring Arbor, Michigan. As the associate editor of *Guideposts for Kids*, he won a national award for children's nonfiction from the Educational Press Association of America in 1996. He has a Ph.D. in interdisciplinary studies (English, communications, and religious studies) from Michigan State Univeristy and an M.S. in education from the University of Tennessee.

Linda Kerr Causey has been teaching grades K-5 for over 20 years. She has contributed over 300 articles to such publications as *Good News Newspaper*, *The Lighthouse*, *Tips for Teachers*, and *ACSI Today*. Her books and poetry have won several Gold Medal awards from the association of Christian Schools International.

Gary Burge, Ph.D., is a professor in the department of Biblical and Theological Studies at Wheaton College. He holds a Ph.D. in New Testament from King's College, the University of Aberdeen in Aberdeen, Scotland, and a Master of Divinity degree from Fuller Theological Seminary. He is a member of Bibilical Archaeological Society, the Society of Biblical Literature, and the Institute for Biblical Research.

Picture credits:
Animals Animals: E.R. Degginger: 253 (top); Mickey Gibson: 248 (right); Gérard Lacz: 250 (right); Joe McDonald: 257 (top); Ralph A. Reinhold: 260 (right); Noah Satat: 256 (right); Richard Shiell: 254 (right); Leen Van Der Glik: 261 (top right); **Art Resource:** Galleria Palatinea, Palazzo Pitti, Florence/Scala: 306 (right); Scala: 259 (top); **Biblical Archaeology Society:** 151 (right); Courtesy of the Israel Museum: 301 (top); Zev Radovan: 303 (left); Gail Rubin: 293; John Trever: 315 (center); **The Crosiers:** 313 (left); **FPG International:** Carson Baldwin: 261 (bottom right); David Bartruff: 309 (top); Marcus Brooke: 157 (right); Ron Chapple: 297 (right); Tom Craig: 298 (right); Richard Johnston: 198 (right); Michael Krasowitz: 266 (left); Barry Rosenthal: 159 (right); Gail Shumway: 9 (left); Telegraph Colour Library: 109 (left); **Image Select Interantional:** Chris Fairclough Colour Library: 19 (right); **International Stock:** Warren Faidley: 67 (right); Buddy Mays: 49 (right); Wood Sabold: 124; Stockman: 157 (left); **Richard T. Nowitz:** 31 (right), 68, 71 (top), 79 (right), 80 (left), 103 (left), 110, 120, 125 (right), 166 (bottom), 171 (right), 190 (right), 191 (left), 203 (bottom), 264 (left), 279 (left), 280 (right), 282 (bottom), 283 (right), 289, 290 (right), 292, 298 (left), 305 (bottom), 307 (right), 309 (center), 311 (left), 315 (left & right); Sam Avnisan: 95; **PhotoEdit:** Bill Aron: 311 (right); **Photri:** 71 (bottom), 99 (center); **Zev Radovan:** 16 (right), 23 (left), 27 (left), 54, 69 (right), 81, 83 (right), 85 (top), 93 (left), 96 (left), 114, 116, 117 (left), 121 (right), 138 (right), 153 (right), 169 (bottom), 173 (top), 175 (right), 181 (right), 189 (left), 197, 251 (right), 277, 278 (right), 284 (right), 286 (right), 287 (left), 291 (left), 300, 302; **SuperStock:** 115 (right), 184 (right), 305 (top), 307 (left); Sistine Chapel, Vatican, Rome/Bridgeman Collection: 297 (left); **Transparencies, Inc.:** J.G. Faircloth: 55 (right).

Illustrations: **Thomas Gianni; Randall Hamblin; Michael Jaroszko; Barbara Kiwak; Yuan Lee; Carol Lundberg; Stephen Marchesi; Lyn Martin; Wayne Parmenter; Karen Pritchett, Cheryl Roberts; Sally Schaedler; James E. Seward; Richard Stergulz; Gary Torrisi; Brian Warling.**

Louis Weber, C.E.O., Publications International, Ltd.
7373 North Cicero Avenue, Lincolnwood, Illinois 60712

Ground Floor, 59 Gloucester Place, London W1U 8JJ

Customer Service: 1-800-595-8484 or customer_service@pilbooks.com

www.pilbooks.com

Permission is never granted for commercial purposes.

p i kids is a registered trademark of Publications International, Ltd.

ISBN-13: 978-0-7853-7808-2
ISBN-10: 0-7853-7808-1

8 7 6 5 4 3 2 1

Contents

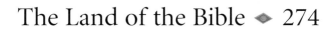

Introduction

◆ ◆ ◆

A thorough knowledge of the Bible is worth more than a college education.
—THEODORE ROOSEVELT

THE BIBLE is a very important book, a book that has provided the core values of western civilization for many hundreds of years. Unfortunately, many people today think of this book as inaccessible for themselves and more so for their children. It can appear to be far removed from our daily lives. The *Children's Book of the Bible* is designed to help bridge that gap by exploring both the content and the context of the Scriptures. As you and your children use this book, you will be delighted and amazed. Not only will you learn about Bible characters, you will learn about how they dressed and what they ate. You will learn about their customs and their concerns.

This background will make the Bible come alive and launch your children toward a lifelong understanding and appreciation of the greatest book ever written. Intriguing facts and helpful background should engage their minds and imaginations. Their faith will be encouraged, and so will yours.

Each topic is beautifully illustrated and supported with several related facts. Because of its breadth and scope, you will find many ways to use this book: quiet reading on a road trip, research for homework or Bible studies, trivia and truths for family entertainment and discussion.

The book begins with exciting stories of Bible heroes, kings and prophets, fishermen and farmers, godly men and women. These stories should be part of every child's education—and enjoyment. But then there are entire chapters on religious customs, miracles, everyday life, family life, parables, plants and animals, and geography. There's even a chapter that answers the question, "How did we get our Bible?"

In fact, lots of questions are answered here. How long did people live? How were they buried? What games did kids play back then? What weapons did the soldiers use? Why are people baptized? What did the women do? What were houses like? What is a synagogue?

There is more here than just information, however. Important moral principles such as gratitude, obedience,

and honesty are illustrated and explained. This is easily and effectively accomplished without being preachy or dogmatic through the use of stories.

In most cases, this book answers questions and explains topics by telling stories or referring to stories you can look up on your own. This is because children retain and comprehend material better in story form. Kids love trivia, too—and there is lots of it here. They love to surprise others with what they know. As they share the things they learn from this book with you and with their friends, they will be building a foundation for their future grounded in the wisdom of the past.

After a hard day's work in the field, the ancient Hebrews gathered in the evening to eat, talk, and tell stories. This is how they taught their children what was important and what was true. The stories they told are the same ones told here in the *Children's Book of the Bible*. We invite you to tell them again, and for the same reason.

Heroes of the Bible

❖ ❖ ❖ ❖

IBLE HEROES came in all shapes and sizes. A young boy named David killed a giant. A woman named Deborah led the Israelite army to victory. A prophet named Jonah was sent by God to Ninevah. They were poor and rich, strong and weak, young and old. But they had one thing in common. They wanted to know God and obey him. So God used them to show his power. And his love.

The First Humans

◆ ◆ ◆

AT FIRST there was nothing: no earth, no ocean, no sky, no stars. But God began to make things, and he did it by speaking. He would say "let there be light" or "let there be sky," and it just happened.

That's how he made the sea, the land, the plants, the sun, the moon, the fish, and the birds. And that's how he also made all the other creatures, like elephants and lizards and kittens. After he made something, he would say: "That's good."

Finally, he scooped up some dust and made it into his own image. When he breathed into it, it became the first man. His name was Adam. "That's good, too," God said. "That's very good."

God placed Adam in a beautiful garden called Eden. Adam had a lot to do. He named all the animals. He took care of the garden, just like God told him to. But Adam felt lonely. So while Adam was sleeping, God took one of his ribs and made the first woman. She was beautiful, and Adam loved her very much. He named her Eve.

THE FIRST KIDS

Adam and Eve lived a very long time and had many sons and daughters. One son, Abel, was a shepherd. Another son, Cain, was a farmer. Cain got angry with Abel and killed him. Then Cain left home. Adam and Eve were very sad, but they eventually had another son named Seth. Before long, their children and grandchildren began to build cities and fill the earth.

God told Adam and Eve they could eat any of the lovely fruits and vegetables that grew in the garden, anything except for the fruit of one special tree.

One day, a serpent tried to get Eve to eat from the special tree. He said if she ate the tree's fruit she would know the difference between good and bad. She would be just like God. Eve looked at the tree, and the fruit looked very good. So she took a bite and gave some to Adam.

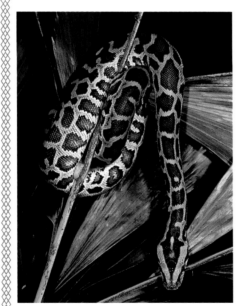

NO LOVE LOST

Adam and Eve had to leave the garden after they disobeyed God, but the serpent didn't get off the hook. God put a curse on it and made it crawl on its belly. He also said there would be trouble between the serpent and Eve's children. No wonder most people don't like snakes!

Immediately, they felt guilty and ashamed. Adam tried to blame it on Eve, and Eve tried to blame it on the serpent. But God said they both knew what they were doing. They had disobeyed him and must be punished.

So they had to leave the garden. Thorns and weeds began to grow, and Adam had to work even harder to grow food on the land. Eve had babies, and these children fought with each other and disobeyed God, too.

But God gave Adam and Eve hope. He said one of their offspring would destroy the serpent, who was really God's enemy, Satan.

But that's another story.

TAKE A BREAK

The Bible says God made everything in six days, and on the seventh day he rested. Later, God would ask the Israelites to do the same thing. They were to take one day off each week to rest and worship him. It is one of the Ten Commandments, a special set of rules God gave his people.

A PERFECT WORLD

The story of Adam and Eve disobeying God is called The Fall. The results of this first sin include death and sickness and pain for everyone. The results also include thorns and tornadoes and everything bad that happens to the earth. According to the Apostle Paul and the Apostle John, God will someday create a new and perfect world.

The Big Flood

◆ ◆ ◆

THE WORLD had become an evil place. After Adam and Eve died, people even began to forget about God. They spent their time thinking of wicked things to do. And when they did them, they weren't sorry.

But God was sorry. He was sorry he had made these people, and he decided to destroy them all. There was one man, however, who still loved God and tried to obey him. His name was Noah.

One day, God came to Noah. "I'm going to send a huge flood to destroy the earth," God said. "So I want you to build a big ship, an ark. You can take your entire family on the ark and be saved. And I want you to take at least two of every kind of animal."

So Noah did just what God said. He and his sons began to build the ark. He tried to warn others, but they laughed at him. Finally the ark was finished.

Then the animals came to Noah in pairs. There were chickens and rabbits and giraffes and dogs. There were

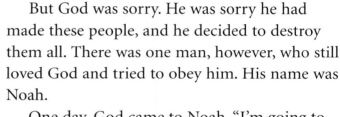

A LONG LIFE

Before the flood, people lived a long time. Adam, for example, lived to be 930, and Noah lived to be 951. Noah's grandfather Methuselah lived longer than anyone else in the Bible—969 years. After the flood, people did not live as long. Noah's son Shem only lived 600 years and his grandson only lived to be 438.

horses and lions and turtles and butterflies. All of them began to enter the ark. That took a whole week. Then Noah and his family went inside, and God closed the door. It rained for 40 days and 40 nights, and the water covered the earth for six months. Everything was destroyed.

When the flood was over, Noah sent a raven out the window to find dry land, but it couldn't find anything. Twice he sent out a dove. It finally returned with a freshly plucked olive leaf. Noah then knew it was safe to leave the ark. When Noah and his family left the ark, they saw a rainbow. Noah built an altar and thanked God for saving him and his family.

God was pleased that Noah had obeyed him. He told Noah the rainbow was a promise that he would not destroy the earth with a flood again. "Never again will I destroy all living creatures," God said. "Seasons will come and go, and day and night will never cease."

TONGUES AND TOWERS

After the flood, everyone spoke the same language. All the people got together and decided to build a big tower that would reach all the way to heaven. They wanted to all stay in the same place. But God was not pleased with this idea, so he came down and gave the people several different languages. Then they got together with people who talked like them and spread out across the whole earth.

A BIG BOAT

God told Noah how big to build the ark. It was pretty big, big enough to hold almost 50,000 animals. It was as long as a football field plus another half a football field (450 feet) and almost as wide as a football field (75 feet). It was taller than a four-story house (45 feet) and had three decks, or levels.

Special Son

◆ ◆ ◆

ONE DAY, God spoke to a man named Abraham and told him to leave his home. "Go to a land I will show you, and I will make you into a great nation."

So Abraham did what God said. It was a long trip, a couple of thousand miles across the desert. And it was a hard trip, too. Abraham had to move cattle and servants. He also brought his nephew Lot. They all lived in tents along the way.

Finally they came to the place where God wanted them to be. After a few problems—like a famine and a fight with his nephew—Abraham settled down to wait for God to keep his promise. He wanted to have children so his descendants could become a great nation.

Abraham was married to a very beautiful woman named Sarah. She was so beautiful that as they traveled two different kings had wanted her to be their wife.

But Sarah was not able to have a baby. Abraham and Sarah were worried. Sarah was getting too old to have a baby, and they didn't know how God would give them a child. Sarah suggested that Abraham have a baby with her servant girl, Hagar. He did, and a son named Ishmael was born. But this was not what God wanted.

God spoke to Abraham again and promised him that he and Sarah would have a son. He even sent some angels to Abraham to

A GREAT HONOR

Sarah was the first woman to be listed in the Hall of Faith, a special list of great men and women of the Bible. You can read the list in Hebrews 11. The list celebrates people like Abraham and Sarah who believed God and did what he asked them to do.

tell him when. Sarah laughed at the very idea. She was 90 years old and Abraham was 100, much too old to have a child.

But God kept his promise, and Sarah had a baby. She named him Isaac, which means laughter, because he made her very happy, and because she had laughed when God made his promise.

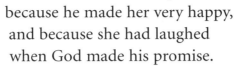

Abraham loved Isaac very much. But several years later, God tested Abraham's love for him by telling Abraham he had to sacrifice the boy. So Abraham obeyed God, just as he had when God told him to leave his home.

He gathered some wood and started to build a fire on the altar where sacrifices were made. When God saw that Abraham was doing as he had been told, he knew Abraham's faith was real. God stopped Abraham just in time and provided another sacrifice, a ram caught in a nearby bush.

Isaac had two sons, and one of them, Jacob, had 12 sons. Soon there was a nation. God had kept his promise, just like Abraham knew he would.

A PRIEST AND KING

Once, Abraham's nephew Lot was kidnapped. Abraham had his own private soldiers, so he went to rescue Lot. He defeated the kings of several small cities. On the way home, he met a king named Melchizedek, who was also a priest of the Most High God. The priest gave Abraham bread and wine and blessed him. He reminded him that God had helped him win the battle. Abraham thanked God for his help and gave Melchizedek part of everything he had captured. That was one way he could show how grateful he was.

A BEAUTIFUL BRIDE

When Isaac was old enough to get married, Abraham sent his servant to Mesopotamia to find a wife for his son. Mesopotamia was where Abraham had been born. When the servant got there, he was tired and thirsty. A young woman named Rebekah gave him some water to drink. She even ran to get some water for his camels. The servant knew that this kind girl was the right wife for Isaac. After he talked with her family, she decided to return to Canaan and marry Isaac, even though she had never seen him.

Lot of Trouble

◆ ◆ ◆

AFTER ABRAHAM and Lot arrived in Canaan, both men became very wealthy. They had so many sheep and cattle that herdsmen began to argue about where the animals should graze.

Abraham didn't want to argue with Lot, so he gave Lot first choice. "Let's not have any quarreling between you and me," he said. "If you go to the left, I'll go to the right." Naturally, Lot took the best land. It was lush and green, with plenty of water for the animals. Abraham was left with the stony hillsides.

But Lot began to get into trouble. To start with, he was kidnapped and Abraham had to rescue him. And then Lot moved to Sodom, a city where the people were very wicked. The people there were so wicked that God had decided to destroy the entire city. But first he warned Abraham, who prayed for God to spare his nephew Lot.

So God sent two angels to Sodom to warn Lot. "Get your family out of the city, for God is going to destroy it," the angels said. "Run for your lives and don't look back." So Lot fled from the city, along with his wife and two daughters. God rained fire and burning tar, destroying all the people and all the plants. But Lot's wife looked back, and God turned her into a pillar of salt.

SALT CITY

Sodom and Gomorrah (another evil city) were both totally destroyed, and the place where they once were is now under the Dead Sea between Israel and Jordan. The sea is very salty—so salty that even fish can't live there—and surrounded by bare and rocky land. A number of minerals are mined there, and there are oil wells nearby.

The Birthright

◆ ◆ ◆

ISAAC MARRIED Rebekah and had twin sons, Jacob and Esau. Esau was born first. That meant he would receive a special blessing, called a birthright. He would get most of his father's land and wealth, and he would be the leader of the family.

When he grew up, Esau became a hunter, a rugged man who liked to be outdoors. Jacob, on the other hand, liked to stay around the house and help his mother. Rebekah and Jacob were very close, but Isaac liked Esau best.

One day, Esau came home from the hunt so hungry he made a serious mistake. Jacob was cooking some stew, and Esau wanted some so badly he traded his birthright to Jacob for a bowl of stew.

When Isaac was very old, he called Esau in to give him his blessing. Because Isaac was nearly blind, Rebekah and Jacob were able to trick him into blessing Jacob instead. While Esau was out hunting for deer to make a special meal for his father, Rebekah fixed goat meat to taste like deer meat. She also put a goat skin on Jacob's arms so he would feel hairy like his brother.

So Isaac blessed the wrong son. God had important plans for Jacob, however. He would have 12 sons, and his family would grow big enough to form a whole nation. This is what God had promised his grandfather Abraham.

ANOTHER TRICK

After Jacob tricked his father into blessing him instead of his brother, Esau was so angry that Jacob left home and traveled to Mesopotamia, to his mother's relatives. While he was away, he fell in love with a beautiful girl named Rachel. But he had to work for her father, Laban, seven years before he could marry her. The day after the wedding, Jacob realized Laban had tricked him. He had married Rachel's sister Leah instead. He had to work seven more years before he could marry Rachel.

A Young Dreamer

◆ ◆ ◆

JACOB HAD many children, but Joseph was his favorite. Even though Jacob had 11 other sons, he gave Joseph a beautiful, very special coat.

Joseph's brothers didn't like him. They thought he was a tattletale. He had dreams in which his brothers served him and bowed to him.

One day, when Joseph was out in the fields helping take care of the goats, his brothers grabbed him and threw him in a deep pit. They were going to leave him there to die. But some slave traders were passing by, going to Egypt, so they took him and sold him instead.

Joseph's brothers ripped his coat and dipped it in blood and showed it to their father. "Joseph must have been eaten by wild animals," Jacob said. He was very sad.

Meanwhile, Joseph became the slave of a wealthy man in Egypt. Joseph was a good worker and became the chief

A KING'S RING

When Pharaoh made Joseph ruler over Egypt, he put a gold chain around his neck and had him dressed in fine white linen. He also gave him his gold signet ring. The signet ring was used to stamp the Pharaoh's signature in wax. This made letters and orders official. Even though few people could read and write, everyone recognized the Pharaoh's stamp.

servant, but he was accused of a crime by his master's wife and sent to jail. There, too, he was trusted and put in charge.

Then the king of Egypt, Pharaoh, had a troubling dream. Someone remembered that Joseph could tell people what their dreams meant so Pharaoh sent for Joseph in jail.

Joseph told the Pharaoh what the dream meant. For seven years there would be lots of food, but after that there would be seven years of very little. The crops would fail and there would be no rain. This is called a famine. "Someone should gather food now and save it for later," Joseph said.

The Pharaoh liked the idea. He liked Joseph, too. So he put Joseph in charge of the whole country.

Years later, the famine did come to Egypt and lots of other countries, too. Joseph's brothers heard that there was food in Egypt. They went there to buy bags of grain, not knowing that their brother had become the governor.

When they met him, they didn't even recognize him. He knew them, though. He asked them questions about their father. He sold them food. Then he took one of his brothers prisoner and told the rest of them not to come back without their little brother.

They were afraid and didn't want to come back, but they needed food and finally did return, and they brought their little brother with them. When Joseph saw his little brother, Benjamin, he broke down and cried. He told his brothers who he was and forgave them. "God sent me here to save lives," he said.

His brothers were amazed. They went home to get their father, and they all returned to Egypt, where Joseph took care of them. Jacob was very happy. "I can see my son before I die," he said.

JACOB'S BLESSING

Before Jacob died, he gathered his sons together and blessed them, telling a little about the future of each family. His sons would become the 12 tribes of Israel. Except for the family of Levi, the sons' families would each receive a portion of the land God had promised Abraham. Levi's family would become the priests and keepers of the temple. After Jacob died, his sons returned to Canaan to bury him, and then they went back to Egypt.

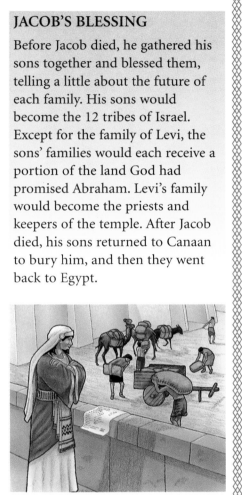

FOOD FACTS

For the first seven years that Joseph was ruler in Egypt, he collected one fifth of all the grain and stored it in granaries, much like modern silos. When the famine came, he was able to feed the people by trading them food for their land. Eventually, the Pharaoh owned almost all the land.

Moses Frees God's People

◆ ◆ ◆

FOUR HUNDRED YEARS after Joseph was a ruler in Egypt, there was a new Pharaoh. He was afraid the children of Israel, called Hebrews, would multiply and join his enemies. So he made them slaves. He even passed a law that all their boy babies were to be killed.

One mother hid her baby, but when he got too big to hide, she put him in a wicker basket and set it afloat on the Nile River. His sister, Miriam, hid nearby to see what would happen.

The Pharaoh's own daughter was walking along the Nile and found the baby. He was so adorable that she wanted to keep him, even though she knew he was a Hebrew boy. Then Miriam came up and asked the Princess, "Would you like me to find a Hebrew mother to take care of the baby?"

The princess said yes, and of course Miriam went and got her own mother. When he was older, she took him to the Princess, who named him Moses, and raised him as her own son in the palace.

One day, when Moses was grown up, he saw an Egyptian beating a Hebrew slave. Moses killed the Egyptian to save the Hebrew and then went to the wilderness to hide. He stayed there for many years until God spoke to him from a burning

A BASKET BOAT

Moses' mother put him in the Nile in a basket made of papyrus reeds and waterproofed with tar. These reeds can be found all along the river and sometimes grow as tall as 16 feet, twice as tall as any NBA star. The Egyptians used the reed to invent paper.

AARON'S TALENT

Even though Moses was a great leader, he had trouble talking. He spoke slowly and stuttered. But his brother Aaron was good with words and could talk easily with crowds. God let Aaron speak for Moses, and so the two brothers worked together to do God's work.

bush. "I will send you to Pharaoh so that you may bring my people out of Egypt," God said.

At first, Moses was afraid to go, but God gave him courage and power. Moses went to Pharaoh and demanded that he let the children of Israel go free. The Pharaoh refused, so God sent ten plagues.

First he turned the river into blood. Then he covered the country with frogs, and later with swarms of insects. Next the cattle all died and then the people were covered with ugly sores. Then there were thunderstorms with large hail, and then grasshoppers ate up all the crops. But the Pharaoh was stubborn, and each time he refused to let the people go.

Finally, God sent the angel of death to kill all the first-born sons, even the Pharaoh's. The Hebrew families were protected from this plague. All the Egyptians were very sad, and finally Pharaoh agreed to let the Hebrews go. They packed their wagons and carts and headed for the wilderness, praising God and Moses for their deliverance.

The Pharaoh changed his mind and followed them with his army. But when they got to the Red Sea, Moses stretched out his rod and God parted the waters. The children of Israel just walked across. When Pharaoh's army tried to follow them, the waters came together again and all his army was drowned.

God's people were finally free.

THE PASSOVER

Hebrews today are called Jews. On Passover, a Jewish holiday, they remember the night the death angel "passed over" their first-born children while the children in Egypt died. The Hebrew families marked their doorposts with lamb's blood, which saved their children. In today's Passover celebration, the children ask why the night is special, and the father tells the story of how the Hebrew people were freed from Egypt. This custom has been going on for 3,000 years or more.

In the Wilderness

❖ ❖ ❖

WHILE THE CHILDREN of Israel were in the wilderness, God gave Moses special instructions about a Tabernacle where the people could come to worship him. The Tabernacle was a tent, but the instructions were very detailed—and skilled people were needed for the job.

A man named Bezalel was put in charge. He was a very talented craftsman who could design things out of gold or silver or bronze. He was a woodcarver and a jewelry maker. He was even an expert at weaving and engraving.

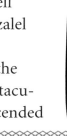

He hired others to help him. Then the people donated materials. They brought gold, silver, bronze, animal skins, leather, oil, spices, precious gems, and purple cloth. They brought so much that Bezalel finally had to tell them to stop. Then Bezalel went to work.

When they put up the Tabernacle, it was spectacular. A cloud of fire descended

THE ARK OF THE COVENANT

The Ark of the Covenant was a wooden chest covered with gold. Two cherubim, also made of gold, covered the Ark with outstretched wings. The priests could stick poles through rings on the sides and carry the Ark without touching it. Inside the Ark were the two stone tablets with the Ten Commandments. The priests carried the Ark before the people when they moved from place to place.

on the Tabernacle, and God was there. When the cloud stayed over the Tabernacle, the people stayed where they were. But when the cloud lifted and began to move, they followed it. They were headed home, back to the land that God had promised Abraham.

Later, as the Hebrews camped near Mount Sinai, God sent thunder and lightning. A thick cloud covered the mountain, and there was a loud noise, like a trumpet. The people were afraid. God called Moses up to the top of the mountain and gave him the Ten Commandments, which God had carved in stone with his own finger.

These were very important laws for God's people, laws that would help them show their love to God and each other. Moses was on top of the mountain for 40 days, and God gave him many other rules, too. While he was gone, the people became impatient and they built a god that reminded them of Egypt.

When Moses came down from the mountain, the people were singing and dancing and worshiping a calf made of gold. Moses was very angry and threw the tablets of stone on the ground, breaking them. He asked the men who had not worshiped the calf to join him, and they killed 3,000 men who had. Then they asked God to forgive them all.

Later, Moses took another set of stone tablets to the top of the mountain. God wrote down his laws again—and he forgave the people. "I am slow to anger, and full of love," God said.

A LITTLE HELP FROM HIS FRIENDS

Moses once held up his hands for an entire day. The Israelites were fighting the Amalekites, a hostile and evil nation. Moses stood on a hill watching the battle. As long as he held up his hands, the Israelites were winning. But when he rested his hands, the Amalekites began winning. Aaron and Hur, another Israelite, brought him a stone to sit on. Then they stood on each side of him and held his hands up for him. By sunset, the Israelites had won the battle.

THE BIG TEN

While Moses was on Mount Sinai, God gave his people a special set of rules called the Ten Commandments. They were not to worship other Gods or swear using his name. They were to set aside one day each week to worship him and rest. They were to honor their parents. They were not to murder, or steal, or lie, or envy. These laws have been used as the basis for other laws ever since.

The Walls That Fell

❖ ❖ ❖

JOSHUA HAD BEEN Moses's second-in-command for many years. Finally, it was time for Joshua to take his place. "Be strong and courageous," God said. "Be careful to obey the law I gave Moses and you will be successful. I will be with you wherever you go."

So Joshua led the people across the Jordan River. It would be his job to lead the Hebrews into Canaan, the land God had promised them. People were already living there, so there would be many battles. The first one took place at Jericho. It was a strong city, with a wall around it 25 feet high and 20 feet thick.

Joshua sent two spies to Jericho to check it out. While they were there, a woman named Rahab risked her life by hiding them from the king. Her house was next to the city wall, so she helped them escape through a window. She made them

A GOOD REPORT

Caleb was one of Joshua's best friends. As young men, the two of them were sent with a group of spies to Canaan to see if it was safe for the Hebrews to enter. The other spies came back with bad reports—they thought it was too dangerous. They even claimed that there were giants in the land. But Caleb said they should do as God commanded and go forward. Joshua agreed. Of all the men alive that day, only Joshua and Caleb eventually entered the land.

promise to spare her when they conquered Jericho. "We have heard how your God parted the Red Sea," she said. "The people have melted away because your God is God in heaven and earth."

Joshua had an army of 40,000 men, and he was ready to go. "Everyone is afraid of us," the spies told him. "Let's take the city." But God wanted the Hebrews to know that he would help them conquer the whole land. So God gave them some unusual directions about how to conquer Jericho. He told them to march around the city once a day for six days. Priests carrying trumpets were to lead the march. Then, on the seventh day, they were to march around the city seven times, blowing on the trumpets. When they finished, the priests were to blow the trumpets for one long, loud blast. Then the men were to shout.

So that's exactly what they did. When they had marched around the city for seven days and blown the trumpets on the last day, Joshua commanded the people to shout. And the walls came tumbling down.

The men marched straight into the city and destroyed everyone except Rahab and her family. Then all the other people in Canaan were afraid. God had helped the Hebrews.

Jericho

THE OLDEST CITY IN THE WORLD

People have lived in Jericho longer than in any other city in the world, about 11,000 years. It is an oasis in the Jordan Valley, and it was called the City of Palms. After it was destroyed by Joshua, it lay in ruins for over 1,000 years before it was rebuilt.

MUSIC AS A WEAPON

Like Joshua, Jehoshaphat used an unusual battle tactic. A choir marched in front of his army singing a hymn to God. When the enemy soldiers heard the music, they started fighting each other and destroyed themselves. Jehoshaphat had depended on God and believed him when God promised victory.

THE PROMISED LAND

When the Hebrews left Egypt, they returned to Canaan, the land God had promised Abraham. It was the promised land. The spies they sent ahead described Canaan as a country "flowing with milk and honey." They returned with a bunch of grapes so large two men had to carry it.

A Woman of War

❖ ❖ ❖

AFTER THE HEBREWS had settled in Canaan, they were led by rulers called judges. Sometimes Israel's enemies would defeat them, and other times the judges would lead Israel to victory.

Only one of these judges, Deborah, was a woman. The people respected her and followed her advice. They came to her home near a palm tree on Mount Ephraim and asked her what to do. The Canaanites had been attacking their villages and burning their fields for 20 years. Those troops were led by a brutal general named Sisera.

Deborah told Barak, the leader of Israel's army, to attack Sisera and his men. Barak was afraid because Sisera had 900 iron chariots and he had none. Barak told Deborah he would only attack Sisera if she went with him. "I will go," she said. "But you will not get the credit for destroying Sisera. The Lord will use a woman instead."

So Deborah and Barak led 10,000 men down the slopes of Mount Tabor. Sisera's army became frightened. As they tried to get away, the Kishon River flooded, and their chariots became useless. Israel's army killed every one of them, except Sisera himself, who jumped off his chariot and ran away. He hid in the tent of a woman named Jael, who killed him while he slept.

VICTORY SONG

In celebration of their great victory, Deborah and Barak sang a song. In it they praised God and gave him the credit for their success. Some of the words to the song are:
Praise the Lord!
Israel's leaders bravely led;
The people gladly followed!
Yes, bless the Lord!
Listen, O you kings and princes,
For I shall sing about the Lord,
The God of Israel.

The Uncertain Soldier

◆ ◆ ◆

ONE OF ISREAL'S JUDGES was named Gideon. One day, an angel came to Gideon while he was working on his father's farm. "The Lord is with you," the angel said. "You will save Israel from the Midianites." Gideon was not sure. "Show me a sign that what you say is true," he said. So the angel touched a piece of meat and bread with his staff and it burst into flames. Then the angel disappeared.

That night, Gideon took his father's bull and pulled down an altar to Baal, the god of the Midianites. The Midianites were very angry and began to gather their army. So Gideon asked God for another sign that he should lead the army. He laid a piece of wool on the ground. In the morning if the wool was wet and the ground was dry, he would be sure. That's exactly what happened.

Gideon was ready to lead the army. But first God told him his army was too large. He started with over 30,000 men, but he sent all but 300 of them home. He gave each of them a trumpet and a jug with a torch inside. In the middle of the night, they surrounded the Midianite army. At a signal, they all blew their trumpets at the same time and smashed their jugs, so that the light blazed in the night. "A sword for the Lord, and for Gideon," they all shouted. The Midianites were so scared that they began to run away, fighting with each other in the dark.

A SMALL ARMY

Gideon started out with over 30,000 soldiers, but that was too many for what God had in mind. So Gideon sent home everyone that was afraid. That left 10,000. Then Gideon took his army down to the water for a drink. Everyone who knelt down and scooped up water in their hands he sent home. Only 300 lapped up the water with their tongues, "as a dog laps." These were the ones chosen for the battle.

A Very Strong Man

◆ ◆ ◆

ONE OF ISRAEL'S JUDGES, Samson, was famous for his great strength. Before he was even born, an angel told his parents that Samson would deliver Israel from the Philistines. They were not to let Samson drink wine or cut his hair. When the boy grew up he would be very strong, the angel said.

And it was true. Samson once tore a lion apart with his bare hands. Another time he caught 300 foxes and tied torches to their tails, destroying the Philistines' fields. He even killed a thousand men with the jaw-bone of a donkey. He tore a huge gate off a city wall and car-ried it off and left it on a mountain.

But then he fell in love with a beautiful Philistine woman named Delilah. The leaders of the Philistines offered her 1,100 pieces of silver if she could find out the secret of his strength.

A VISIT FROM AN ANGEL

In the Bible, angels often were thes bearers of good news. An angel visited Samson's mother, who could not have children, to tell her that she would have a son. He promised that her son would deliver the Israelites from the Philistines. She told her husband, Manoah, the amazing news, but he wanted to talk to the visi-tor himself. The angel did return to talk to Manoah.

"If you really love me you would tell me," she said. He told her if he was tied with fresh green vines or new ropes he would be weak like any other man. He told her if she braided his hair he would lose his strength. Each time she did what he told her, and each time when the Philistines burst into his room thinking he was weak, he would still be too strong for them.

Finally, he told her the truth. If his hair was cut, he would be just as weak as any other man. (His long hair represented a secret vow of faithfulness he had made to God.) So while he was sleeping, she had his hair cut.

This time, the Philistines seized him and poked out his eyes. They chained him in prison, and he had to grind wheat.

But his hair began to grow back. One day, the Philistines had a big party. They called for Samson so they could make fun of him. They praised their god Dagon. "Our god has given Samson into our hands," they said.

They tied Samson to the pillars that held up the house and laughed at him. But he prayed and asked God to help him one more time. Then he pushed down the pillars with all his strength, and the house fell down, killing him and all the Philistines who were there.

Baal

PAGAN GODS

The people of Canaan worshiped gods made of stone or metal, called idols. The main god was Baal, who hurled lightning bolts and spoke in thunder. Canaanites often sacrificed their own babies to Baal. Cities and families often had their own idols, too. God was very unhappy with the Canaanites.

THE PHILISTINES

The Philistines were a warrior people who lived along the coast. They had more experience fighting and better weapons than the Hebrews, so they collected taxes from the Hebrews and took away their weapons. They also took all the blacksmiths prisoner so they could not make new weapons.

HERE COMES THE JUDGE

Between Joshua and Israel's first king, Saul, the children of Israel were led by a series of 12 judges. These were either wise leaders or military heroes, like Deborah, Gideon, and Samson. Other judges include Elud, who made a special two-sided sword to kill the king of Moab, and Jephthah, who identified his enemies by their inability to say a certain word. The last judge was Samuel, a priest.

The Last Judge

◆ ◆ ◆

DURING THE LAST days of the judges, things were not going well for Israel. The Philistines had ruled over the land for many years. But one woman, Hannah, had her own reasons to be sad. She wanted a child, but she had been unable to have one. Her husband had another wife who had several children. She teased Hannah all the time.

So one day, while they were at the temple, Hannah prayed and wept and asked the Lord to give her a son. "If you do, I will give him back to you to serve you all of his life," she told the Lord.

She did have a son, and she named him Samuel. When he was old enough, she took him to the temple and left him there to help Eli, the high priest. Eli loved Samuel, because his own sons were evil men who did not love God. But Samuel did love God, and he helped Eli take care of the temple.

One night, the Lord called Samuel. Samuel thought it was Eli and ran to his room. But Eli said he had not called. This happened three times, and Eli realized it was the Lord who was calling Samuel. He told him to go back to his bed and wait for God to speak again.

So Samuel lay back down on his bed and waited. When the Lord called his name, Samuel said "Speak, Lord, for your servant listens." The Lord told Samuel what would happen to Eli and to his sons.

The people were excited that the Lord had spoken to Samuel because he had not spoken to any of their leaders for many years. When Eli died, Samuel became the high priest and the last judge of Israel. The people came to him for advice. They allowed him to settle their arguments. He even defeated the Philistines in one battle by calling on the Lord, who frightened the Philistines with thunder.

But the people decided they wanted a king instead of a judge. Samuel warned them that this was a bad idea. A king would force their sons to join his army, and he would charge taxes. He would take whatever he needed whenever he wanted. "The Lord should rule over you instead," Samuel said.

But the people insisted on having a king. "We want to be like all the other countries," they said. So the Lord helped Samuel pick a king. All his life, Samuel prayed for the people, and he tried to help them do the right thing.

BAD NEWS

When the Lord called to Samuel in the night, the message he had was bad news for Eli, the priest. Because the priest had not controlled his sons, two selfish and wicked men, God said they would both die on the same day. Both sons later died in battle. When he heard the news, Eli fell backward off a bench and broke his neck and died.

THE LOST ARK

While Eli was the high priest, his sons took the sacred Ark of the Covenant into battle against the Philistines. They lost the battle, however, and the Philistines captured the Ark. The Lord punished the Philistines by destroying one of their temples and sending a plague. Eventually they sent the Ark back to Israel.

SCHOOL DAYS

Because many of the priests—like Eli's sons—had become selfish and had begun to steal from the people, Samuel started four schools for prophets. For over 300 years, men would be trained to hear God's voice and tell the people and the kings what God said. Later, more famous prophets were Nathan, who was an advisor to King David, and Elijah and Elisha.

The First Kings of Israel

❖ ❖ ❖

ONE DAY, a young man named Saul came to Samuel, the prophet and judge. Saul had lost some of his father's donkeys and wanted to know if Samuel had seen them.

But when Samuel saw Saul, God told Samuel the young man was to become the first king of Israel. Samuel took the young man aside and poured some oil on his head. Then he prayed that God would help Saul rule the people wisely.

God did help Saul. When the Ammonites attacked one of the Hebrew cities, Saul called the people together to fight, and they easily rescued the city. Then the people wanted to make Saul king.

Before this time, Israel only had an army when one of the judges called the people together to fight, but as king, Saul had an army all the time. With the help of his son Jonathan, Saul began to drive the enemies of Israel out of the land, even the dreaded Philistines.

But Saul disobeyed the Lord. Once, he offered sacrifices to God without Samuel's help. Another time, he defeated the Amalekites but did not destroy all the people and cattle, as God

ARMOR BEARERS

Warriors were often accompanied by a young man who carried their extra weapons. Jonathan and his armor bearer once climbed up a cliff and surprised a group of Philistines. When King Saul was finally defeated in battle, he asked his armor bearer to kill him so the enemy would not capture him alive, but the boy refused.

DAVID'S SONGS

When he was afraid, David often wrote songs, known as psalms. In Psalm 54:4–7, he wrote "God is my helper; the Lord is the upholder of my life. He will repay my enemies for their evil. In your faithfulness, put an end to them.... I will give thanks to your name, O Lord, for it is good. For he has delivered me from every trouble, and my eye has looked in triumph on my enemies."

DAVID, THE GIANT-KILLER

Everyone was afraid of the giant Goliath. This Philistine was over nine feet tall and was dressed head to toe in heavy armor. But David knew that God would help him fight Goliath. He took one smooth stone, put it in his sling, and flung it at his enemy. The stone hit Goliath on his forehead, and the giant fell over. The soldiers of Israel then won a great victory over the Philistine army.

had commanded. So Samuel told Saul that God would take the kingdom from him and give it to someone else.

That someone else was David, Jonathan's best friend. As a shepherd boy, David had played his harp for King Saul. But as he grew older, David became a mighty warrior. When Saul and Jonathan were killed in battle, the people made David king.

David was a good, strong king. He loved the Lord, and he loved the people. He defeated the Philistines. He defeated the Moabites. And the Syrians, and the Edomites, and the Ammonites, and the Amalekites. Israel at last became a strong, united country, spread out all across the land that God had promised Abraham. He even brought back the Ark of the Covenant, which had been captured by the Philistines.

But everything was not well. One of David's own sons turned the hearts of the people away from the king. The son gathered an army and marched against his father, but the son's army was defeated and he was killed. David was very sad.

But God was pleased with David. He was a friend to God, a shepherd to his people. "Your throne will be established forever," God said.

Jerusalem

THE CITY OF DAVID

David made Jerusalem the capital of his kingdom. The city was on a hill called Zion and had strong walls. He conquered it by climbing up the water shaft with a few of his closest friends and surprising the people who lived there. After that, it was often called the City of David.

SAUL AND THE WITCH OF ENDOR

After Saul disobeyed him, God never spoke to Saul again. So Saul decided to consult a witch, even though he knew it was wrong. Right before a battle, he went to see her after dark and wore a disguise. The witch called up the spirit of Samuel, who told Saul he would lose the battle and die the very next day. And that's exactly what happened.

A Singer of Songs

◆ ◆ ◆

DAVID WAS A GREAT KING. But he was also a great musician. He played different instruments. Once he even danced in the streets, worshiping and praising God.

The Book of Psalms is a collection of songs, and David wrote at least half of them. His songs were very honest. He wrote about being sad and about being happy. He wrote about being afraid, even though he was a mighty warrior.

Many of the songs were also prayers. Some of the words he used a lot were "trust," "praise," and "rejoice." He used the word "mercy" hundreds of times. He was so glad that God was kind and patient with his people.

Here is one of David's songs:

"I waited patiently for the Lord,
  and he inclined to me and heard my cry.
He drew me up from a horrible pit,
out of the muck and the clay,
and he set my feet upon a rock,
making my steps secure.
He put a new song into my mouth,
a song of praise to our God.
Many shall see and fear
and trust in the Lord."

With all of his heart, and with all of his soul, and with all of his might, King David loved the Lord.

LISTEN TO THE MUSIC

Music was very important to the Hebrews. Instruments included the lyre, harp, timbrel, and flutes. A trumpet called a shofar was made from a ram's horn. Trained choirs sang in the temple. Dancing was part of every celebration. The Hebrew word for dance means "to leap like a lamb."

David's Sin

◆ ◆ ◆

ONE EVENING, while his armies were away at war, King David took a walk on the roof of his palace. Glancing down, he saw a beautiful woman taking a bath. Her name was Bathsheba.

Immediately the king fell in love with her. There was just one problem. She was already married to a soldier named Uriah. That did not stop King David. When King David learned that she was going to have his baby, David sent for her husband. He was hoping Uriah would sleep with his wife. Then no one would know the baby was David's. But Uriah refused. "Why should I sleep with my wife when all my soldier friends are sleeping in a field?" he asked.

So David sent a letter to the commander of his army. "During the battle, retreat and leave Uriah to die," he wrote. So Uriah died and David married Bathsheba.

Later, the prophet Nathan told David about a rich man who had many sheep of his own, but who killed a poor man's only lamb to feed his guests. David was very angry. "That man should die," he said. "You are like that man," Nathan said. "You already have many wives, but you killed Uriah so you could have his wife, too." David was very sad. Guiltily he bowed his head. "I have sinned against the Lord," he said.

Later the baby got sick and died. But God forgave David and Bathsheba. They had another baby, Solomon. After David died, Solomon became king.

TRUE STORIES

The Bible is different from other books written during that time because it tells the truth about leaders. In other books, the king was always made to look good. But in this story of David and Bathsheba, we are told the king did wrong. The mistakes of the judges, priests, prophets, and other kings are also recorded.

Solomon's Temple

◆ ◆ ◆

AFTER DAVID DIED, his son Solomon became king. Soon after that, the Lord appeared to him in a dream. "What can I give you?" the Lord asked.

Solomon asked for wisdom so he could lead the people. This pleased the Lord. "I will give you wisdom," he said. "But because you did not ask for riches or honor, I will give you those, too."

Since Solomon did not have to fight many wars, as his father had, he was able to use his wisdom to make the nation great. He made friends with other countries and began to trade with them. He built ships. He made chariots for his army.

As he became richer, he was able to do something his father David could not do: He built a temple for the Lord in Jerusalem. "By the kindness of God, I have not had any trouble," he said. "I will build a house to the name of the Lord my God."

It was a magnificent building. Although it was only 90 feet long and 30

WISE JUDGMENT

Once, two women brought a baby to King Solomon, each claiming it was her own. Solomon said to cut the baby in two and give half to each woman. But one woman cried out, "No! Give her the child—don't kill him!" In this way, Solomon had discovered who the real mother was and gave the baby to her. The real mother would not have allowed her baby to be harmed.

feet wide, the walls were made of huge stones. Inside, everything was made of fine wood, much of it covered with gold or jewels or carvings. There was a huge bronze basin that could hold over 13,000 gallons of water. Over 150,000 men helped build the temple. It took them seven years.

When it was finished, the priests brought the Ark of the Covenant into the temple. There was a great celebration, and a thick cloud filled the temple. It was the glory of God.

"But will God dwell in the earth?" Solomon prayed. "The heavens cannot contain him, how much less this house that I have built. But Lord, look at this place night and day, and always listen to the prayers that are offered here."

Solomon built a palace for himself, too. People came from all over to see the city. Solomon was wise and rich and famous, just as God had promised.

A FOOLISH KING

Solomon was very wise, but as he grew older he did some foolish things. He married many wives. Some of them were from other countries, and they worshiped other gods. He began to worship their gods, too. He also taxed the people heavily and forced them to work on his buildings. When he died, the kingdom split into two parts—Israel and Judah—because many of the people did not trust Solomon's sons.

QUEEN OF SHEBA

Rulers all over the world heard of Solomon and his wisdom. One of them decided to visit him herself. The Queen of Sheba traveled to Jerusalem bringing gifts. She asked Solomon many difficult questions and visited the temple. "The truth was told me before I came," she said. "You are wiser and richer than I imagined."

A BOOK OF WISDOM

Solomon did not keep all his wisdom to himself. He collected many wise sayings in a book to share with the people. You can read these in the Book of Proverbs. Here is one of his wise sayings: "Trust in the Lord with all your heart and lean not on your own understanding. In all your ways acknowledge him and he will direct your path."

Jonah's Mission

◆ ◆ ◆

NINEVEH WAS the capital of Assyria, and it was a very wicked city. No one in Israel liked the Assyrians. So the prophet Jonah was both surprised and scared when God told him to go to Nineveh and preach. "Tell them to turn from their sin or else I will destroy their city," God said.

But Jonah decided not to go, and he got on a ship headed in the opposite direction. When the ship was out to sea, there was a terrible storm. The sailors were afraid they would drown. But Jonah knew the storm was his fault because he was running from God. He told the sailors to throw him in the ocean and the storm would stop. At first they didn't want to, but the storm continued.

Finally, they threw Jonah overboard. As soon as they did, the storm stopped. But Jonah did not drown. The Lord sent a big fish to swallow him alive. Jonah spent three days inside the fish. He prayed for God to help him. The fish spit him up on dry land, and Jonah went to Nineveh to preach.

To his surprise, the people heard his message and turned to God. Even the king was sorry for his sins. Jonah was upset. He wanted God to punish the Assyrians, not forgive them. "Should I not have compassion on Nineveh?" the Lord asked. "There are many small children there. And animals, too."

A CRUEL PEOPLE

Jonah didn't want to go to Assyria because the Assyrians were very cruel. When they conquered a city, they would level it completely, killing all the people or taking them as slaves. Conquered countries had to pay high taxes, and people who refused to pay were tortured.

Elijah's Contest

◆ ◆ ◆

MANY KINGS ruled in Israel who did not serve God. Often, they would worship idols—especially Baal. But there were always a few prophets who tried to turn the people back to God. One of these was Elijah.

Elijah told the wicked king Ahab that it would not rain until the people repented. Then, for three years, the prophet hid by a small brook, where the ravens brought him bread and meat. Finally, the grass was so dry the cattle began to die. Elijah went to the king and told him to bring the people and the prophets of Baal to the top of Mount Carmel.

"How long will you serve two gods?" Elijah asked the people. "Choose one or the other." Then he had two bulls killed and laid on two altars. "You call to your god and I will call to mine," he told the prophets of Baal. "Whoever answers with fire, he is God."

While Elijah teased them, the prophets of Baal cried to their god all day. But nothing happened. "Maybe your god has gone to sleep?" Elijah asked. Finally Elijah had the people pour 12 jugs of water on top of the other altar. "Now, oh Lord, show that you are God in Israel and I am your servant," Elijah said. Immediately, the fire of the Lord fell, burning up the bull and the wood and the stone and even the water.

The people fell on their faces. "The Lord, he is God," they said. Soon after that it began to rain.

CHARIOTS OF FIRE

When he was very old, Elijah anointed Elisha to take his place. Elisha was walking with Elijah near the Jordan River one day when a chariot of fire and horses of fire came between them, snatching Elijah up in a whirlwind into heaven. Only his cloak was left behind.

A New Temple

◆ ◆ ◆

BECAUSE THEY had sinned against the Lord, the people of Judah were defeated by the Babylonians. The city of Jerusalem was destroyed, including Solomon's magnificent temple.

Many of the wealthy and educated were taken to Babylon. They longed to return to their own land, to rebuild the temple of the Lord. Seventy years later, a new king who had conquered the Babylonians offered to let some of them go home and rebuild the temple. The trip was long and difficult. When they arrived, Jerusalem was in shambles.

But the people began to rebuild the city. When they finished the foundation, they were so happy many of them cried for joy. But there were many problems, and it took many years to finish everything.

Ezra came from Babylon to lead the people. He had studied God's law, and he came to teach them how to worship God. They had been gone so long that they had forgotten how to worship God correctly.

He called the people together and read to them from the Book of the Law. Then he prayed, and he confessed his sins and the sins of the people, and he encouraged them to rebuild God's temple. Every day for a whole week, he read from the book all morning while the people stood and listened. The people wept for joy to hear the word of the Lord.

THE BOOK OF THE LAW

The Old Testament tells about the laws, religion, and history of the Hebrew people. It was written by different leaders, priests, and prophets over a long period of time. The oldest copies were found in a cave near the Dead Sea in 1947. The Dead Sea Scrolls are about 2,000 years old.

A New Wall

◆ ◆ ◆

ONE OF THE LEADERS who returned from Babylon was a man named Nehemiah. He was not a priest, but a wise man who knew the people would not be safe until the wall around Jerusalem was rebuilt. Many of those who lived in nearby cities and countries did not want Israel to be strong again.

So one night, while everyone else was asleep, he took a band of soldiers and walked around the city, checking to see where the wall needed to be rebuilt. After carefully measuring the wall, he called the leaders of the city together and told them his plan.

At first their enemies just laughed, but as the walls got higher and higher, they began to plan an attack. But Nehemiah divided his men into two groups—workers and soldiers. Even the workers had a short sword. Nehemiah carried a trumpet wherever he went. "If there is trouble, I will blow the trumpet," he said. "Come to that place and fight, and God will fight for us."

No one left the city. No one took off their clothes to sleep. They just kept working on the wall and finished it in only 52 days. "All our enemies knew that God had helped us," Nehemiah said.

THE WESTERN WALL

All together, three different temples were built in Jerusalem. The last one was built by King Herod about 20 years before Jesus was born. It was destroyed about 90 years later. The western wall of that temple is still standing. Hebrews (called Jews today) still go there to pray.

Daniel and the Lion's Den

❖ ❖ ❖

WHEN DARIUS was king of Babylon, Daniel was his special helper. In fact, the king wanted to put Daniel in charge of his whole kingdom. Some men were jealous of Daniel. He was from a different county, and he could speak a different language. They didn't think he should be allowed to tell them what to do.

These men knew that Daniel loved God. So they asked the king to make a new law. For 30 days, anyone who prayed to any god or human except Darius would be thrown into a den of hungry lions. Without even thinking about Daniel, the king agreed. The law was written down, and the king stamped it with his ring. He wanted all the people to think about their king.

Daniel did think about the king. And he thought about God. Daniel loved God more

A NEW NAME

Daniel was probably a relative of the king in his own country, Judah. But Judah was conquered, and many young men were taken to Babylon to serve the king there. They were given new names. Daniel's new name was Belteshazzar, which means "the king's attendant" or "the king's favorite."

A GREAT CITY

Babylon was one of the greatest cities in the world in its time. Writers who lived back then said the city was surrounded by a wall that was 80 feet wide, wide enough for chariots to race along the top. The wall was 60 miles long, 15 miles on each side of the city, with 250 guard towers, and 100 gates. Babylon was known for its beautiful hanging gardens.

GOOD FRIENDS

When Daniel was a young man, he had three Hebrew friends. Together they promised each other that they would follow God's laws. King Nebuchadnezzar made a huge statue of himself and ordered everyone to worship it. Because they refused, Daniel's three friends were thrown into a furnace. But not even a single hair on their heads was burned. God brought them out of the furnace completely unharmed.

than he loved anyone else. So Daniel went to his room three times a day and prayed to God—just like he always had.

Of course, his enemies ran to tell the king. At first, the king was upset with himself. Daniel was his friend. But even the king had to obey the law. So he ordered his soldiers to tie Daniel up and throw him into a den of lions. "Your God will deliver you," the king said, hoping it was true. Then a huge rock was placed over the opening.

The king went back to his palace, but he couldn't eat or even sleep. Early the next morning, he ran to the opening and called to Daniel. Imagine his excitement when Daniel answered. "My God sent an angel to shut the lions' mouths," Daniel said. The king was very glad. The soldiers moved the stone and lifted Daniel out of the den. There wasn't a scratch on him. Everyone was amazed.

The king had Daniel's enemies thrown into the lions' den. Then he passed a new law. The new law said all the people in the kingdom should worship Daniel's God, the only true God. "He is the living God," the king said, "because he has delivered Daniel from the lions."

AN OLD MAN

Daniel was probably an old man when he was thrown in the lion's den—perhaps as old as 90. He had already been an advisor to five or six kings. One reason the kings liked him was because he could often tell them what their dreams meant. Nebuchadnezzar dreamed of a large statute of a man made of gold, silver, bronze, iron, and clay. Only Daniel could tell the king what the dream meant.

A Savior Is Born

ONE DAY, an angel appeared to a young Hebrew woman named Mary. "You are favored by the Lord," he said. "You will have a son named Jesus, the Son of the Most High." "How can this be?" she asked. "I'm not even married." "The Holy Spirit will come upon you, and the child will be the son of God," the angel said.

Mary did have a fiancé named Joseph, and he was upset by the news. But an angel came to him, too, and he agreed to marry her and take care of her and her special child.

About this time, the Emperor in Rome made a law that everyone had to register to pay taxes in their hometown. Since Joseph was a descendent of King David, he had to go to Bethlehem, the city where David was born. They arrived late at night, the night Mary was ready to have the baby.

There were no rooms available, but a family allowed them to stay in a room with animals. It was there, surrounded by the smell of animals and hay, that Jesus was born. Mary wrapped him in a blanket and placed him in a feeding trough.

A PROMISE TO KEEP

Mary was not surprised when the angel told her a Savior would come. Ever since God promised David that his throne would be established forever, the Hebrew people had looked forward to a promised king, the Messiah. Many of the prophets had promised that this day would come and that the Messiah would save his people from their sins.

That same night, an angel startled shepherds in a nearby field. "Do not be afraid," the angel said. "I have good news. A Savior is born in Bethlehem tonight. He is Christ the Lord. Go and see." Suddenly, the whole sky lit up with angels singing, "Glory to God and peace on earth!" The shepherds hurried to town to see the baby, laughing and shouting that a Savior had come.

A few weeks later, Mary and Joseph took the baby to the temple to be blessed. An old man and an old woman both asked to hold the baby. They knew he was the Savior, and they rejoiced. "My own eyes have seen the bright salvation God has sent for all people," the old man said.

Mary and Joseph stayed in Bethlehem for a few years, and while they were there some wise men, called Magi, came to see the baby. They had traveled a long way, following a star. They brought the baby gifts and worshiped him.

Finally, the Savior had come.

A VERY SAD DAY

When the Magi came to Judea, they stopped to see the king in Jerusalem, a wicked man named Herod. They told him they were looking for a new baby, the "King of the Jews." Herod was afraid the new baby might steal his kingdom, so he ordered his soldiers to kill all the young children in Bethlehem. God warned Mary and Joseph, so they escaped and fled to Egypt. But the Bible says many mothers were weeping the day the soldiers killed their babies.

BOW DOWN BEFORE HIM

It must have looked strange—shepherds bowing before a little baby. But this was no ordinary baby. Kneeling, or even falling face down on the ground, was a way of showing respect to a king. Many people also pray on their knees, showing their respect for God.

JESUS' BROTHER, JAMES

James was the brother of Jesus. He may have doubted Jesus at first, but later he became a disciple and a brave leader in the early church. He also wrote a letter, or epistle, to Jewish Christians giving them helpful instructions on how to live. This letter is found in the New Testament.

Jesus as a Boy

❖ ❖ ❖

WHEN JESUS WAS 12, his parents took him to Jerusalem to celebrate the Passover, a special time each year when the people remembered how God had delivered them from Egypt. The family camped outside the city with friends and relatives. Each day, they would go into the city to the temple, where thousands of people were worshiping and celebrating.

The festival was over. Mary and Joseph joined a caravan back to Galilee. Since the men traveled together and the women and children were together, it was hard for families to keep track of children. Mary thought Jesus was with Joseph, and Joseph thought Jesus was with Mary! Mary and Joseph were worried when Jesus was missing.

They hurried back to the city, a whole day's walk. They searched for him for three days. They finally found him in the temple, sitting with the priests and elders, listening and asking questions, talking with wisdom far beyond his age. In fact, the priests and elders were amazed.

"Don't you know your father and I have been worried?" Mary scolded. "We've been looking for you everywhere." "Why were you looking for me?" Jesus asked. "Don't you know I must be in my Father's house."

His parents were confused. They didn't realize he was talking about his heavenly Father. But he returned home with them and obeyed them. He grew stronger and wiser, and everyone who knew him admired him.

JESUS' EARTHLY FATHER

Joseph was Mary's husband and Jesus' father on earth. Joseph worked as a carpenter, and as Jesus grew older his father taught him how to build things out of wood. Joseph may have died early in life, because the Bible does not mention him after Jesus' childhood.

Jesus Is Baptized

❖ ❖ ❖

JOHN THE BAPTIST was Jesus' cousin. He was also a prophet. "The Kingdom of God is at hand," he said. "The Messiah will soon appear." John preached in the wilderness near the Jordan River, warning people to turn from their sins and be baptized. He wore camel hair and ate wild honey. Many people came from Jerusalem to hear him.

John baptized the people to show that they were sorry for their sins and wanted to be washed clean. One day, Jesus came to him. "Baptize me," he said to John. "Oh, no," said John. "You are the one who should baptize me." But Jesus insisted. "It is fitting that we do the right thing," he said. Jesus did not need to be baptized for his sins. But he did want to show all people that he obeyed God.

So John baptized Jesus. When Jesus came up out of the water, the heavens opened up and the Spirit of God descended like a dove. Then a voice came from heaven. "This is my son," God said. "He pleases me."

After that, Jesus began to preach, too. He traveled around the country with his followers, teaching everyone how to love God and to love each other.

THE TEMPTATION

After Jesus was baptized, he went out into the wilderness alone, where he was tempted by Satan. He was there 40 days without food. Three times Satan tried to trick him into doing something wrong, and each time Jesus answered him with words from Scripture. Finally, Satan gave up and left Jesus alone. Then angels came and comforted Jesus. Remember how Adam and Eve were tempted? Jesus was tempted just as they were—except he didn't sin.

A Man of Miracles

◆ ◆ ◆

WHEN HE BECAME a man, Jesus began to teach in the towns and villages of Galilee. "The Kingdom of God is here. Repent and believe the good news!" Crowds gathered around him, eager to hear his message. "He talks with authority," they said.

One day, he stood up in the synagogue at Nazareth, his hometown. "The spirit of the Lord is upon me," he said, reading from the book of the prophet Isaiah. "He has anointed me to preach good news to the poor. He has sent me to proclaim release to the captives, sight to the blind, freedom to those who are oppressed."

He closed the book and sat down. "This is talking about me," he said. The people were shocked and angry. "Isn't this the carpenter's son?" they asked. They thought he was making too much of himself.

But Jesus began to show that the words were true. He did make blind people see and crippled people walk. He moved to Capernaum and went about the countryside, healing people and helping them. He even raised a little girl from the dead.

SPIRITUAL HEALER

A paralyzed man asked Jesus to heal him. But when Jesus saw how much faith the man had, he not only made him well but also forgave his sins. This amazed the religious leaders. It showed them that Jesus could heal the spirit, too.

TEMPLES VERSUS SYNAGOGUES

The Jewish people first met in the temple for worship. But, while in exile, they began worshiping at synagogues. The synagogue had no priests, and no sacrifices were offered. The synagogue also served as a place to study Jewish teachings, as a school to teach Hebrew, and as a community gathering place.

He gathered 12 men around him and taught them. These men were his disciples, and they saw him do wonderful things. Some of them were fishermen, and he told them where to cast their nets. When they did what he said, the nets were so full they could not pull them into the boat.

One night, Jesus was asleep in the boat when a great storm came up. The wind and the waves were fierce, threatening to turn the boat over in the angry sea. The disciples woke Jesus up. "Help us," they cried. He just spoke to the storm. "Peace, be still," he said, and it was. "What kind of man is this?" the disciples asked each other. "Even the winds and the waves obey him."

He was the man Isaiah had promised would come.

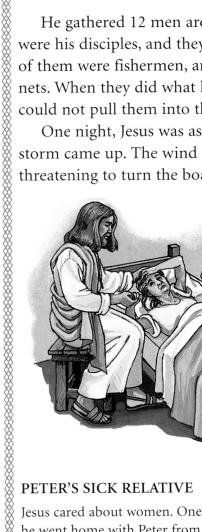

PETER'S SICK RELATIVE

Jesus cared about women. One day, he went home with Peter from the synagogue. There they found Peter's mother-in-law sick in bed with a high fever. Jesus spoke to her and, taking her by the hand, helped her up. Immediately, the fever left her, and she felt well enough to help serve a meal.

ONLY ONE WAS GRATEFUL

Once, Jesus healed ten men who had leprosy (a very serious and crippling skin disease), but only one returned to thank Jesus for making him well again. We don't know that man's name, but he was a hero for remembering to give proper thanks and praise to God.

SURPRISE CATCH

One day, when Peter arrived in Capernaum, the temple tax collectors came to him asking if Jesus paid taxes. All Jewish males were required to pay a temple tax. Peter mistakenly answered that Jesus did not have to pay taxes. Just as a king pays no taxes, Jesus the King owed no taxes. When Jesus learned of Peter's answer, he told him to cast a hook into the sea and to open the mouth of the first fish he found. In it was a coin! Peter used the coin to pay the temple tax for both himself and Jesus. Jesus did not want to offend those who did not understand that he was truly a king.

A Special Sermon

❖ ❖ ❖

ONE DAY, Jesus gathered around himself many of the people who loved him and followed him. He took them up on the side of a mountain and sat down, and he began to teach. First, he told them how to be happy. "Blessed are the poor in spirit," he said. "For theirs is the kingdom of God." There were many blessings, enough for everyone—for the meek, for the merciful, and for the pure in heart. "Blessed are the peacemakers, for they shall be called the children of God," he said.

But then he began to say some things that were not quite so easy to understand, or to appreciate. He said they would be blessed even if people joked about them, or hurt them, or lied about them, because they loved him. He told his disciples that they should be like a candle, giving light to a dark world. But it would not be easy. In every instance, Jesus said, they were to treat others like they wanted to be treated.

All day he sat and taught, explaining how they should live. They were not to be angry,

JESUS' MANY NAMES

In the New Testament, Jesus has many names. Some of them include the Living Water, the Bread of Life, and Emmanuel, which means "God with us." He is also called the Way, the Truth, and the Life. Another of his names is Messiah, or "Promised One," because he is the one who God promised would die and rise again to take away people's sins.

or try to get even. If someone slapped them on the cheek, they were not to slap back—but were to turn the other cheek. "Love your enemies," he said.

"And pray for them." He even taught them to pray.

"Ask, and it will be given to you, seek and you will find," he said. "And don't worry so much. Look at the birds and the lilies. God takes care of them, and he will take care of you. So don't worry about your clothes or your food. Your heavenly Father knows you need these things. Seek his kingdom, and be like him. Then all these things will be added to your life."

Finally, it was night. Jesus stood to return to town. He had one more thing to say: "Anyone who hears my words and obeys them is like a wise man who builds his house on a rock. But anyone who hears them and does not obey them is like a foolish man who builds his house on the sand. When the rain comes, and the flood comes, and the wind comes, his house will fall down flat."

EXTRA MILE

In Jesus' time, Judea was ruled by the Romans. The law said if a Roman soldier asked a Jew to carry his luggage, he had to carry it one mile—but no further. Jesus said if a soldier asked you to carry his luggage for a mile, you should carry it two.

LORD'S PRAYER

While Jesus was teaching the Sermon on the Mount, his disciples asked him to teach them to pray. He gave them an example of how to pray; it is called the Lord's Prayer. It is only 65 words long. Most churches today still use this simple but important prayer. Many Christians have memorized it.

Church of the Beatitudes

MANY BLESSINGS

The blessings Jesus talked about at the beginning of this special sermon are called the Beatitudes. There are nine of them. You can read them in the Book of Matthew, chapter 5. The sermon itself is Jesus' most famous sermon. It is called the Sermon on the Mount.

Special Friends

❖ ❖ ❖

JESUS HAD MANY special friends. One group of friends was his disciples. These 12 men traveled around Galilee with him, listening to him teach and watching him heal many people. Sometimes, they would sit around a campfire late at night, and he would answer their questions. These men were called apostles.

He spent extra time with three of them; James, who was his brother, John, who was the youngest, and Peter, who was the biggest and strongest and loudest of the bunch. Sometimes, Jesus would go off by himself and take only these three men along.

Many women were his friends, too. Mary and Martha were sisters who lived in Bethany, near Jerusalem. When he visited that city, he would stay at their house. Martha was always very busy, cleaning house and preparing meals. Mary liked to just sit and listen to Jesus teach.

Mary and Martha had a brother who died. His name was Lazarus. A few days after his death, Jesus came to see the sisters. "If you had been here our brother would not have died," Mary said. But Jesus said it was all right. "Now everyone can see how great God is," he said. Then he called Lazarus'

A KIND ACT

Mary and Martha were two sisters who were very devoted to Jesus. Once, Mary wanted to show Jesus how important he was to her. She took costly scented oil and poured it on Jesus' feet and wiped his feet with her hair. This kind act pleased Jesus and surprised everyone.

CHILDREN ARE SPECIAL

One day, when Jesus was very tired, some children came up to see him. The disciples shooed them away, thinking he wouldn't want to be bothered. "Let the children come to me," Jesus said. Then he held the children, talked to them, and blessed them. Children were important to Jesus, and he loved them.

name. "Come forth," Jesus said, and Lazarus came out of the grave alive, even though he had been dead for four days.

Jesus was even friends with people others did not like or trust. He made friends with several sinful women. He even made friends with Zacchaeus, a short man who collected taxes.

When Jesus was traveling through Jericho, Zacchaeus climbed up in a tree to get a better look.

Jesus stopped by the tree and looked up. "Zacchaeus, come down," he said. "I want to stay at your house today." Many people were shocked. No one liked Zacchaeus, because he often cheated them when he collected their taxes. But after Jesus visited with him, Zacchaeus gave half his money to help the poor, and he gave everyone back four times the money he had stolen.

"I want to help everyone," Jesus said. "Even those who make mistakes." That's why he had so many friends.

POWER OF FAITH

A woman had been bleeding for 12 years, but the doctors could not help her. One day, she saw Jesus in a crowd. "If I could just touch the hem of his garment, I would be healed," she thought. As soon as she touched his robe, she knew she was well. Jesus also knew something had happened. He told the woman her faith had healed her.

TRUE FOLLOWER

Nicodemus was a leader in Jerusalem who had heard of Jesus and his miracles. He wanted to find out more, but he was afraid to be seen with Jesus. He came to Jesus at night. Jesus answered his questions clearly, explaining to Nicodemus that he had to be born again to enter the kingdom of Heaven. Later, Nicodemus would show everyone he loved Jesus. He helped bury Jesus after he died on the cross.

The Day Jesus Died

◆ ◆ ◆

As PEOPLE BEGAN to flock around Jesus, the leaders and priests became jealous and nervous. If the people tried to make Jesus king, the Romans would destroy the temple—and them, too.

In fact, some people did want to make Jesus king. One Sunday, crowds from Galilee accompanied Jesus into the city, singing and shouting, laying palm branches under the feet of his donkey. "Blessed is the King," they shouted.

But Jesus did not want to be king, at least not on a throne in Jerusalem. The kingdom of God is in our hearts. This disappointed the people, including one of his disciples, a man named Judas. Judas decided to hand over Jesus to the leaders and priests, who wanted to kill him.

One night after dinner, Jesus went to a garden to pray. While he was there, Judas brought soldiers who arrested him and took him to the high priest. The priests accused him of trying to be like God. He didn't disagree with them, which made them angrier.

The priests were not allowed to put someone to death, so they took Jesus to Pilate, the

THE KISS OF DEATH

When Judas brought the soldiers to the garden, he kissed Jesus on the cheek. That was his way of showing the soldiers whom to arrest. "What are you doing, friend?" Jesus asked. The priest had given Judas some money for helping them find and arrest Jesus. Later, he tried to return the money. Then he hanged himself.

Roman governor. "This man claims to be the King of the Jews," they said. Pilate questioned Jesus and didn't want to have him killed. But the priests insisted. They stirred up the people of the city who had not watched Jesus heal the sick among the hills of Galilee. "Crucify him," they all shouted.

Finally, Pilate gave in to their demands. He turned Jesus over to the soldiers, who stripped off Jesus' clothes and beat him. Then they made Jesus and two criminals carry heavy wooden crosses to a hill outside the city. There they nailed them to the crosses and waited for them to die.

Many of the people in the crowd made fun of Jesus. "Save yourself," they called. Jesus was on the cross all day. It was hard for him to breathe. He was thirsty and weak. But even then he tried to help others. He asked John to take care of his mother. He talked to one of the criminals about heaven, and he promised to take him there.

He talked to God, too. "Father forgive them, because they don't know what they are doing," he prayed.

Then Jesus died. The sky turned black and the earth shook. Lightening flashed across the sky. Even the soldiers were afraid. "This must be the Son of God," one said.

A CRUEL DEATH

The Romans often put people to death by nailing them to a cross. This was called crucifixion and was sometimes used for murderers, terrorists, and thieves. It was most often used for people who rebelled against Rome. The Romans once crucified 500 Jewish rebels in a single day.

HOLY GRAIL

The Holy Grail was the cup supposedly used by Jesus at the Last Supper. It became the subject of many legends during the Middle Ages. In King Arthur's court, an empty seat was reserved at the Round Table for the knight who found the Grail. The cup has never been found.

A SPECIAL SUPPER

Before Jesus was arrested, he had a special meal with his disciples. After he asked the blessing, he served them bread and wine. He said the bread should remind them of his body and the blood should remind them of his blood. They were to do this as a way to remember him. Churches today still remember him this way. It is called the Lord's Supper, or the Eucharist.

Jesus Is Alive Again!

◆ ◆ ◆

Jesus' Garden Tomb

WHERE IS THE TOMB?

Jesus was crucified and buried outside the city walls of Jerusalem. It was along a road so travelers could see it and be warned. About 35 years after Jesus died, Jerusalem was destroyed by the Romans. They completely leveled the temple and most of the city. This is why the exact site of the tomb is difficult to find.

SOME OF JESUS' FRIENDS took his body off the cross and laid it in a tomb. The tomb was a gift from one of his friends. But there was no time to clean his body and prepare it for burial, because the Passover had begun.

His enemies were busy, however. They asked the governor to have soldiers guard the tomb and to put a huge stone in front of it so no one could steal the body. He agreed. "Make it as secure as you know how," he said.

That next Sunday morning, three women went to the tomb, hoping to take care of Jesus' body. "Who will roll the stone away?" they wondered. But when they got there they were amazed. The stone was already rolled away. And the tomb was empty. Suddenly two angels appeared. "Why do you look for the living among the dead?" they asked. "He is not here. He is risen, just as he told you."

Mary Magdalene ran to get two of the disciples, Peter and John. They couldn't believe their eyes. The cloths they had wrapped his body in were lying in the tomb, but Jesus was not there. They thought maybe the soldiers had stolen his body. But the soldiers had fled out of fear when an earthquake had opened the tomb.

John and Peter returned to the city, but Mary stayed near the tomb, crying and wondering where Jesus was. Then Jesus came to her. "Why are you crying?" he asked. At first, she thought he was the gardener. But once he called her name, she knew it was Jesus. He sent her to tell the others that he was alive.

Christian Easter service

A BIG, IMPORTANT WORD

Resurrection is the word we use to describe Jesus coming back from the dead. Christians celebrate his resurrection on Easter. Most believe the story of the resurrection is the most important story in the Bible. The Apostle Paul wrote that if the resurrection were not true, there would be no reason to be a Christian at all.

THE GOSPEL

The word gospel means "good news." The Bible says the gospel is that Jesus was born, that he died, and that he rose again from the dead. Because of this, God can forgive people for their sins, since Jesus took their punishment. Now we can go to heaven to live with him forever.

Meanwhile, the soldiers went to the temple. They told the priests that during the night there was an earthquake, and in a blinding light angels had moved away the stone. "Tell everyone that his disciples stole the body," the priests said. But soon everyone would know the good news. Jesus was alive!

Many Witnesses

❖ ❖ ❖

AFTER JESUS came back from the dead, he appeared to many of his followers. For example, two men were walking home from Jerusalem that same afternoon. Even though they had heard that Jesus was alive again, they did not believe it or understand it. But Jesus appeared beside them and showed them how the Scriptures promised he would die for the sins of the people.

They did not recognize him at first. But when they got to the place where they were going to spend the night, they invited him to stay. He came in for dinner, and as he asked the blessing on their meal, they knew who he was. He immediately disappeared.

That same night, the disciples gathered in a locked room. They weren't sure what to do or what to believe. Suddenly, Jesus appeared in the middle of the room. "Peace be with you," he said. But one of the disciples, Thomas, was not there. When the others tried to tell him Jesus was alive, he didn't believe them. "I won't believe it unless I see for myself," Thomas insisted.

A week later, Jesus appeared again. He told Thomas to place his finger in the nail prints. Then Thomas believed. "You have seen and believed," said Jesus. "Blessed are those who believe even though they do not see."

A TRUE STORY

After his resurrection, Jesus appeared to over 500 of his followers. Sometimes he appeared to one or two at a time, sometimes to a small group or a large group. Later, some of these followers would be killed for insisting that this story was true. If it were not true, they could have said so and saved their own lives.

Jesus Goes Back to Heaven

◆ ◆ ◆

FOR 40 DAYS after his resurrection, Jesus appeared to his followers, teaching them about the Kingdom of God. Then he gathered his disciples together on the Mount of Olives, just outside Jerusalem. "Wait here in Jerusalem," he said. "John baptized you with water, but I will baptize you with the Holy Spirit very soon."

"Then you will tell everyone about me, not just here in Jerusalem, but across the country and across the world. You should go everywhere and teach everyone what I have taught you. Then baptize them in the name of the Father, and of the Son, and of the Holy Spirit. Now go, and remember, I am always with you."

After he told them this, he was lifted up in a cloud. As the disciples watched, he became a small speck, rising up to heaven. The disciples just stood there, wondering what to do. Then two angels appeared. "Why are you standing here looking at the sky?" they asked. "This same Jesus who has gone away to heaven will return in just the same way."

Then the disciples returned to Jerusalem, shouting and praising God.

GREAT COMMISSION

Jesus commanded his disciples to go everywhere and teach everyone to follow him. This command is called the Great Commission. This is the command churches are following when they send missionaries to tell people about Jesus. Many heroes of the church have been missionaries.

The Church Begins

❖ ❖ ❖

JESUS RETURNED to heaven, and Peter and the disciples returned to Jerusalem. There they began to wait, as Jesus had commanded them. As they waited and prayed, thousands of devout Jews poured into the city to celebrate Pentecost. There were Jews from many countries, and they spoke many languages. Suddenly, there was a noise like a violent, rushing wind, and it filled the house where the disciples were.

The people began to gather outside. Inside, flames appeared on the heads of Jesus' followers. They all began speaking in different languages, languages they had never spoken before. It was the baptism of the Holy Spirit that Jesus had promised.

The people outside were amazed. They all heard the disciples speaking in their own language. Then Peter got up and began to preach. He reminded them that the prophet Joel had promised that God would send his Spirit. He reminded them that David had said the Messiah would die but rise again.

Then he told them about Jesus: "Jesus walked among you and did many miracles. You nailed him to a cross, but God raised him up again. We have seen him, and he has sent his Holy Spirit to be among us."

That day, 3,000 people heard the good news, believed it, and were baptized. It was the day the church was born.

DORCAS'S RETURN

Dorcas was renowned for doing kind things for people, especially the poor. She made robes and coats for people who had no money. When she died, the people were very sad. They showed Peter all the wonderful clothes she had made them. God helped Peter bring Dorcas back to life. After that, many people believed in the Lord.

In Jesus' Name

◆ ◆ ◆

ONE AFTERNOON, Peter and John went to the temple to pray. As they entered the temple, a lame man sitting by the gate called to them, begging for money. Peter and John both stopped and looked at the man.

"I have no silver or gold," said Peter. "But I have something better. In the name of Jesus Christ—walk!" Then Peter took him by the hand and raised him to his feet. The man had never walked in his life. Suddenly, he had strength in his legs. He stood on his own and followed Peter and John into the temple, leaping and praising God. The people recognized him and were amazed. For 40 years they had seen him sitting beside the gate, begging. "Why are you so amazed?" Peter asked. "It is the name of Jesus that has strengthened this man."

This caused such a stir that the temple guards grabbed Peter and John and put them in jail. "By what name have you done this?" the priests asked the next day. "By the name of Jesus," Peter said. The priests didn't know what to say, especially since the lame man was standing there, praising God. So they told Peter and John not to speak or teach in the name of Jesus again. "We can't help ourselves," Peter said. "We cannot stop talking about what we have seen and heard."

So the priest let them go, and the church continued to grow.

THE FIRST MARTYR

Stephen was a wise Christian who loved to talk about God. But many people—especially religious leaders—hated his message. While he was speaking one day, an angry crowd stoned him to death. Stephen was the church's first martyr, that is, a person who is killed for his beliefs.

Paul Takes the Good News to Everyone

◆ ◆ ◆

AS THE CHURCH continued to grow, the priests became more and more concerned. The followers of Jesus would have to be stopped before the new church became more important than the temple itself. One of the leaders in Jerusalem was a man named Saul, a smart young man who understood the problem. He had been taught the Law since he was a young boy, and he hated the church.

SPECIAL HELPERS

The 12 disciples were the leaders of the church in Jerusalem. They would come to be called apostles, which means "messengers." The church grew so fast the apostles had to appoint other people to help them. The helpers were called deacons. As churches grew, they needed their own leaders. These were called elders. Eventually, as the priests tried even harder to stop the church, the people moved to other cities. This is one way the gospel was spread to all the world.

The leaders sent Saul out to find members of the new church—called Christians. He was to break up their churches and put their leaders in jail. Once, he even stood by as angry Jews threw huge stones at a Christian named Stephen until he died.

One day, Saul left Jerusalem to go to Damascus and arrest the Christians there. But on the way, a bright light struck Saul down, leaving him blind and helpless. "I am Jesus," a voice said. "I want you to stop persecuting me and my people. I want you to follow

me, and go tell the Gentiles about me."

This was an amazing thing. The Gentiles were not Jews. Why would God care about them? But Saul obeyed God, and then changed his name to Paul. At first, the Christians did not trust Paul. But God showed a man named Ananias that Paul was his special servant. Ananias prayed for Paul, and soon he could see again.

Paul began to tell everyone the good news, traveling from place to place and writing letters to encourage the churches. He reminded them that Jesus would return. He used his education to help the church, not to destroy it.

He made four trips, taking the message of Christ across Galatia and Greece and eventually to Rome. He had many adventures. He was beaten several times, shipwrecked three times, and bitten by a snake.

Eventually, he became the most powerful leader in the church. The priests he used to work for hated him and had him put in jail. Since he was a Roman citizen, he asked to be tried in a Roman court. So he was taken to Rome, where he spent his last days in jail, writing letters that eventually became part of the Bible.

"I have finished the race and kept the faith," he wrote. "Now the Lord will give me a crown of righteousness, and he will give one to everyone else who loves to think about his return."

PAUL'S SHIPWRECK

The Apostle Paul once had a frightening experience at sea. On his way to Rome to stand trial for his beliefs, Paul's ship ran into a storm and broke apart. God told Paul that he and his fellow travelers would make it to shore safely. Indeed, all were saved.

EPHESIANS

One of the letters Paul wrote was to the church at Ephesus, a major city in the Roman state of Asia. In the Bible, the letter makes up the Book of Ephesians. In this letter, Paul tells about God's purpose and plan for the world. Two chapters explain how husbands, wives, and children should act.

Questions & Answers

◆ ◆ ◆

Q: Which disciple denied knowing Jesus?

A: When Jesus was arrested, Peter followed along in the crowd. Three times people accused him of being a follower of Jesus, and three times he said he wasn't—just as Jesus said he would. Later, Jesus forgave him. Peter became an important leader in the early church.

Q: What's the safest way out of town?

A: Some people in Damascus were so angry with Paul they wanted to kill him. That night, his friends helped him escape by letting him down in a basket through a window in the city wall. Rahab also helped two Hebrew spies escape from Jericho by letting them down through a window with ropes.

Q: Who were some of the bad guys of the Bible?

A: The Bible tells about the deeds and the destruction of many evil men. One of them was Haman, an official in Persia who tried to have all the Jews killed because one of them would not bow down to him. King Herod tried to get rid of Jesus by having all the babies in Bethlehem killed.

Q: What's so important about a name?

A: Sometimes God changed peoples' names to show that he had a new relationship with them. He changed

Paul is lowered to the ground to escape the angry people of Damascus.

Jacob's name, which means "deceiver," to Israel, which means "he struggles with God." Abram became Abraham, and Sarai became Sarah. The Book of Revelation says all Christians will have a new name in heaven.

Q: Who was the most wicked woman in the Bible?

A: The worst woman in the Bible was probably Jezebel, the wife of King Ahab. She forced her husband and the entire nation of Israel to worship the pagan god Baal. She had Naboth killed so her husband could steal his land. She ordered God's prophets slaughtered.

Q: Were women important in the early church?

A: Many women helped the church begin. Lydia, for example, was one of Paul's first converts. This seller of purple cloth opened her home to Paul and Barnabas so they could preach to the people in Phillipi. Phoebe was a woman from Corinth who helped take care of many people, including Paul. Paul called her a sister.

Q: Who was the most beautiful woman in the Bible?

A: It might have been Esther. She won a beauty contest, and she was picked to be the queen by the king of Persia. Later, she helped save the Jews from being destroyed by a wicked man named Haman. She believed God made her queen—and made her beautiful—for that very reason.

Q: How were the prophets treated?

A: Jesus pointed out that prophets were often mistreated. Jeremiah, for example, was thrown in a well—and people came by and laughed at him. Other prophets were stoned, thrown to the lions, and killed with swords. Prophets were not very popular, but they continued to preach God's word.

Ahasuerus chooses Esther to be his queen.

will take them with him to heaven.

Q: Are there any great love stories in the Bible?

A: The best love story is about Ruth and Boaz. Ruth was a foreign widow who came to Israel to take care of her mother-in-law, Naomi. Boaz, a relative of Naomi's, was so impressed with Ruth's kindness that he married her—and they lived happily ever after. Another love story is found in the Song of Solomon.

Q: What is a deacon?

A: When the church first started, the apostles were very busy. They needed to study and preach, so some men were chosen to take care of the widows and help in other ways. These people were called deacons, which means "to wait on." One of them, Stephen, was the first person to be killed for telling others about Jesus.

Q: Does everybody have to die?

A: Only two men never died. One of them was Enoch, a man who lived before the flood. He walked and talked with God—and God took him directly to heaven. God did the same thing with the prophet Elijah, sweeping him away in a chariot of fire. Christians who are alive when Jesus returns to earth will not die either. Jesus

Q: How many kings ruled in ancient Israel?

A: Forty-one different kings ruled over all or part of Israel. After Saul, David, and Solomon, the kingdom was split in two. Some of the kings, like Josiah, tried to honor God. Others did not. Some worshiped idols and killed God's prophets. One of them, Zimri, killed himself after being king for only one week.

Q: Did Jesus have a hero?

A: Jesus said no one had ever been born greater than his cousin John. John was a prophet who lived in the desert. He wore camel hair and ate wild locust. John preached that everyone should turn from their sin because the Savior was about to come. He baptized many people—including Jesus—in the Jordan River.

Religious Customs

◆ ◆ ◆ ◆

THE ANCIENT HEBREWS were very serious about their faith, and some of the ways they showed it seem strange to us today. For example, they offered sacrifices and took baths as part of their worship. But some things weren't different at all. They prayed and studied the Scriptures, both at home and at the temple. They expected God to speak to them and to show them what to do. That's exactly what he did, and what he still does today.

A Special Stick

❖ ❖ ❖

MANY MEN in Bible times carried a long stick called a staff. They used it to help walk in the rocky wilderness, to defend themselves, and to help control cattle or sheep.

Moses and his brother Aaron had staffs that showed their power and authority. When God chose Moses to lead his people out of Egypt, Moses was afraid. Moses was not sure the people would listen to him or follow after him.

God showed Moses that he would help him. "What is that in your hand?" God asked. "A staff," Moses replied. "Throw it on the ground," God ordered. Moses did, and it became a snake. Moses started to run away. "Pick it up by the tail," God told him. When he did, the snake became a staff again. "This is so people will believe that I have sent you," God said.

Later, Moses would use his staff to show God's power to the people—and to Pharaoh. Moses struck the Nile River with his staff and it became blood. When Pharaoh's

CELEBRATION OF SEVENS

Seven was an important number to the Jews. One day out of every seven they rested. One year out of every seven they let their land rest, and they did not grow crops on it. The fiftieth year—the year after seven periods of seven years—was the year of jubilee. There was no planting or harvesting. Any land that had been sold was returned to its original owner and slaves were freed.

POWER AND PROTECTION

The staff was a symbol of power. But it was also a symbol of protection. Shepherds used it to protect their sheep. King David was a shepherd when he was a boy. He said God was like our shepherd. "Your rod and your staff, they comfort me," David prayed. You can read this prayer in Psalm 23.

army followed the Hebrews out of Egypt, Moses stretched his staff out over the Red Sea. The waters parted, and the people walked across on dry land. Later, when the people complained of thirst, he struck a rock with his staff and water flowed out.

God also chose Aaron to help Moses. Aaron used his rod to do miracles, too. One day, some of the people complained about Aaron being the chief priest. So God told Moses to have the leader of each tribe give him a staff. Then Moses placed the twelve staffs in the Tabernacle where the people worshiped. "The staff belonging to the man I choose will sprout," God said.

The next day, Aaron's staff had sprouted. Flowers and almonds had grown on it, too. The people were amazed. Moses took the staff back into the tabernacle and put it in the Ark of the Covenant, a special box for the stone tablets on which God had written the Law. The staff reminded the people that God wanted Moses and Aaron to be in charge. It was a symbol of authority.

THE RAINBOW'S PROMISE

After the great flood, in which all on earth but those aboard the ark perished, Noah said a prayer of thanks to God for allowing him and his family to be saved. God then pledged that he would never again send such a devastating flood. As a sign of his promise, God created a rainbow in the sky.

A HIGH PLACE

When the Hebrews entered the Promised Land, Joshua built an altar on Mount Ebal. Half the people stood on Mount Ebal and half the people stood on Mount Gerizim as they pronounced the blessings and curses Moses had written in the Law. The people often worshiped on top of mountains. The mountains represented the presence of God.

The Cross of Christ

◆ ◆ ◆

THE ROMANS often executed murderers and thieves by nailing them to a wooden cross. This was called crucifixion. They would do this near a crowded highway, so others would see the victim and be afraid to do what he had done.

Often, the victim was beaten with a whip and then made to carry the cross to the place where he would die. Then his clothes were stripped off, and he was nailed to the wood. A list of his crimes was posted on the top of the cross. It would take several hours to die. Sometimes soldiers would break the victim's legs so he could not push himself up to breathe better. With broken legs, he would die faster.

Jesus was not a murderer or a thief. He did nothing wrong. But some of the leaders in Jerusalem were afraid of him. They thought the people would follow Jesus and make him king. It also made them angry that Jesus said he was the Son of God. So they arrested Jesus and sentenced him to die. Then they got the Romans to crucify him on a cross.

Jesus was beaten and forced to drag his cross through the

SIGN OF THE FISH

Early Christians were sometimes put in jail or even killed because of their beliefs. So they developed secret ways to identify each other. One of these was to draw a picture of a fish. They used this symbol because the first letters of the Greek words for "Jesus Christ, God's Son, Savior" spelled *ichthus*, the Greek word for fish.

THE LAST SUPPER

Before Jesus was crucified, he had one last meal with his disciples. During the meal, he told them that he would die. He gave them bread to eat and said it should remind them of his body. He gave them wine to drink and said it should remind them of his blood. "Do this to remember me," he said.

Putting on a phylactery

crowded city streets. Then he was crucified on a hill outside the city, which was also used as the dump. While they waited for Jesus to die, the soldiers tossed dice and gambled for his cloak.

But Jesus forgave the priests and elders and soldiers who crucified him. While he was on the cross, he prayed: "Father, forgive them." He also asked one of his disciples to take care of his mother. Then Jesus died. The soldiers did not break his legs like they usually did. Instead, they stuck a spear in his side—to make sure he was dead.

Later, Jesus came back from the dead. The cross has become a powerful symbol. Today, when Christians see a cross they are not afraid. They are reminded that Jesus died for their sins and that he forgives them.

WORDS OF THE LAW

Some Jews wore and still wear small leather boxes containing portions of Scripture on their forehead and elbow when they pray. These boxes are called phylacteries, and they show that the wearers are very serious about their religion. In Jesus' time, some of the religious leaders made the bands that held the boxes very wide so others would notice them. Jesus said they were doing it just to show off, not because they loved God's Word.

Power and Prayer

◆ ◆ ◆

THE BIBLE is filled with stories about men and women who prayed. Moses, for example, prayed for almost an entire day—with his hands raised toward heaven. The Israelites were fighting the Amalekites. Moses stood high on a hill watching the battle. As long as he held his hands up in prayer, Israel was winning. But when he rested his hands by his sides, the Amalekites began winning.

Keeping his arms raised was hard work, but Moses did not give up. Aaron and Hur brought a stone for him to sit on. Then they stood on each side of him, and held his hands up as he continued to pray. By sunset, Israel had won the battle.

Some prayers are very personal. The Book of Psalms contains many of King David's prayers. The prophets also prayed long and often. Jonah prayed from the belly of a great fish. Elijah prayed that it would not rain. Daniel was even thrown into the lions' den for praying.

TRUE CONFESSION

One of the reasons to pray is to tell God about sins you have committed and ask him to forgive you. King David did this with his own sin in Psalm 51. Some of the prophets confessed not only their sins, but the sins of all the people. Three of these prayers are in Ezra 9, Daniel 9, and Nehemiah 9.

Because prayer is so important, Jesus' disciples wanted to know more about how to pray. He taught them that they should pray simply and in secret. "Go into your room and close the door. Then your Father will reward you," he said.

Later he told this story: Two men went to the temple to pray. One of them was a Pharisee, a religious leader. He stood up and prayed loudly so others could hear him. "I'm glad I'm not like other men," he said. "I go without food so I can pray more, and I give a tenth of all my money to help feed the poor." There was another man, a tax collector, also praying. Everyone hated tax collectors because they worked for the Romans and stole from the people. But the tax collector prayed like this: "Lord, have mercy on me, because I am a sinner."

God was pleased with the tax collector and not with the Pharisee, Jesus said. Prayer is not proud; it is for the humble. But as Moses showed, it can be very powerful.

Garden of Gethsemane

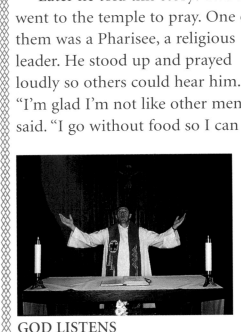

GOD LISTENS

The Bible says that prayers are important to God, who always listens to them. It even says prayers smell sweet to God, like perfume. According to the Book of Hebrews, we can go boldly before God's throne when we pray. There we can find help when we need it.

A PATTERN FOR PRAYER

Throughout his life, Jesus often went off by himself to pray. He did this for 40 days at the beginning of his ministry. He did it several times after he taught and healed the people in Galilee. He also did it the night before he died on the cross. He went to the Garden of Gethsemane, where he prayed for God to give him strength.

A GOOD ATTITUDE

The Apostle Paul taught his young disciple Timothy that attitude was important in prayer. He said that people should pray, "lifting up holy hands without anger or argument."

Special Assignment

❖ ❖ ❖

ANGELS ARE God's heavenly servants and soldiers. They do special tasks for him. For example, after Adam and Eve disobeyed God, he sent them away from the Garden of Eden. Then he sent an angel with a fiery sword to stand guard over the garden and keep them from returning.

Sometimes God uses angels to rescue people from danger. Once the Apostle Peter was in prison for preaching. King Herod had already killed the Apostle James, and Peter was next. But the night before Peter was to be executed, God sent an angel to help him. Peter was asleep, chained between two soldiers. More soldiers were guarding the gate. The angel woke Peter and told him to get up. The chains slipped off him, and Peter followed the angel out of the prison.

Shadrach, Meshach, and Abednego were three Hebrew slaves who refused to worship the pagan gods of King Nebuchadnezzar. Because of this, the king threw them into a fiery furnace, but another being was seen in the furnace, who had "the appearance of a god" (Daniel 3:25). Not a hair on their heads was burned, despite the burning heat. After

NO BOWING

No one should bow down to or worship angels. The Apostle John learned this after he had a vision of heaven. He wanted to worship the angel who was guiding him, but the angel said not to. Only God should be worshiped, the angel said.

that, King Nebuchadnezzar ordered everyone to worship the God of the Hebrews.

God also used angels to bring messages to people. Angels came to Abraham and told him he would have a son. An angel came to Mary and told her she would have the baby Jesus. And angels announced the birth of Jesus to shepherds in a field.

Sometimes, however, God uses angels to punish people. When Moses was trying to lead the children of Israel out of Egypt, Pharaoh refused to let them go. When an angel killed the first-born child in every home one night, Pharaoh finally changed his mind. An angel once destroyed an entire army camped outside Jerusalem.

Angels have one very special job. They protect God's people. When Elisha was fleeing from an angry king, he went to Dothan with his servant. The king sent an army, however, and surrounded the city. "What shall we do?" the servant asked. "Open his eyes so he can see," Elisha prayed. Then the servant saw that the hills around the city were full of chariots and horses of fire. God had sent his angels to protect them.

That's their job.

UNDERCOVER AGENT

People do not always recognize angels. Three angels came to Abraham to tell him that God was going to destroy the city where his nephew lived. Abraham welcomed them as guests and gave them food and drink. Before they left, one of them told him that he would have a son the next year. Only then did he know that they were angels.

NUMBERS AND NAMES

At least half of the books in the Bible talk about angels. The word, which means "messenger," occurs 275 times. The Book of Hebrews says there are so many angels we can't count them. Two angels in the Bible have names: Michael, the archangel, and Gabriel, the angel who brought the news of Jesus' birth to Mary.

Where Are the Wings?

◆ ◆ ◆

NOT ALL ANGELS have wings. In fact, there are several different kinds of angelic beings, and each kind has different responsibilities. They don't all look the same.

There are seraphim, fiery angels with six wings. The name seraphim means "to burn." Isaiah saw these angels circling the throne of God. Their voices were like thunder and shook the walls, Isaiah said. They were calling to one another saying, "Holy, holy, holy is the Lord Almighty." That may be their whole job—to worship God around his throne.

Cherubim are fearsome creatures with four faces and four wings. Ezekiel describes these angels. Each face is different: one was like a man, one like an eagle, one like a lion, and one like an ox. They travel in a cloud of fire, surrounded by lightning. Their job is to guard God and his holiness.

As far as we know, the rest of the heavenly hosts have no wings at all. The angels who appeared to men and women in the Bible with messages from God did not look that unusual. Often, they were not even recognized as angels. No one comments on their having wings. They may be spirit beings who

JUDGING THE EARTH

Angels will have a role in the end of the world when God judges and punishes sin. The Book of Revelation tells how angels will take part in a series of judgments in the last days. They will fight with God against Satan. Then they will cast Satan and his angels into a lake of fire, along with all the people who rebelled against God.

ANGELIC REJOICING

Angels are heavenly beings created by God to serve him. The work of good angels—those who obey God—includes standing in his presence and worshiping him. Also, as ministering spirits, they actively assist and protect creation. In the parable of the lost sheep, Jesus indicates that the angels rejoice each time a sinner turns to follow God.

just take on bodies to do certain tasks on earth.

In the Old Testament, there is a specific angel called the Angel of the Lord. He appeared to different prophets and judges in Israel, and he looked just like a man. He often did miracles and made special promises on behalf of God.

There are many, many angels, apparently organized like an army with captains and other officers. One of the most powerful angels we know about is Michael, the archangel. He appears to be a commander, whose chief responsibility was to guard the children of Israel.

One angel with a special job is Gabriel. He made special announcements about God's plans to the prophet Daniel, and he announced Jesus' birth to the virgin Mary. He did not have wings. But like all God's other angelic creatures, he was powerful and wise.

CARING FOR CHRIST

Angels had a special interest in Jesus when he was on earth. They announced his birth and protected him as a baby. After he was tempted in the wilderness, they came and comforted him. They also strengthened him when he prayed in the Garden of Gethsemane, rolled away the stone from his tomb, and announced his resurrection.

NOT HUMAN

Some people think angels are people who have died. This is not true. Angels are specially created spiritual creatures. They are not like people. They do not sin. They do not get married or have babies. They do not die. Angels existed before humans were created.

Prophets and Predictions

GOD USED DREAMS and visions to speak to his people. God used dreams to speak to people when they were asleep. When God used a vision, the person was awake. For example, God spoke to Abimelech in a dream. This Philistine king wanted to take Abraham's wife and marry her, but God warned him not to.

On the other hand, God once appeared to Abraham and promised him that he would have a son. This was a vision. Later, as the sun was going down, Abraham fell into a deep sleep. Then God appeared as a smoking firepot and a blazing torch, passing between the pieces of a sacrifice. This was a dream.

Dreams were often used to reveal the future. Joseph got in trouble for a dream in which he saw himself ruling over his older brothers. It made them jealous, and they sold him into slavery. But later he became a ruler in Egypt, and he did rule over his brothers.

Joseph also explained one of Pharaoh's dreams, which warned of a future famine.

Daniel also explained the dreams of the kings he served in Babylon. He had visions, too,

TIMELY DREAM

Joseph dreamed that he should take Mary and young Jesus to Egypt to escape King Herod's wrath. After Herod died, the family returned and settled in Nazareth.

WHAT'S FOR DINNER?

The Apostle Peter had a vision in which a sheet with pigs and other "unclean" animals was lowered from heaven. He was told to eat the animals, even though Hebrew law did not allow it. Later, he understood that he should regard everything God made as good. It also helped him see that God loved everyone, even people who were not Jews.

and he explained the visions of others. One night, King Belshazzar had a great banquet. His city was surrounded by the Persian army, but he was not afraid. He and his friends laughed and danced and mocked God, using golden goblets from the temple in Jerusalem to drink their wine.

Suddenly, the fingers of a human hand appeared and wrote on the wall. That made the king afraid! He sent for Daniel and asked him what it meant. "Tell me what it means and I will put a gold chain around your neck and make you an important officer," the king said. "Keep your gifts or give them to someone else," Daniel told him. "You have not honored the God who holds your life in his hands. The writing says your kingdom is at an end and will be given to someone else."

That very night, the king was killed, and the Persians took over his kingdom. Later, Daniel had a vision of his own about the future of Israel and all the kingdoms of the earth. Like the other prophets, he had learned to listen to God speak through visions and dreams.

JACOB'S LADDER

One night, Jacob used a stone for a pillow. As he slept, he saw a stairway to heaven, with angels going up and coming down the stairs. The Lord spoke to Jacob and promised to help him and bless him. Jacob was once blessed by an angel, too. He wrestled with the angel all night long, until the angel struck him on the thigh. Then the angel blessed him.

A TERRIBLE STORM

In the Book of Revelation, John has a vision about the future when God will punish those who have disobeyed him. Seven "bowls" of God's wrath will be poured on the earth. The first will cause an outbreak of terrible sores. The second will cause the oceans to become like blood; everything in them will die. With the third, the rivers and springs will become blood. The fourth bowl will cause the sun to scorch and burn. The fifth will turn the earth completely dark. The sixth bowl will unleash evil spirits and demons. God's seventh bowl of wrath will cause a terrible storm, with lightning, thunder, and 100-pound hailstones.

Servants of the Temple

❖ ❖ ❖

ISRAEL WAS MADE of 12 tribes, descendants of the 12 sons of Jacob. One of these tribes was set apart to serve God. When the land was divided among the tribes, the tribe of Levi did not receive a share. Instead, they took care of the Tabernacle and later the temple. The other tribes gave ten percent of their income to support the Levites. This included a share of their crops and livestock.

Any Levite could clean or guard the temple. They could help organize the people. They could sing and play musical instruments. But only the ones descended from Aaron could be priests. The priests could perform the sacrifices and other special duties of temple worship.

The rules about who could be priests were very strict. A priest's hair could not be too short or too long. They could not drink wine. They could not touch anything that was "unclean," which included dead bodies and certain kinds of animals.

WOMEN PRIESTS

There are no women priests mentioned in the Bible. This does not mean that women were inferior to men, but in those days there were very clearly defined roles for men and women. In the New Testament, women began gaining more equality with men in ministering in the church.

Each day, the priests woke up before dawn and bathed. Then their duties were assigned, such as offering sacrifices, cleaning the altar, lighting the lamps, or teaching the people. Then they were called to morning worship by the clash of a gong. The morning service included music and singing—and lasted for several hours. Then there were sacrifices and prayers.

There was also a high priest. Aaron was the first high priest. During Jesus' time, the high priest was a descendent of Zadok, the high priest who served in Solomon's temple. The high priest wore special garments. He only ministered on the Sabbath, new moons, and special festivals.

The most important of these festivals was the Day of Atonement. Once a year, the high priest would go into the Holy of Holies. He made three trips, one with burning incense, one with the blood of a bull, and one with the blood of a goat. He would sprinkle the animals' blood on the altar, both for his own sins and for the sins of all the people.

THE BIGGER THEY COME

Abiathar was a priest who won great favor, only to lose it all. He was high priest during David's reign, and he stayed loyal during Absalom's rebellion. Later, however, he conspired to crown David's son Adonijah king even before David was dead. Instead, Solomon became king and punished Abiathar by removing him from his post.

RICH ROBES

The high priest wore special clothes when offering sacrifices to God. The outer garment was called an ephod, and it was made of richly embroidered linen. High priests also wore a breastplate encrusted with 12 jewels. Each stone bore the name of one of Israel's tribes.

Rabbi teaching

RABBIS AND PRIESTS

Jewish priests worked in the temple, holding worship services and offering sacrifices. But a priest's most important duty was to teach the law of God to the people. In the same way today, rabbis teach people the Jewish law and how to apply it to their lives. Rabbi means teacher.

THE HIGH PRIEST

The high priest was chosen from the family of Zadok. Under King Herod and the Romans, the high priest was picked from this family by the king or the governor. Usually the high priest kept his job until he died, but during the time Jesus was alive a new high priest was chosen more frequently.

Keeping Clean

◆ ◆ ◆

Pool of Siloam

A BEGGAR IS MADE TO SEE

Jesus once healed a blind beggar by making a lump of mud from saliva and dirt. He put it on the man's eyes, then told him to go wash in the Pool of Siloam. The beggar's neighbors were stunned to see him walking around, able to see.

PETER'S PREACHING

Once, the Apostle Peter gave a long and powerful sermon. He had just received the Holy Spirit, who gave him wisdom and just the right words to say to glorify God. Peter told the audience to turn to God for forgiveness and salvation. That day, the 3,000 people who had become believers were baptized!

KEEPING CLEAN was very important to the Hebrews, even though they lived before bathtubs and sinks. If someone touched a dead animal, or did certain things, or had certain diseases, they were unclean. Others could not touch them. They had to bathe in certain ways or wait a certain number of days before they could enter the Tabernacle or the temple. This was especially true of the priests, who had to take elaborate baths before they could offer sacrifices.

One of the diseases for which there were specific rules was leprosy. This was a terrible skin disease, and it spread easily from person to person. If someone had the disease, they had to live alone, outside the city or town. If they got better, they had to go to a priest before they could return to live with others. The priest sprinkled them with a mixture of blood and water seven times. Then the person had to wash their clothes, shave their head, and take a bath. All this sprinkling and washing did not cure them; they were already cured. They did it to show they were clean and to obey the Law.

Once a man named Naaman learned to obey God. He was a mighty man, the commander of the Syrian army. But he had leprosy. He came to the prophet Elisha with gifts, hoping to be healed. Elisha did not meet with him, but sent a message with his servant instead. "Go wash yourself in the Jordan River seven times and you will be healed," he said.

Naaman was furious. He said, "I thought he would call on the name of the Lord, wave his hand over me, and cure me." Naaman refused to go to the river and wash. He went home instead. "We have our own river in Damascus," he said.

But his servants encouraged him to go back and do what the prophet said. "If he asked you to do some great thing would you have done it? Why not do some little thing?" they asked.

So Naaman went and washed seven times in the Jordan River. His skin became like that of a young boy, clean and clear. Naaman learned that being clean was not just about water. It was about being obedient.

REPENT AND BE BAPTIZED

John the Baptist told the people to repent. If they did, he baptized them in the Jordan River. The water did not really wash their sins away or even make them clean. Being baptized just showed that they were willing to be clean and obedient. Later, the early church would require that new members be baptized.

WATER IS SYMBOLIC

Baptize comes from a Greek word that means to "dip." A person being baptized is often dipped completely under the water and then brought back up. Some churches today only sprinkle water on the person. Baptism reminds us of the death, burial, and resurrection of Christ.

Offerings to God

❖ ❖ ❖

A SWEET SMELL

One of the offerings made by the priest was incense. A special blend of spices was placed on the fire of a small altar just outside the Holy of Holies each morning and evening. The incense had a sweet smell, unlike the smell of blood and burning animals.

GOD COMMANDED the children of Israel to bring sacrifices and offerings to him. The most important of these sacrifices was the burnt offering. An animal was killed as a payment for sin. It could be a male bull, sheep, or dove, depending on how wealthy or poor the person was. The priest laid his hands on the head of the animal and then slit its throat. The blood was collected and sprinkled on the altar. The animal was then burned. In some cases, part was kept as food for the priests.

Grain was also offered as a sacrifice on the altar. It was a sacrifice of thanksgiving, reminding the people that their food came from God. The grain could either be cooked or ground into flour to make bread. The bread that was made as a sacrifice included oil but no yeast. It was not light and fluffy, but heavy and dense. It was called unleavened bread.

Sometimes the grain offering was simply parched green grain. Oil, spices, or salt might be added. The grain was given to the priest, who sprinkled some of it on the altar with the burnt offerings and kept the rest. People were expected to bring their very best to

FOUR HORNS OF THE ALTAR

One type of altar used for making sacrifices was a square pillar with four horns at each of its upper corners. A part of the blood from the sacrifice was placed on each of these horns. Both Israelites and Canaanites used altars, but an Israelite altar would have been more rounded.

THE FINAL SACRIFICE

Jesus is called the Lamb of God. The New Testament teaches that he was the last, great sacrifice for sin. Since he died for our sins, there is no need to sacrifice animals any more. The Book of Hebrews was written to explain to Jewish Christians how all of the Old Testament sacrifices and rituals were needed until Christ came to become our High Priest.

the altar. They could not bring an animal with spots or any wounds or sores. The grain could not be old and moldy. This was one way the people showed their awe of God.

Each day, offerings were made for all the people. Individuals could bring an offering at any time. They did this either to show God their sorrow or joy. Sometimes, they brought an offering when they made a promise to God to show they were serious.

At Passover, every family tried to bring a sacrifice to the temple in Jerusalem. The most important day of the year was the Day of Atonement. The people would not eat or drink all day, but they prayed for cleansing from their sins.

On that day only, the high priest entered the Holy of Holies, the place where God dwelled. The high priest offered a sacrifice for his own sins and then for the sins of the people.

Censers

HOLY OBJECTS

Censers were used to carry the coals upon which incense would be burned. Priests used these tools in the temple, and they were considered holy objects. The first censers were made of brass, but the ones in Solomon's temple were made of gold.

A Special Task

◆ ◆ ◆

ANOINTING WITH OIL was a special custom. A small amount of oil was poured on someone's head to show that he had been chosen for a special task. Only certain people could be anointed. Usually they were kings, prophets, or priests.

Samuel anointed the first two kings of Israel. One day, a handsome young man named Saul came to him, looking for some lost donkeys. God told Samuel that this would be Israel's first king. Samuel took Saul aside and poured some oil on his head. "You will be the king," he said. First Saul had to prove himself in battle. Then he became king. Samuel anointed him again, in front of all the people.

Later, Saul disobeyed God. God wanted a new king. "Fill your horn with oil and be on your way," God said to Samuel. "I am sending you to Jesse of Bethlehem. I have chosen one of his sons to be king."

When Samuel got there, he found that Jesse had eight sons. He didn't know which one to anoint. The oldest, Eliab, was a fine young man. "Surely this is the one," thought Samuel. "You look on the out-side, but I look on the inside," God said. "This is not the one."

So seven of Jesse's sons passed before Samuel. "The Lord has not chosen these," said

THE ANOINTED ONE

The word Christ means "anointed one." Jesus' followers called him by this Greek name so others would understand who he was. The name told people that Jesus had been chosen by God for a special task.

THE OIL OF JOY

Sometimes people used oil to refresh themselves in the hot, dusty climate. They rubbed it on themselves after a bath, or used it when a bath was not possible. The Psalms say that when brothers work together, it is like oil running down their face and off their beards. The Epistle to the Hebrews says God anointed Jesus with "the oil of joy."

Samuel. "Do you have any more sons?" "Just the youngest," said Jesse. "His name is David. He is out in the field taking care of the sheep." They sent for David. "Arise and anoint him," God said. "He is the one."

David had to prove himself, too. He killed a giant in battle and became a mighty warrior. When Saul died, David became Israel's greatest king. He was chosen for a special task.

Jesus was anointed, too, but not by a priest or prophet. Shortly before he died, a woman poured expensive perfume on his head and feet. Some people were offended. "Why didn't you sell the perfume and give the money to the poor?" they asked. "Leave her alone," Jesus said. "She has done a beautiful thing. She has poured perfume on me to prepare my body for burial." He knew that he would soon die for our sins. He had been chosen for a special task.

Olive trees

OIL'S MANY USES

Olive oil was used for anointing, but it had many common uses as well. The oil was used for cooking, for grooming a person's hair and skin, and as fuel for lamps.

ANOINT A PILLAR?

Jacob, a famous leader in the Old Testament, once anointed a stone pillar. When Jacob came to Bethel, God appeared to him and said his name would be changed to Israel, which means "one who struggles with God." To commemorate this event, Jacob built a stone pillar on the spot where the vision had appeared. He then poured wine over the pillar as an offering and anointed it with olive oil.

False Gods

◆ ◆ ◆

WHEN THE HEBREWS entered the promised land, the Canaanites already lived there. These people had their own customs and gods. God told the Hebrews not to marry these people or to copy their ways. Unfortunately, they didn't listen.

One of the things they copied was a way of worshiping, or at least a place of worshiping. These places were called high places. The high places were platforms built on the top of a hill or mountain where the Canaanites sacrificed to their gods. Although the Hebrews sacrificed animals to God, the Canaanites sometimes sacrificed humans, even babies.

Sometimes the Hebrews would try to worship both God and idols. This made God angry. He would send prophets to warn the people that he was going to judge them.

When David became king, he destroyed many of the high places. But after he died, other kings built them up again. One of these kings was Jeroboam, who built high places in Bethel and Dan. He made a golden calf for each place. One day, a prophet came to Jeroboam. "A new king will tear down these high places," he said. The king reached out to grab him, but the king's arm shriveled up.

"Pray for me," the king begged. So the prophet prayed, and God healed the king's arm. But the king did not repent. Many of the kings who followed him also worshiped in the high places and led the people away from the true God.

THE GOD OF THUNDER

The Canaanites worshiped many gods, but the main one was Baal, who they called the "Lord of all the Earth" and the god of weather. His voice was the thunder, and he hurled lightning from the sky. The Canaanites believed he made the rain come so the crops would grow.

The True God

◆　◆　◆

THE HEBREWS were different from their neighbors because they had only one God, a God who spoke to them and gave them rules to live by. "I will come down on Mount Sinai in the sight of all the people," God said to Moses. Then he did. There was thunder and lightning and the sound of a trumpet. The mountain shook, and fire came down from heaven.

Then God called Moses to the top of the mountain. There God gave Moses the Ten Commandments. He gave Moses other rules, too, about how the people should worship God and live together. Then God wrote these laws with his own finger on two tablets of stone.

Moses was on the mountain for 40 days. When he came down, the people had made a golden calf and begun to worship it. Moses was angry. He threw the stone tablets down and shattered them on the ground.

God wanted to destroy the people, but Moses prayed for them, and God forgave them. So Moses went back to the mountain, and God made new tablets. When Moses came back, his face was glowing, reflecting the glory of God. The tablets were kept in the Ark of the Covenant, which was carried by the priests.

The Lord had spoken to Moses face to face, as a man speaks with his friend. He was not like the false gods. He was a God who spoke to his people.

GOOD FRIENDS

God had an especially close relationship with three men in the Old Testament. The Bible says Moses "spoke to God face to face, as a man does with a friend." The Bible calls King David "a man after God's own heart." Abraham was called "a friend of God."

A Tent of Meeting

❖ ❖ ❖

THE CHILDREN of Israel wandered in the wilderness for 40 years. During this time, they lived in tents. They worshiped in a tent, too. It was a special tent called the tent of meeting, the Tabernacle.

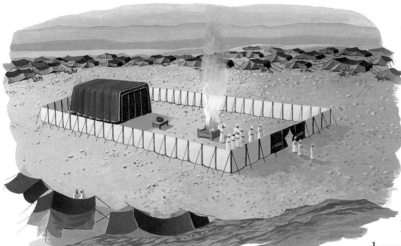

The Tabernacle was made of gifts from the people. These included gold, silver, and bronze, as well as blue, purple, and scarlet linen. God gave Moses very specific instructions about how the tent was to be made.

There was a courtyard around the Tabernacle. It was 150 feet long by 75 feet wide, made of fine linen curtains fastened to wooden poles with silver hooks. In the courtyard, there was a bronze altar and a basin of water so Moses and the priests could wash their hands and feet before they entered the Tabernacle.

The Tabernacle had two rooms; the outer room, called the Holy Place, and the inner room, the Holy of Holies. The walls were made of curtains, embroidered with angels in blue, purple, and scarlet thread. The whole thing was hung on gold-covered poles and overlaid with a goat hair tent. In the outer room, there was a table for bread, a lampstand with seven lamps, and an altar for burning incense. These were all made of acacia wood covered with pure gold.

A TEMPORARY HOME

The children of Israel worshiped in the Tabernacle or a tent like it for hundreds of years. Most of the time, the Tabernacle was at Shiloh. Finally, a temple was built in Jerusalem. Even though the temple was a magnificent structure made of stone and gold, it was still built with the same plan as the Tabernacle.

BEFORE THE TABERNACLE

Before the Tabernacle was built, Moses went up to Mount Sinai to meet with God. While he was there, the people grew tired of waiting for Moses, and they decided to build a golden calf to worship. Aaron told them to bring him their gold, and he built an idol out of it. The people offered sacrifices and danced around the altar the next day. God was very angry about this, but Moses pleaded with him to have mercy on the people.

CAMP MEETING

When the Hebrews were in the wilderness, the Tabernacle was in the center of the camp. The Levites camped on the north, west, and south sides. Moses and the priests camped on the east side. Around them camped the 12 tribes, three tribes on each side of the Tabernacle.

The inner room contained only one thing: the Ark of the Covenant. This was the most precious thing in the Tabernacle. It was a wooden chest covered with gold. Inside were the two tablets of the Ten Commandments, Aaron's rod, and a pot of manna. The Ark was covered with a solid gold lid, with a special altar called the Mercy Seat—this is where God sat. A golden cherubim was made for each end of the altar. Once a year, on the Day of Atonement, the high priest entered the Holy of Holies and sprinkled blood on the Mercy Seat.

The first time the Tabernacle was set up, a cloud came down and settled over it. The cloud was so bright that Moses could not even enter the tent. The glory of the Lord had filled the Tabernacle. The people had a place to meet with God.

ARK OF THE COVENANT

The Ark of the Covenant was a holy object that could not be touched. Even priests had to carry it with long poles. One day, while the Ark was being moved, the oxen carrying it stumbled. A man named Uzzah tried to catch the Ark and died instantly.

SHOWBREAD

Bread kept in the Tabernacle was so special that it was carried on gold trays and eaten only by priests. Called showbread, it was replaced every Sabbath with fresh loaves. There were 12 loaves, one for each of the 12 tribes of Israel.

A House for God

◆ ◆ ◆

THE CHILDREN OF ISRAEL worshiped God in a tent, called the tabernacle, for many years. But King David wanted to build a temple, a building where the people could always come to God. King David had bought land for the temple.

But God said David could not build the temple. "You are a man of war," he said. "Your son will build me a house." So when David's son Solomon became king, he did what his father had wanted to do. He built a magnificent temple for the Lord.

Solomon spared no expense in building the temple. He traveled to other nations for materials and advice. He used cedar wood from Lebanon. These huge trees had to be floated down the coast and then carried almost 40 miles up the mountains to Jerusalem. Huge stones were cut and dragged to the construction site, where they were fitted perfectly in place.

The temple itself was only 90 feet long and 30 feet wide. But everything was done with great care by skilled craftsmen. The basin in the courtyard held over 10,000 gallons of water. It

A HEAVY TAX

Solomon taxed the people heavily to pay for the temple and for his own expensive palace. He also forced many men to work on these projects. When his son became king, some of the people rebelled. They thought he would charge high taxes, too. The kingdom split in two, although for a long time both sides still came to the temple to worship.

WHAT'S IN A NAME?

There were two bronze columns outside the temple. They were about 30 feet high. Solomon named the two columns Jachin and Boaz. Jachin means "he establishes" and Boaz means "in him is strength." He wanted the people to know that God had helped to build it, and that he had blessed the temple.

stood on 12 bulls made of bronze. The walls inside the temple were covered with wood, carved with palm trees and flowers, and decorated with gold and jewels. Even the floor was covered with gold.

Solomon hired skilled craftsmen to help him build the temple, and he forced many of his people to help carry the logs and stone. Over 150,000 men helped build the temple. It took seven years.

Finally it was finished. The people gathered to dedicate the temple. They sacrificed so many sheep and cattle that no one could count them. Then the glory of God filled the temple and the people rejoiced. "Praise the Lord," Solomon said. "He has kept every one of his good promises."

God had brought the children of Israel home to the land he had promised Abraham. Now he had a house of his own, the temple.

A THRILLING SPECTACLE

The dedication of Solomon's temple was a thrilling event, for the building was the first permanent place of worship for the Jews. After the festivities and King Solomon's prayer, fire issued from heaven and consumed the sacrificial meat on the altar. God then filled the temple with bright light and smoke, showing that he was present.

BABYLON'S INVASION

Solomon's spectacular temple was destroyed almost 400 years later when the Babylonians invaded Jerusalem in 586 B.C. They robbed the temple of much of its gold and silver and burned both city and temple to the ground. The temple was rebuilt in a much simpler style about 80 years later.

A Place to Study

◆ ◆ ◆

AFTER THE TEMPLE was destroyed by the Babylonians, the people had no place to worship. Many of them were carried off to Babylon, where they sometimes met together to worship and pray.

When the Jews returned to their land and rebuilt the temple, they still liked the idea of gathering on their own to study the Law. Eventually, many towns and villages built a place where everyone could meet for prayer and instruction. These buildings were called synagogues.

There were no priests at the synagogue, and no sacrifices. The Sabbath service began with one man praying before a cupboard (called the ark) that contained a copy of the Law. Then everyone joined in the prayers. After that, a scroll was taken from the cupboard and someone was chosen to read parts of the Law. When he was finished, the man sat down and gave a sermon on what he read.

Jesus often did this when he began to teach and preach. One of his first sermons was at the synagogue in Nazareth, his hometown. He read from the

SCHOOL DAYS

Boys started school at the synagogue when they were five and continued until they were 13. They were taught to read. By the time they finished school, they knew most of the Old Testament by heart. There were also classes at the synagogue for adults. Girls did not go to school.

prophet Isaiah about the Messiah, the promised king and deliverer of Israel. "This is talking about me," he said. The people were furious because they thought he was only the local carpenter's son. They tried to throw him off a cliff, but he escaped.

An ark

INSIDE THE SYNAGOGUE

Synagogues were usually built so that the front door was facing Jerusalem. There was a section for women and children, who were not allowed to sit with the men. There was usually a raised platform for the reading of the lessons. The cupboard containing the Scriptures is called an ark. The Scriptures themselves are called the Torah.

Several times he healed people in the synagogues. This also made people angry because they believed no one should do any work on the Sabbath. But Jesus said it was more important to do good on the Sabbath. "If your ox fell in a ditch, wouldn't you pull it out?" he asked. He thought people were more important than cattle.

Later, the Apostle Paul would also preach in synagogues. As he traveled to different countries, he would go into a new city and go to the synagogue. There he would find Jews who already knew the Scriptures about the Messiah. Then he would tell them about Jesus. If they did not believe what he had to say, he would begin to tell those who were not Jews.

A NEW CHURCH

When the Apostle Paul went to Corinth, he stayed with Aquila and Priscilla for a year and a half. During the week, Paul worked as a tentmaker, but on the Sabbath he would go to the synagogue and teach. Many people believed the gospel and were baptized, including Crispus, the leader of the synagogue. This is how the church at Corinth began. Later, Paul wrote two letters to this church. These letters became part of the New Testament.

Seven Celebrations

◆ ◆ ◆

EACH YEAR the Hebrews had seven different festivals, or feasts. These special times were explained to Moses by God in the Book of Leviticus.

Three of them were all the same week, beginning with Passover. At Passover, the Jews remembered how Moses led them out of slavery in Egypt. The next day began the Feast of Unleaven Bread. For seven days, no one ate any bread made with yeast. Yeast was a symbol of evil. Just a little bit would make a whole loaf of bread rise. God wanted them to think about how even a little sin might affect a whole family or nation.

The day after that was the Feast of Firstfruits. Before they had any for themselves, they brought part of the new barley harvest to the Tabernacle or the temple. Then they poured wine on it. This was to praise God for the harvest.

Pentecost was 50 days later. The people brought two loaves of bread at the end of the wheat harvest to thank God for his blessing.

Six months after Passover, there were three more festivals. At the Feast of Trumpets, a special trumpet, called a shofar, was blown. Then the people

A SCAPEGOAT

On the Day of Atonement, a goat was sacrificed for the sins of the people. Then the high priest laid his hands on the head of another goat and confessed the sins the people had committed. This goat was called a scapegoat. It was led into the wilderness and released. Then the people shouted for joy. They believed the goat had carried their sins away. They would be so happy they would sing and dance.

THE LIVING WATER

Jesus went to Jerusalem to celebrate the Feast of Tabernacles. Each day of the festival a priest carried a silver basin of water around the altar and then climbed to the top and poured it on the altar. On the last day of the festival, Jesus said in a loud voice so everyone could hear: "If anyone is thirsty let them come to me and drink." He wanted to satisfy their thirst for spiritual things.

examined themselves to see if they had sinned. They did this for ten days.

The tenth day was the Day of Atonement, when the priest offered a sacrifice for all the people. Five days after that was the Feast of Tabernacles. The people built shelters out of branches and camped out for seven days. This was so they could remember when the children of Israel lived in tents in the wilderness.

For three of these festivals—Passover, Pentecost, and Tabernacles—Jews traveled to the temple in Jerusalem if they could. That's why there were so many Jews in Jerusalem when Jesus was crucified during Passover. And that's why there were so many Jews from different countries in Jerusalem when Peter preached at Pentecost.

By the time Jesus was born, the Jews had added two more festivals, the Feast of Lights and the Feast of Purim. At the Feast of Lights, they lit a candle every night of the feast. This is to remember the rededication of the temple under the Maccabees. The Feast of Purim remembered how God delivered them during the time of Queen Esther.

The festivals were special times for the people to remember God's blessings. During each festival, the people brought other sacrifices to God. They decorated their homes, read the Scriptures, and praised God. Jewish people today celebrate in much the same way.

Dressed up for Purim

A COSTUME PARTY

The Feast of Purim is the most fun of all the Hebrew holidays. Sometimes children wear costumes and go from house to house asking for a penny. When the scroll of Esther is read in the synagogue, the crowd jeers and stamps its feet when the name of wicked Haman is read. Haman tried to have all the Jews in Persia killed, but Queen Esther stopped him.

FARMING FEASTS

The Jewish festivals were designed to help the people remember that they had been slaves in Egypt. The festivals also marked the beginning (Firstfruits) and end (Tabernacles) of the harvest. Homes were often decorated with flowers. During the Feast of Tabernacles, the people marched around the altar waving palm branches.

The First Passover

GOD SENT MOSES to lead his people out of slavery in Egypt, but Pharaoh would not let the people go. So Moses turned the river into blood. Then he called on God to cover the land with frogs, then lice, and then flies. Still Pharaoh refused to free the people.

God sent more trouble. The people were covered with boils. Locust and hail destroyed their crops. The sky was black for three whole days. God sent nine plagues, but Pharaoh stubbornly refused to let the people go.

Finally, God said he would send one more plague, the worst of all. The oldest son in every family would die. The oldest calf, the oldest lamb, and the first born of the cattle would die, too. Moses warned Pharaoh that this would happen. "There will be loud wailing throughout Egypt," he said.

Ancient scroll

RENEWING A CUSTOM

How exciting to find something you've lost! King Josiah of Judah learned about Passover from old scrolls his high priest found. He held the festival for the first time in many years.

PASSOVER AND EASTER

The Christian Easter is always held on the first Sunday after the Jewish Passover. Passover's date varies, but it always comes at full moon in March or April.

But the children of Israel would be spared if they did what God commanded. Moses called the people together and told them what to do. They had to kill a lamb and roast it, smearing some of the blood over the door with a hyssop branch. They were to eat very quickly, with their cloak tucked up in their belt and their sandals on, ready to flee from Egypt. The people bowed and worshiped God. Then they returned to their homes to do what he had told them to do.

At midnight, an angel struck down all the firstborn in Egypt, from the oldest son of Pharaoh to the oldest sons of the prisoners in the dungeons. Pharaoh woke up in the middle of the night. Everyone was crying. There was

not a house without someone dead, except the houses of the Hebrews. The angel had passed over every home where the doorpost was smeared with the blood of a lamb.

Pharaoh called for Moses. "Go, take your people and leave," he said. And so the children of Israel left Egypt, free at last. For thousands of years, they have remembered this event with a special meal and a special celebration. It is the Passover. The Lord "passed over" their homes and set them free. Jews still celebrate it today.

THE HEBREWS' "THANKSGIVING"

The Passover meal was the most important one for the Hebrews, much as Thanksgiving would be for us. Everything had to be just right. The roast lamb would serve 10 to 20 people. Four cups of red wine were used. Bitter herbs and bread made without yeast reminded the people of how hard it had been to live in Egypt. Scriptural passages from the books of Exodus and Psalms were read to recall the first Passover.

A FAMILY CELEBRATION

After the temple was destroyed by the Babylonians, there was no place for the Hebrews to offer sacrifices at Passover. Passover became a family celebration; families would hold a special service of prayers, stories, and songs to recount the events of the first Passover.

A Day of Rest

◆ ◆ ◆

THE SABBATH was an important day for the Hebrews. It was the last day of the week, a day to rest from all their work, as God had instructed them in the Ten Commandments. The Sabbath reminded them that God had created the world in six days. On the seventh day he, too, had rested.

The Sabbath began on Friday evening when the sun went down. Supper was served, with prayers and songs and blessings. There was a service in the synagogue the next morning, followed by dinner. The Sabbath continued until Saturday evening.

Many rules governed what someone could and could not do on the Sabbath. They could not prepare food, light a fire, carry something heavy, buy or sell things, or travel. Some Jewish soldiers would not even fight on the Sabbath, not even to defend themselves. Eventually there were so many rules they were hard to keep track of.

A SABBATH REST

In ancient Israel, even the land got a rest. Every seventh year the people were not allowed to plant or harvest the land so it could be renewed. During this time, any food that grew on its own could be picked by anyone, including the poor and those who did not own land.

A SABBATH DAY'S JOURNEY

Jews were allowed to travel only about half a mile on the Sabbath, a distance called a Sabbath day's journey. This had been the distance between the Ark of the Covenant and the people when they traveled in the wilderness. It was also the distance allowed for pasture land outside the cities and towns.

One day, Jesus was walking through some grainfields on the Sabbath. His disciples were hungry and began to pick some of the grain and eat it. "Look," said some of the religious leaders. "Your disciples are breaking the Sabbath." But Jesus reminded them that when King David and his soldiers were hungry, they had entered the temple and eaten the special bread belonging to the priests. The priests themselves worked in the temple on the Sabbath. "The Sabbath was made for man, not man for the Sabbath," he said. "I am Lord of the Sabbath, too."

This made the religious leaders angry. But Jesus continued to challenge their rules. He healed a man with a withered hand on the Sabbath. And he healed others on the Sabbath, too. "It is right to do good on the Sabbath," he said.

A CHRISTIAN SABBATH

Christians do not celebrate the Sabbath, which is the last day of the week. Instead, they meet and celebrate on the first day of the week, Sunday. This is the day Jesus was raised from the dead. Many Christians try to set the day aside for rest as well as worship.

A SABBATH MIRACLE

When the children of Israel were in the wilderness, God sent bread from heaven, called manna, to feed them. Each day, they were to pick up just enough for that day. If they picked up more, it would spoil. But on the sixth day, they picked up enough for two days and it did not spoil. There was no manna on the seventh day. It was the Sabbath, a day of rest.

A SABBATH BLESSING

A common practice on the evening the Sabbath began was for the father to bless his children. He also often sang a hymn taken from the Book of Proverbs about a godly wife and mother. Women were more highly regarded by the Hebrews than by most other nations in those times.

The Lord's Supper

MANY NAMES

The celebration of the Last Supper has different names. It is called Communion, the Lord's Supper, and the Eucharist. (Eucharist is a Greek word that means "thanksgiving.") One church calls it the Love Feast—and includes an entire meal. Regardless of its name, all Christian churches observe this special meal that Jesus shared with his disciples.

A SACRED PROMISE

At the Lord's Supper, Jesus used the word covenant to describe the wine, which represented his blood. A covenant is a sacred promise God makes with those who love him and obey him. The Lord's Supper is a sign that God promises to forgive the sins of those who follow Jesus.

JESUS AND HIS DISCIPLES had come to Jerusalem for the Passover. It had been a busy week. Jesus had gone to the temple every day to teach. Now, he was alone with his disciples in a borrowed room, ready to share a special meal.

But first Jesus did something very unusual. He took a towel and a basin of water and washed his disciples' feet, which were caked with dust from the city streets. The disciples were shocked. This was something a servant or even something a slave did. "I am setting an example for you," Jesus said. "You must serve one another."

The disciples were confused. They did not know that Jesus would soon die. But Jesus knew he would die soon. He told them that one of them would betray him, and that Peter would deny even knowing him. They were even more confused.

Then Jesus took the bread and blessed it. He broke it in pieces and gave it to the disciples. "Take this and eat it," he said. "This is my body, which is broken for you." Next he took a cup of wine and passed it around the room. "Drink this," he said. "It is my blood, which will be shed for the forgiveness of sins." They passed the cup around the room and drank the wine, wondering what it all meant.

"I will not drink wine with you again until we drink it together in my Father's kingdom. But until then, do this to remember me," Jesus said. Then he tried to calm their fears. "Don't be troubled. I'm going to prepare a place for you in my Father's house," he promised.

The Cenacle in Jerusalem, where Jesus may have celebrated the Last Supper.

A PASSOVER LAMB

The Lord's Supper was celebrated at the Passover. The Apostle Paul later compared Jesus' death on the cross to the lamb each family sacrificed at Passover. John the Baptist called Jesus "the Lamb of God, who takes away the sins of the world." The Apostle John describes Jesus as a lamb in the Book of Revelation.

AN ORDERLY TABLE

In the early church, the Lord's Supper was a whole meal, not just the bread and wine. The Apostle Paul wrote a letter to the church at Corinth and scolded them for the way they ate this meal together. Some people took more than others, and some drank too much wine. He said they should be serious about this important ceremony.

After that, he prayed for them. They sang a song together and went out to a garden where Jesus prayed. That same night, soldiers arrested him. Later, he was crucified. Three days after that, he came back from the dead. Then he returned to heaven to keep his promise.

The disciples remembered what he said. They shared wine and bread. It helped them remember he had died for them.

Promises to Keep

❖ ❖ ❖

A NAZIRITE WAS a man or woman who made a special promise to God. This promise is called a vow. They showed their devotion and service to God by following three rules. First, they could not cut their hair. Second, they could not eat or drink anything made from grapes—including raisins or wine. Finally, they could not touch a dead body, even if it was their own parents.

They made this promise for a certain period of time, but at least for a month. Sometimes they took this vow for the rest of their lives. Usually they volunteered, but parents could set their child apart as a Nazirite for life.

If the vow was a temporary one, they brought a sacrifice to the Lord at the end of their vow. Then their head was shaved, and the hair was burned on the altar.

The most famous Nazirite in the Bible is Samson, whose parents had made him a Nazirite from birth. His mother even avoided drinking wine before he was born. Because of this vow, God gave him great strength. He was a mighty warrior, who defeated the Philistines single-handed.

KEEP YOUR PROMISES

The Hebrews were very careful about keeping their vows because of a commandment in the Law. It says: "If a man makes a vow to the Lord, he must not break his word, but must do everything he said."

NO SWEARING

An oath was a special promise made before God. It involved using God's name and was usually made in front of a prophet or priest. Sometimes people did this on their own. Jesus said to be very careful about using God's name in this way. "Just say yes or no," he said. "Anything more will get you in trouble."

But Samson fell in love with a Philistine woman who talked him into telling her the secret of his strength. She had his hair cut off, and he became as weak as any other man.

The prophet Samuel was also a Nazirite. He did not cut his hair or drink wine. Like Samson's mother, Samuel's mother promised him to God before he was born.

Modern Hasidic Jew

BEARDS AND HAIR

The Hebrews cared a great deal about their beards and hair. Hebrew men did not cut their hair at the temples nor trim the corners of their beards. Modern Hasidic Jews still wear their hair like this.

There are many other examples of vows in the Bible. Some vows were simply bargains with God or someone else. Jacob vowed to worship God and give him a tenth of everything if God would take care of him. Sometimes vows were promises that showed how serious someone was. These vows often involved not eating or sleeping. Vows were very important promises. The Book of Ecclesiastes says it is better not to make a vow than to make one and not keep it, especially if the vow is made to God.

DANCING IN THE STREET

When King David decided to bring the Ark of the Covenant to Jerusalem, he vowed not to go home or go to bed or even go to sleep until the job was done. David was so happy that he danced in the streets when the Ark was brought into the city.

A RASH VOW

Jephthah was one of the judges of Israel. He made a rash vow, one he soon regretted. If God would give him victory, he promised to sacrifice whatever came out of his house to meet him when he returned from battle. He did win. But he was heartbroken when his only daughter came out to meet him, dancing to the sound of tambourines. In Old Testament times, animals as well as people stayed in the house. Jephthah thought an animal would come out.

Questions & Answers

◆ ◆ ◆

Q: Where did the devil come from?

A: Satan was an angel who decided he wanted to be like God. He rebelled and was thrown out of heaven with some of his followers. These fallen angels are called demons. Satan and his demons have great power, but the Bible says some day they will be defeated and destroyed.

Q: What should a king wish for?

A: God asked Solomon in a dream what he wanted most. Solomon, as a new king, asked for wisdom to rule his people fairly. God was so pleased with Solomon's request that he granted his wish—and God gave him wealth and fame as a bonus.

Q: How important was a synagogue?

A: Very important. Because the synagogue was the center of the community, it was used for more than worship. Sometimes it was used for a court, a school, and a place to talk about politics. Some synagogues had a place for visiting teachers to stay.

Q: Why did an altar have horns?

A: The altar of burnt offering had pointed corners called horns. This was the ultimate place of safety, like home base in a really serious game of tag. First Kings tells of

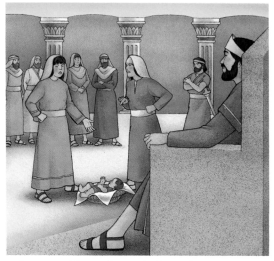

Solomon used his wisdom to find out who a baby's real mother was.

two men who clung to the horns for protection. When the prophet Amos said the horns of the altar would be cut off, he was saying there would be no place to hide.

Q: How long was Jesus dead?

A: Jesus was dead from Friday afternoon, when he was crucified, until Sunday morning, when he was resurrected. It totaled about 36 hours. This was considered three days because the Jews counted any part of a day as a whole day.

Q: Who has the keys to heaven?

A: Jesus said he would give Peter the keys to the kingdom of heaven. Peter became the leader of the early church, showing thousands of people the way to God. The Book of Revelation says Jesus has used the "key of David" to open a door to God that no one can shut.

Q: What was the most serious job in the Bible?

A: Once a year the High Priest had to enter the Holy of Holies, the place of God's awesome power and presence. The priest wore golden bells so he could be heard—and a rope tied around his foot so he could be pulled out if he fainted or died!

Q: Did prophets have crystal balls?

A: Sometimes prophets told the people what was going

to happen, but they didn't need a crystal ball. God spoke to them directly and told them what to say. That wasn't their main job, however. Most of the time, prophets warned the people and the kings of God's coming judgment of their sins. Needless to say, prophets weren't very popular.

Q: Can anyone predict the future?

A: The priests and prophets of other gods tried to tell the future by consulting the stars, analyzing smoke, or even studying the livers of dead animals. The Bible condemns these practices as idol worship and witchcraft. Only God can say what the future holds.

Q: How valuable was gold?

A: The value of gold depends on how common it is. King Solomon brought in about 50,000 pounds of gold a year—2.5 billion dollars worth. Gold was so plentiful that silver was considered almost worthless. There's a lot of gold in heaven, too, where it may even be used to pave the streets.

Q: What did Solomon do with all that gold?

A: He used a lot of it to build the temple, where even the walls were covered with gold. He also used silver, bronze, and iron, along with all kinds of jewels, purple

Daniel prayed to God, even though he knew he would be thrown into the lions' den for doing it.

and red fabric, stone blocks, and the wood of cedar, olive, and cypress trees. When he was done, he built a palace for himself and several for his wives.

Q: When is the best time to pray?

A: Anytime. Daniel prayed three times a day in his bedroom, but Nehemiah prayed while he worked—often quick prayers under his breath during a crisis. Jesus prayed early in the morning and late at night. The Apostle Paul said we should pray to God constantly!

Q: Did children run in the synagogue?

A: Probably not. They likely got in trouble for doing it! The Talmud said a Jew should not run when he leaves the synagogue—but it's all right to run to the synagogue. That's because we should be eager to hear God's Word.

Q: What's the most famous prayer in the Bible?

A: For Christians, the most famous prayer is the Lord's Prayer, which Jesus taught his disciples when they asked him how to pray. For Jews, it is the Shema, a prayer used in all their religious services. The name comes from the first word of the first sentence— "Hear, O Israel, the Lord your God is one."

Miracles

◆ ◆ ◆ ◆

I F YOU HAVE FAITH, you can and should expect the unexpected. Turning water into wine, taking Elijah to heaven in a fiery chariot, raising the dead: These miracles are no problem for God. He often used his followers, and sometimes his angels, to do great and wonderful things. He is an amazing and awesome God who shows his power to those who believe him. So expect great things—because these stories are true.

The World Begins

◆　◆　◆

THE CREATION of the world was one miracle after another. First there was only cold and shapeless darkness spread out over the surface of a deep and silent sea. But the Spirit of God was there, hovering and waiting.

Then God spoke. "Let there be light," he said. He saw that the light was good, and he separated it from the darkness. Then there was day and night. And that was the first day.

The next day he made the sky, and the day after that he made the dry ground. He filled the earth with trees and plants—all beautiful shades of green, with flowers of every color. And he saw that it was good.

On day four, sunlight flooded the morning sky, and the moon and stars began to rule the night. "Let there be lights in the sky," God said. And it was so.

Then he filled the sea with fishes and the sky with birds. There were porpoises and angelfish and whales. There were trout and bass and salmon. And above them eagles soared, as white doves cooed in the cool, dark trees and nightingales broke into song. "Very good," God said. "Very, very good." And that was the fifth day.

The sixth day he made animals: rabbits and rhinoceros,

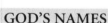

GOD'S NAMES

The Old Testament was written in Hebrew. The Hebrew name used for God in the very first verse of the Bible is Elohim, which means "Strong One." Other names used for God in the Old Testament are Adonai, which means "Lord," and Yahweh, which means "I am the One who is."

IN THE BEGINNING

Like the first book of the Bible, Genesis, the Gospel of John starts with "In the beginning." But John's focus is on Jesus, calling him the Word that "became flesh and dwelt among us."

horses and hippopotamuses, cats and kangaroos, lizards and llamas. Suddenly the world was alive with creeping, crawling creatures. But there was still something missing.

"I will make man in my own image," God said.

So he leaned down and picked up some dust from the ground, and he fashioned it into a human shape. He breathed into it, and it became a man. Now that's a miracle!

He named the man Adam. But still something was not quite right. "It is not good for man to be alone," God said. So while Adam was asleep, he took a bone from Adam's side and made a woman. Her name was Eve.

It was the end of the sixth day. Finally God was done. He looked across the earth at all he had made. He saw the waterfalls crashing down the mountain sides. He saw the young deer leaping through the meadow. He saw the fish splashing in the lakes and ponds.

"It's very good," God said. And then he rested. It was the seventh day.

GARDEN OF EDEN

After God created Adam and Eve, he placed them in the Garden of Eden to take care of the plants and animals. No one knows exactly where the garden was. Later Adam and Eve displeased God, and he made them leave the garden. An angel with a flaming sword guarded the garden to keep them from coming back.

HEAVEN'S MEANINGS

The word heaven can mean three things: the atmosphere; the sky with stars, moon, and sun; and the place where God dwells.

In the Wilderness

◆ ◆ ◆

THE CHILDREN OF ISRAEL were slaves in Egypt, until one day God sent Moses to lead them to freedom in the promised land. This escape from Egypt is called the Exodus. Many miracles were part of the Exodus.

As the people fled, Pharaoh chased after them with more than 600 chariots and horsemen. The people were walking or running, pulling carts with all their belongings. They came to the edge of the Red Sea and huddled there—they were unable to go on.

But Moses told the people not to be afraid. "The Lord will fight for you," he said. Then Moses stretched his hand out over the sea, and a strong wind began to blow. It blew all night, drying a path between walls of water. The next morning, the Israelites marched through on dry land.

Pharaoh and his army were close behind. "After them!" Pharaoh commanded. But as his army crossed, the wind stopped and the walls of water slammed down on top of them, drowning them all. The people of God cheered, and the women danced, and Moses' sister Miriam sang a song: "Sing to the Lord, for he has triumphed.

Jordan River

ENTERING THE PROMISED LAND

Another miraculous parting of the waters occurred at the Jordan River when the Israelites entered the promised land. The priests carried the Ark of the Covenant. When they stepped into the water, the river parted, and the Hebrews crossed safely to the other side.

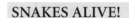

SNAKES ALIVE!

One day, God punished the people because they complained so much. He sent poisonous snakes, and people began to die. "We have sinned," they said. Then God had Moses hang a brass snake on a pole in the middle of the camp. If the people looked at the pole, they would live. If they refused, they died.

ONE OMER

When God provided manna, he told everyone to gather what they needed—one omer for each person in the family. An omer was a measurement equal to about two quarts. The people who disobeyed and gathered more than an omer had none left over, but the people who gathered what they were told always had plenty!

He has thrown the horse and rider in the sea."

But there were more miracles to come. A pillar of cloud went before them, leading them. At night, the pillar became a cloud of fire.

When the cloud moved, the people moved. When the cloud stopped, they camped and waited. It was a long trip. It took 40 years.

During this time, the people often complained. "What shall we drink?" they asked. Moses tossed a branch into a pool of bitter water, and it became sweet. Twice he struck a rock with his staff, and fresh, cool water poured out on the dry desert ground.

"What shall we eat?" they asked. God rained bread down from the sky each night. "What is it?" they asked. And that's what they called it—manna, which means "what is it?" Each morning, the children of Israel gathered the honey-tasting wafers from the ground and used it for baking or ate it like cereal.

But then they complained about that, too. "We want meat," they said. So God sent quail, millions of them. Some people gathered and ate so many of the small birds that they became sick. Still the people complained, even though they lived in the midst of miracles.

TELLING NAMES

Moses called the desert place where he struck rock with his staff Massah and Meribah, meaning "testing" and "quarreling," because the people complained so much. They had found fault with their leader and cried, "Is the Lord among us or not?"

The Power of the Prophets

❖ ❖ ❖

WHEN THE PEOPLE of Israel did not love and serve God, he often sent prophets to warn them before he punished them. Sometimes the people listened. Sometimes they did not. Often God helped the prophets do miracles to get their attention.

For example, when King Jeroboam reached out to keep one prophet from destroying an altar, the Lord shriveled the king's hand. But when the prophet prayed, the king's hand was healed.

Sometimes the prophets could tell what would happen in the future. When King Jehoshaphat's army was stranded in the desert with no water, Elisha told him to dig ditches because there was going to be a flood—and there was, the very next day. The prophets could even tell what would happen a long time in the future. Micah predicted where Jesus would be born hundreds of years before it happened.

Because the prophets often warned the people about their sins, they were not very popular. Sometimes people threw rocks at them, or the kings tried to put them in jail. But God protected his prophets and took care of them.

When Elijah was hiding from King Ahab near a small

HEALING BONES

On their way to bury a man, some Israelites saw a gang of bandits. Frightened, they threw the dead man's body into Elisha's tomb. When the dead body touched Elisha's bones, the man came back to life.

THE WOMAN FROM SHUNEM

A woman from Shunem had only one son, who died. She asked the prophet Elisha for help. Elisha prayed and then covered the boy with his body, lying mouth to mouth, eyes to eyes, hands to hands. He could feel the boy's body getting warm. Elisha got up and walked around, then repeated what he had done before. Finally the boy sneezed seven times and opened his eyes.

brook, God sent ravens twice a day with bread and meat. Eventually the brook dried up because there was no rain. God was judging the people for their sin just as Elijah had promised.

Crops were not growing, so there was very little food. God told Elijah to go to a small town where a widow would take care of him. The widow said she had no food, just enough for her to make one last meal for her and her son.

But Elijah told her God would take care of her. So she made Elijah a small piece of bread from her last little bit of flour and oil. But then there was more. In fact, her flour and oil never ran out, not until it began to rain again.

While Elijah was at her house, the woman's son died. But Elijah prayed for him, and he asked God to bring him back to life. Then he carried the small boy to his mother. "Look, your child is alive," he said. She was amazed. "Now I know you are a man of God," she said.

JEREMIAH'S TRIBULATIONS

Jeremiah was another prophet sent to tell people to obey God. But no one listened. Once, some angry people threw him into a deep well and then looked down and laughed at him. But after Jeremiah was rescued, he still continued to preach obedience to God.

AFTER ME!

God had called Elisha to take Elijah's place as God's prophet. But Elisha asked for a double share of God's spirit—double the power that Elijah had. So Elijah told Elisha that if he watched as he was taken to heaven, Elisha would receive that amount of power from God. So when God sent a whirlwind and a chariot and horses of fire to take Elijah to heaven, Elisha watched. Elisha was then God's prophet.

Jonah and the Whale

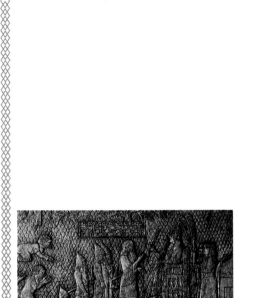

Art of King Sennacherib

THE DESTRUCTION OF SENNACHERIB

One Assyrian king, Sennacherib, tried to conquer Jerusalem. "He will not enter this city or shoot an arrow here," said the prophet Isaiah. When Sennacherib woke up the next morning, his soldiers were all dead. He took down his tent and went back to Nineveh.

WHEN GOD asked the prophet Jonah to go to Nineveh and preach, Jonah didn't want to go. Nineveh was the capital of Assyria, and Assyria was the enemy of Israel.

So Jonah took off in the opposite direction, on a ship headed to Tarshish. But God had other plans. He sent a violent storm, and the sailors were all afraid the ship would break in pieces. They began to throw things overboard, hoping to make the ship lighter.

Jonah knew what must be done. "Throw me overboard and the sea will become calm," he said. At first the sailors did not want to do that, so they rowed even harder to get to shore. But the storm got worse and worse, and finally they pitched Jonah into the angry sea.

Immediately, the sea became calm. That was the first miracle. But then a big fish swallowed Jonah whole, and that was a miracle, too. Jonah lived inside the fish for three days.

On the third day, Jonah prayed for God to deliver him, and the fish spit him up on the shore. Jonah went straight to Nineveh and began to preach. "Forty more days and Nineveh will be destroyed," he said.

To his surprise, they believed him. This was a miracle, too.

THE END OF NINEVEH

Although the people of Nineveh turned to God when Jonah preached, their children and grandchildren did not follow the Lord. A hundred years later, the prophet Nahum told how God would destroy Nineveh because the people there were so violent. "All who hear the news will clap their hands," Nahum said. Nahum's prediction came true in 612 B.C.

These were evil people, perhaps the cruelest who ever lived. "Let everyone call on God and give up their evil ways," the king said. "Maybe God will change his mind and have compassion on us then."

Jonah went outside the city and sat down to wait. When the 40 days were up, nothing happened. "That's just what I was afraid of," Jonah said to God. "I knew you would forgive them."

Jonah sat there waiting, hoping God would change his mind and destroy the city. Overnight, a vine grew up to shade Jonah from the hot sun. He was glad for the shade. But that night God sent a worm that chewed the vine so that it died. Jonah was so angry at the worm—and at God—that he wanted to die, too.

"Why are you so angry?" God asked. "You were concerned about the vine, even though you did not tend it or make it grow. But I made the people of Nineveh—including the children who live there. Shouldn't I be concerned about them?"

So God spared Nineveh. And he taught his prophet Jonah a lesson, too.

Castor oil plant

JONAH'S SHADE TREE

The plant that grew up over Jonah was probably a castor oil plant. This bush grows as tall as a tree. It grows quickly and has very large leaves. Jonah's plant grew up overnight, much faster than usual. Not only did a worm destroy the plant, but a hot east wind made the prophet even more uncomfortable.

PHOENICIAN SHIPS

Jonah left from the port of Joppa on a Phoenician ship. These were small wooden ships propelled by sails, with a crew of rowers just in case of no wind. They sailed near the shore, since they had no way to steer on cloudy nights when they couldn't see the stars. If a storm came up, they would row as hard as they could toward land.

A Festival of Lights

◆ ◆ ◆

BETWEEN THE OLD and New Testaments, the Jewish people were ruled by the Greeks under Alexander the Great. When his empire split up, they were ruled by Syria—including one king who wanted the Jews to act like the Greeks.

He made it against the law for the people to rest on the Sabbath, and he tried to make the people worship Greek gods. He even sacrificed a pig in the temple. The Jews thought pigs were unclean, and they were insulted and angry. Some of them broke the new laws and were killed.

One day, the Greeks came to a small village and commanded the people to sacrifice a pig. Mattathias, an old priest, was angry and killed a Jewish man who tried to do this. Mattathias and his sons fought the Greek soldiers and hid in the mountains, coming down from time to time to attack them.

After Mattathias died, his son Judas became the leader. His soldiers were untrained, and they had simple weapons. But as they fought, they picked up the better weapons of their enemies and had more and more success.

Ancient Roman coins

THE MACCABEANS

Judas had a nickname. He was called Maccabee, which means "the hammer." His followers ruled Jerusalem for about 100 years until the Romans marched into the city, killing thousands of Jews. This happened about 60 years before Jesus was born. The Romans taxed the people heavily, and they often mistreated them. When Jesus was born, many people still remembered what it was like to be free.

A MIRACLE REMEMBERED

According to Jewish tradition, a miracle occurred when Judas and his followers restored the temple. They found a small jar of special holy oil for the temple candlestick, but there was only enough oil for one day. But the candle burned for eight days, long enough for the priests to prepare more oil.

Before each battle, they would go without food and pray. Then Judas would remind his men why they were fighting. "It is better for us to die than to see how the Greeks have treated our temple," he said.

Finally, Judas and his band defeated the Greeks and swept back into Jerusalem. They tore down the Greek idols and cleaned the temple. New priests were trained. And new, clean bowls and jugs and candlesticks were made for the new temple. Judas dedicated the temple again, lighting a special lampstand called a menorah.

Every year on that same day, Jews should celebrate by lighting the first candle of a menorah, he said. Each night they should light a new candle until all eight candles are lit. There should be singing and laughter and joy. Jewish families today still celebrate this.

HANUKKAH

Jews celebrate this story each December. During a holiday called Hanukkah, a candle is lit each night for eight nights. Children play games and sing. Gifts are exchanged, much like Christians do at Christmas. Many Jews eat latkes, a potato pancake, and spin a special top called a dreidl. Hanukkah is also called the Festival of Lights.

A BIBLE STORY?

This story is not found in the Bible used by some Christians. It is found in the Apocrypha, part of the Bible used by the Catholic church. First Maccabees 1–4 tells this true story, one remembered by both Christians and Jews.

Angels We Have Heard on High

◆ ◆ ◆

MANY MIRACLES occurred when Jesus was born. Most of them involved angels.

One angel, named Gabriel, went to an old priest named Zechariah. He told Zechariah that he would have a son, a prophet who would prepare the way of the Lord. Zechariah did not believe the angel because he and his wife, Elizabeth, were too old to have a baby.

Later, Gabriel went to Mary and told her she would have a special son. "You have found favor with God," he said. "You will have a son and call him Jesus, because he will save his people from their sins." This would be no ordinary son, but the Son of the Most High God.

"May it be to me as you have said," Mary said. She was so excited that she went to tell her cousin—who already knew. When Mary entered the room, Elizabeth's own baby leapt for joy, even though he was still inside her.

In the meantime, an angel went to Mary's fiancé, Joseph,

A SON OF DAVID

Matthew lists the ancestors of Joseph, Jesus' legal, earthly father. Luke lists the ancestors of Jesus' mother, Mary. Both lists include David, the king of Israel. God promised David that one of his sons would rule forever.

A MAGNIFICENT PRAYER

When Mary went to visit her cousin Elizabeth, she prayed a beautiful prayer poem called the Magnificat. "My spirit rejoices in God, for he has done great things for me," she said. The prayer, which you can read in Luke 1, shows how much Mary loved God and loved Scripture. She quoted from over 15 verses in the Old Testament in this short prayer.

too. "Don't be afraid to marry her," the angel said. "The baby she is going to have was made by the Holy Spirit."

So Joseph, a carpenter from Nazareth, took Mary as his wife. They went to Bethlehem because Joseph had to register to pay his taxes. They stayed in a room with animals because there were no other rooms available. While they were there, Mary had her baby.

Then there were more angels. Lots of them. One appeared to some shepherds on the nearby hills and told them the Messiah had been born. Suddenly, the night sky was filled with light, as thousands of angels appeared, praising God and singing.

The angels stayed around to protect the baby, too. Later, some wise men came to worship Jesus, bringing him gifts. They had stopped in Jerusalem on the way and told King Herod about the Christ child. "After you visit the child, come and tell me where he is so I can worship him, too," Herod said.

But an angel warned them not to return to Jerusalem because the king really wanted to kill Jesus. And an angel came to Joseph, too, and urged him to take his family and go to Egypt, because the king planned to kill all the young children in Bethlehem.

There were angels everywhere, watching over the young Jesus.

THE GIFTS OF THE MAGI

The wise men who visited the baby Jesus were called magi. They were experts in the study of stars—and they followed one to Bethlehem to find Jesus. We don't know how many magi there were, but they brought gifts fit for a king: gold, incense, and myrrh. Incense is a perfume. Myrrh is a spice that was used to prepare a body for burial.

CHRISTMAS DAY

No one knows when Jesus was born. The early Christians picked December 25 as a day to remember his birthday long after he returned to heaven. It may have been picked because the Romans already celebrated a holiday on that date.

Food for Thought

◆ ◆ ◆

SHORTLY AFTER Jesus picked his disciples, they were all invited to a wedding with his mother, Mary. He must have done some amazing things as a child, because she came to him and whispered, "Jesus, they have run out of wine." Then she told the servants, "Do whatever he tells you to do."

There were six huge water jugs sitting nearby, each one large enough to hold 30 gallons. "Fill them up with water," Jesus said. And so they did just what he said. "Now take some to the master of the feast and ask him to taste it," Jesus said. They did that, too.

The master was amazed. "This is the best wine I've ever tasted," he said. He didn't know what had happened, but Jesus' disciples did. They were amazed, too.

They would be even more amazed before Jesus was through. Some time later, a crowd gathered around him as he traveled through the countryside, and he taught them and healed their sick. As the day wore on, the people became tired and hungry—but there was no place to buy food.

"Give them something to eat," Jesus said. "There is a boy here with five small loaves and two fishes," the disciples

WORRY NOT

Matthew 6:25 states, "Do not worry about your life, what you will eat or what you will drink, or about your body, what you will wear. Is not life more than food, and the body more than clothing?" The Bible also says if God cares enough to provide food for the birds, he will surely provide for us, too.

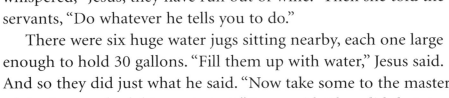

PICKING GRAIN ON SABBATH

The Sabbath was supposed to be a day of rest—not work. But one time on the Sabbath, Jesus and his disciples were walking through a grain field. Because they were hungry, they picked some grain to eat. People immediately accused them of breaking the Law. Jesus reminded them that obeying God was more important than following rules. He was master of the Sabbath, and he had the authority to do what he wanted on the Sabbath.

answered. "But that's all we have." It was enough. Jesus had the people sit down on the grass. There were over 5,000 of them. Then he prayed and had the disciples pass the food to all the people. They kept passing it out and passing it out and the people kept eating and eating until they were full.

That small boy's lunch was enough for all those people. When everyone was through eating, they collected 12 baskets of leftovers. Jesus did the same thing later, with 4,000 people and seven loaves.

LOAVES AND FISHES

The loaves of bread Jesus used to feed the 5,000 were really small round loaves like pita bread we eat today. The fish were small, too, and probably were pickled or smoked. The 5,000 counted only the men, not the women and children.

Soon, people followed him everywhere, hoping he would feed them again. But he didn't, and he said he had something more important than food. "I am the Bread of Life," Jesus said. "Those who come to me will never go hungry." Jesus was talking about the hunger people have in their hearts, not in their stomachs. He can fill us up with love.

Ancient jar used for water or wine

BREAD AND WINE

Christians use bread to celebrate communion, or the Eucharist, in order to remember Jesus' death. The small amount of bread and wine or grape juice are not meant to feed a person's physical hunger but rather they represent spiritual food.

The Great Physician

◆ ◆ ◆

OVER HALF of the miracles the Bible tells about Jesus doing involved healing people. And the Bible says he healed many others, too, who are not mentioned in the Bible.

At least five times he made blind people see. One of these was Bartimaeus, a beggar along the road in Jericho. Like most blind people in the ancient world, he had to ask for money just to survive. There were no jobs and no help from the government.

One day, when Bartimaeus was sitting by the road, he heard a crowd passing. "What's going on," he asked someone passing by. Bartimaeus called to Jesus, but the people yelled at him and told him to be quiet. But he kept shouting, "Jesus, Son of David, have mercy on me."

Suddenly Jesus stopped. "What do you want?" he asked. "I want to see," said Bartimaeus. "Your faith has healed you," Jesus said, and immediately Bartimaeus could see.

This story is like many others. Wherever Jesus went, he healed the sick. He healed ten lepers at one time. He healed people with fevers and people who were deaf.

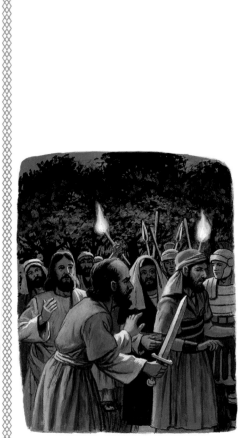

LOVE YOUR ENEMIES

Jesus felt compassion for the sick—even when they were his enemies. When soldiers came to arrest Jesus, Peter tried to defend him. Peter took out his sword and cut off the ear of one soldier who came to get Jesus. Jesus picked up the ear and put it back on the man, healing him completely.

NOT OUT FOR GLORY

Jesus performed miracles to help people, not to impress them. Often, he took only Peter, James, and John with him and told the person he healed not to tell anyone.

AN EXORCISM

Jesus was especially kind to women and children. A Greek woman whose daughter was possessed by an evil spirit begged him to drive the demon out. Jesus tested her faith by saying he should help the Jews first. But she was persistent: She asked for just a crumb of his goodness and power for her child. Jesus told her to go home because the demon had left her daughter. When the woman arrived, she found that her daughter had recovered.

He also healed people who were paralyzed, like a young man whose friends brought him to a crowded house where Jesus was teaching. They tore a hole in the roof of the house and let his stretcher

down by ropes. Jesus forgave his sins and healed him, too. The chief priests and elders were upset that Jesus said he could forgive sin. This was something only God could do.

He healed one paralyzed man without even going to see him. An officer in the Roman army came to Jesus and asked him to heal his servant. Jesus offered to go to his house, but the soldier said, "Just say the word and my servant will be healed." "Go, and it will be done just like you believed it would," Jesus said. The servant was healed at that very moment.

Everywhere he went, Jesus was concerned about sick people, and he healed them. People would bring their sick family members and lay their mats in the streets. If Jesus walked by and they just touched his coat, they were healed.

He is the Great Physician.

PETER'S SICK RELATIVE

Jesus cared about women. One day, he went home with Peter. They found Peter's mother-in-law sick in bed with a high fever. Jesus spoke to her and, taking her by the hand, helped her up. Immediately she felt well enough to help serve a meal.

Walking on Water

◆ ◆ ◆

JESUS LIVED most of his life near the Sea of Galilee. Some of his miracles had to do with water and fish. In fact, one of these miracles is how he "caught" some of his disciples.

One day, as Jesus was teaching, he saw three fishermen cleaning their nets beside two boats at the water's edge. Jesus asked Peter if he could teach from his boat. After he finished teaching, he told Peter to go out and let down his nets again.

Peter and his friends had spent all night fishing without any luck. And he had just finished cleaning his nets. But Peter obeyed Jesus. When he let down his nets, he caught so many fish his nets began to break.

Peter called for his friends to help, and both boats were so full of fish they almost sank. All three men became disciples. "I will make you fishers of people," said Jesus.

Later, Jesus sent all the disciples away in a boat so he could be alone to pray. But as they started across the lake, a storm came up. Strong winds began to blow, and the waves grew rough, crashing over the sides of the little boat.

The disciples rowed hard, trying to get to shore. Suddenly, they were afraid. They saw

WHAT'S REALLY IMPORTANT

Jesus said people look at the sky and predict the weather. (A red sky can mean a storm.) But he said it's more important to know God's Word so they can know what's coming in life.

WHERE IS YOUR FAITH?

Storms didn't bother Jesus. Once, on a trip across the lake with his disciples, Jesus fell fast asleep. A gale blew up, and the boat was in danger of sinking. The disciples were frantic as they saw Jesus peacefully sleeping. They yelled to wake him up, saying they were going to drown. Jesus told the wind and the raging waters to stop, and everything became calm. Then he asked his disciples, "Where is your faith?"

THE ROCK

Simon, one of Jesus' first and closest disciples, was renamed. Jesus called him Peter, or Cephas, which both mean "rock." Later, Peter's strength and growing faith were to make him a leader of the early church.

Fishing on the Sea of Galilee

SKILLED FISHERMEN

At least six of Jesus' disciples were fishermen and knew about boats, lakes, and fishing. The boats they used were small sailboats that they rowed when there was too much or too little wind. The disciples were accustomed to being on the lake after dark since they fished at night.

someone walking toward them on the water—and they thought it was a ghost. It was Jesus. "Don't be afraid," he said.

It was still dark and stormy. Peter said, "If that's you, tell me to come to you on the water." "Come," Jesus said.

So Peter got out of the boat, and he began to walk on the water, too. The storm scared him, and he began to sink. "Save me," he shouted. Jesus reached out and took his hand, and Peter began to walk on the water again.

When they both climbed back into the boat, the storm stopped. Then the disciples worshiped Jesus. "You really are the Son of God," they said.

Power Over Death

◆ ◆ ◆

JESUS SHOWED his power in many ways. He healed the sick, calmed storms, and fed thousands of people with a few loaves and fishes. But the greatest way he showed his power was by raising the dead.

He did this at least three times. Once he saw a funeral. A woman was weeping, the mother of the boy who had died. With her son dead, she had no one. She was a widow, and this was her only son.

This made Jesus sad. "Don't cry," he said. Then he touched the boards that the man was being carried on and said, "Young man, get up." The boy sat up and began to talk. The mother—and Jesus—were glad.

Another time, Jarius, a leader in the synagogue, came and asked Jesus to heal his daughter. Jesus gladly agreed, but before they got to Jarius' house, a messenger came and said the girl had already died. Jarius, of course, was heart-

MORE MIRACLES

Some Old Testament prophets raised people from the dead. Both Elijah and Elisha raised sons of widows who had helped them. In the New Testament, Peter raised a woman named Dorcas, and Paul raised a young man named Eutychus.

AN EYE-CATCHING PHRASE

A figure of speech can get a person's attention. Jesus said that if your right eye makes you sin by looking at evil, you are to "pluck it out and throw it away." He was teaching that sin is so harmful to us that we should do everything we can to avoid it.

A NEW BODY

Many people in the Bible were raised from the dead. But Jesus was the only one who didn't die again later. He had a new body. The Bible promises believers that someday they will come back to life, too—and have a new body like his.

broken. "Don't worry," Jesus said. "Just believe." So they went on to Jarius' house, where everyone was crying. "Don't cry," Jesus said. "The child is not dead, but asleep."

Some of the people laughed. Jesus told everyone to leave the room, except for his disciples and the parents. Then he took the girl's hand and said, "Little girl, get up." She did. Her parents were amazed—and grateful. "Give her something to eat," Jesus said.

The last time he raised someone from the dead, he raised his friend Lazarus. Jesus often stayed with Lazarus and his two sisters when he went to Jerusalem. Jesus heard that Lazarus was sick, but he did not go to him immediately. By the time he got to his house, Lazarus was dead.

His sisters were sad and disappointed. When Jesus saw how sad they were, he cried, too. The sisters took Jesus to their brother's tomb. "Roll the stone away," Jesus told them. At first they did not want to. "He has been dead four days, and his body stinks by now," they said.

But Jesus insisted. When the stone was rolled away, Jesus prayed and shouted: "Lazarus, come out." Then, still wrapped in grave clothes, Lazarus came out of the tomb.

Jesus had not healed his friend when he was sick. He wanted to show his disciples and others that he had power over death.

The Greatest Miracle of All

❖ ❖ ❖

MANY STRANGE and amazing things happened when Jesus died. To start with, the sky turned black, even though it was the middle of the day.

The moment Jesus died, a special curtain in the temple ripped from top to bottom. This was the curtain that separated the Holy of Holies from the rest of the temple. Only the high priest could go behind the curtain, and only once a year. Now everyone could come to God themselves.

At the same time, there was an earthquake and many tombs broke open. The Bible says many holy people who had died were raised to life. They came out of the tombs and went into Jerusalem where many people saw them.

When one of the Roman officers saw the earthquake and all that had happened, he said, "This must be the Son of God."

But there were more strange and wonderful things to come.

Another earthquake shook the city when an angel came down and rolled the stone away from Jesus' tomb. Angels appeared to the women who came to the tomb on Sunday morning. "He is not here," they said. "He has risen, just as he said."

The fact that Jesus had told his disciples ahead of time what would happen was just another miracle in a weekend full of miracles. And Jesus coming back from the dead was the greatest miracle of all.

A SIGN OF DEATH

When Jesus was crucified, the Roman soldiers didn't have to break his legs, as they did with the others, for Jesus was already dead. Instead, they pierced his side with a spear, and blood and water came out—a sure sign of death.

Try, Try Again

◆ ◆ ◆

AFTER JESUS DIED, his disciples were discouraged. Some left Jerusalem and returned to Galilee, unsure of what to do.

One evening, seven of them were together. "I'm going fishing," said Peter. So they got in a boat and went out all night, but they caught nothing.

Early in the morning, they saw a man standing on the shore, but they did not recognize him. He called to them: "Have you caught anything?" "Nothing," they replied.

"Then throw your net on the right side of the boat and you will find some," the man said. When they did, they caught so many fish they could not pull the net back into the boat. John then recognized the man. "It is the Lord," he said.

When he said this, the disciples all knew it was true. Peter jumped overboard and swam to shore, while the others followed in the boat, dragging the net behind them. Jesus had built a fire, and he was cooking some fish and some bread for them to eat.

"Bring some of the fish you just caught," Jesus said. The disciples pulled the net ashore and counted the fish: 153 of them. "Come and eat breakfast," Jesus said.

After they ate together, Jesus helped them understand what they should do next. "Do you love me?" Jesus asked Peter. He asked this question three times. Each time Peter said yes and each time Jesus said, "Then feed my sheep."

He wanted the disciples to lead his followers and to take care of them. Now they knew what to do.

MANY WITNESSES

Jesus appeared to his followers at least 11 different times after he rose from the dead. Sometimes he appeared to just a few at a time. Once he came to over 500 at one time. He told them to go everywhere and teach others about him. And he told them he would return some day. They were excited that he had power over death.

Power in the Early Church

◆ ◆ ◆

FORTY DAYS after Jesus rose from the dead, he went back to heaven. He told his followers to wait in Jerusalem until he sent the Holy Spirit to help them.

The Holy Spirit did come, and the apostles began to preach. Many thousands of people believed that Jesus had died for their sins and had come back to life. The church began to grow.

Peter was the leader of the new church, and he did many miracles, proving that the Holy Spirit was with him and with the new church. One day, several of the apostles were arrested and put in jail. That night, an angel let them out, without opening the doors.

Several men were appointed as deacons. It was their job to help the apostles. Some of the deacons did miracles, too. One of them, Philip, saw a man in a chariot reading from the book of the prophet Isaiah. The man was an important government official from Ethiopia.

"Do you understand what you are reading?" Philip asked. The man said he did not. Philip used the words of Isaiah to explain about Jesus and how and why he died. The man believed what Philip said and asked to be baptized.

They stopped the chariot and went down into some water. After he baptized the man, Philip disappeared. The Bible says the Spirit of the Lord took him away. He appeared in another place, preaching the good news.

Many exciting things were happening as the church began.

A DISHONEST PAIR

Some of the early Christians sold their property and gave the money to help take care of the poor. One couple sold some property and brought some of the money to the apostles. The couple said they were bringing it all. "Why are you lying to the Holy Spirit?" Peter asked. The couple fell down dead.

Paul Preaches the Good News

◆ ◆ ◆

THE APOSTLE PAUL encouraged the Christians in Jerusalem to tell everyone about Jesus—even people who were not Jews. Then he did what he asked others to do. He traveled to Greece and other countries, preaching the good news.

Not everyone understood. In Lystra, Paul healed a man who was crippled, and the crowd thought he was a god. They tried to worship Paul and his friend Barnabas. They wanted to sacrifice an ox in their honor. "Don't do this," Paul said. "We are men just like you. We are bringing you good news."

On the other hand, some of the Jews in that city wanted to kill Paul because they did not believe that Jesus was the Messiah. But Paul continued to travel and preach, often doing miracles as God helped him. He cast out demons and healed a blind man. In fact, handkerchiefs he had touched were taken to the sick, and the sick were healed.

Still, he was hated by enemies of the church. After starting many churches, Paul was taken to Rome as a prisoner. On the way there, his ship was wrecked off the island of Malta. Paul and his guards swam to safety. It was rainy and cold. As Paul built a fire, a deadly snake bit him on the hand. Paul shook it off into the fire. When he did not die, the islanders thought he was a god—just as the people in Lystra had thought.

But Paul was just a man bringing good news.

EUTYCHUS' FALL

Once when Paul was preaching, a young man named Eutychus went to sleep on a window ledge. The unfortunate fellow fell to the ground and died. Paul put his arms around Eutychus and brought him back to life.

Questions & Answers

◆ ◆ ◆

Q: Who was doubting Thomas?

A: When the other disciples told Thomas that Jesus had risen from the dead, he said he wouldn't believe it until he saw the nail holes in Jesus' hand. Later, Jesus appeared to Thomas and offered to let him touch his wounds. Thomas then believed, but Jesus blessed those—like you—who believe without seeing.

Q: What was the hailstorm in Egypt for?

A: The Pharaoh made slaves of the Hebrews and would not let them go. So God sent ten plagues, including the hailstorm and swarms of frogs, mosquitoes, flies, and locusts. When an angel killed the firstborn child in every family—including Pharaoh's own son— the evil king finally let the people go.

Q: Can iron float?

A: Only with God's help. Once the prophet Elisha and his students were building a shelter with a borrowed ax. The axhead slipped off, and it flew into the Jordan River. But Elisha cut a stick and tossed it in the water. The axhead floated up and attached itself to the stick.

Q: Did Elisha do any other miracles?

A: With God's help, Elisha did at least 14 miracles. He parted the Jordan River, multiplied a widow's oil, resurrected a boy, and blinded an army. He gave one

Doubting Thomas needed to see the scars in Jesus' hand to believe that he had risen from the dead.

man leprosy and healed another. God gave him lots of power, and he used it wisely.

Q: Can you feed a lot of people with a little bit of bread?

A: Twice, Jesus fed thousands of people with just a few loaves. But in the Old Testament, Elisha fed 100 hungry men with just 20 biscuit-sized loaves—and there was food left over.

Q: Can the sun stand still?

A: Joshua made the sun stand still during a battle at Gibeon, which added at least a dozen hours to the day. But the prophet Isaiah did something even more amazing. As a sign to King Hezekiah, he made the sun go backward! He did this to show God's promise to heal the king—and his power to do so.

Q: Can animals talk?

A: Not usually, but at least one did. An angel stood in the prophet Balaam's way, but only his donkey could see it. So Balaam beat his donkey three times for refusing to go forward. God then opened the donkey's mouth. "Why are you treating me like this?" the donkey asked. God opened the prophet's eyes and he could see the angel, too.

Q: Why did Jesus do miracles?

A: Christ's miracles were also called "signs" and "wonders." They helped prove that Jesus was the Son of God, the promised Messiah. But he did some miracles, especially his miracles of healing, just because he cared for the sick and the poor.

Q: What was the worst storm ever?

A: Beside the great flood, the worst storm may have been a hailstorm that killed the crops and the livestock in ancient Egypt. But the worst storm ever hasn't happened yet. The Book of Revelation tells about a storm with 100-pound hailstones that will produce an earthquake and even flatten the mountains.

Q: Were all miracles helpful?

A: All the miracles, both in the Old and New Testament, showed God's power. But sometimes they showed his judgment rather than his love. For example, King Agrippa, Ananias and his wife, Sapphira, and Aaron's and Samuel's sons were all struck dead because they failed to honor God.

Q: Does God only judge people?

A: Sometimes God judged entire cities or even countries. That's because he expects everyone to respect him and obey him. He rained fire down on the entire cities of Sodom and Gomorrah because the people there were very wicked.

Noah and his family were the only people to survive the great flood, when it rained for 40 days.

Q: Did Jesus do any miracles like that?

A: Most of Christ's miracles were for healing or helping. But he did send some demons into a herd of pigs, which then ran off a cliff into the Sea of Galilee and drowned. Another time he cursed a fig tree—and it withered and died.

Q: Were all the miracles done by God or his servants?

A: No. Pharaoh's wise men turned sticks into snakes just like Moses and Aaron had. Evil men can use the power of Satan to do amazing things. But Jesus and the prophets used their power to obey God and to do God's will.

Q: Are there more miracles to come?

A: The Bible tells about many amazing things that will happen at the end of the world. Dead people will come back to life. Wonders will fill the earth and sky. The entire earth will be destroyed and then made new. Jesus will defeat Satan in a great battle and all evil will end.

Q: Will there be miracles in heaven?

A: Some pretty amazing things will go on in heaven, but we don't know much about what they will be. However, many of the reasons Jesus did miracles won't exist anymore. There will be no sickness or death or even weeping.

Everyday Life

◆　◆　◆　◆

IMAGINE LIFE with no TV. Or no refrigerator. Or no pants! Life in Bible times seems strange when you first think about it. But if you think about it some more, it's not so strange at all. People dressed up to go to parties. Kids wondered about what they would have for dinner. Everyone enjoyed listening to music. Clothes and food were different, but important. Everyday life in Bible times had both sorrows and surprises—just like life today.

Everyday Dress

◆ ◆ ◆

THE TUNIC was the main item of clothing worn in Bible times. It was a long, simple garment that came down to the knees or to the ankles. In its simplest form, it was merely a rectangle of cloth with a hole cut in the center for the neck. This was fastened at the waist with a cloth or rope belt. A nicer tunic was more like a loose fitting shirt.

The tunic was usually made of wool, and it was often handed down from one generation to another. Both men and women wore tunics, although women's tunics were often made of nicer material. The women added decorative touches, such as designs around the neckline sewn with colored thread.

Although rich people might have several tunics of different colors and fabrics, ordinary people only had one or two. John the Baptist said if a man had two tunics, he should give one to someone who had none. Jesus also talked about clothes. He said if someone took you to court and sued you for your tunic, you should give him your cloak also!

The cloak, or mantle, was a large cloth that could be draped over the shoulder and worn

AN UNFRIENDLY WAGER

After Jesus died on the cross, the soldiers wanted his tunic. They tossed dice to decide who would keep it.

KINDS OF CLOTH

Wool cloth is made from sheep hair. Linen cloth is made from cotton or flax. Because these plants were not often grown in Canaan, linen was usually imported from Egypt or some other country. Sometimes clothes were made of animal skins or the hair of other animals, such as camels.

outside the tunic. Sometimes it had sleeves. This was an important piece of clothing. Men used it to wrap around themselves for warmth or to sleep in at night. They took it off when they were working and sometimes carried things in it.

Women used their cloak as a shawl, a veil, and even a bag. It would cover a woman's head, both to protect her from the sun, and because it was considered disrespectful for a woman not to cover her head. Often, a woman's mantle had a padded ring sewn on top so she could balance a jug of water on her head.

Under the tunic, both men and women often wore a short robe. Men wrapped a cloth around their waist called a loincloth. They might wrap a cloth around their head, too.

Water was not plentiful, and clothes had to be washed by hand. They were nearly always soaked with sweat and soiled with dirt and food. That's one reason why skin diseases—such as leprosy—were so common.

Despite these problems, some people were still too concerned about their clothes. In the Sermon on the Mount, Jesus said not to worry about clothes. "Look at the lilies," he said. "See how beautiful they are. If God takes care of them, he will take care of you, too."

WARM AND SNUG

The Bible says that baby Jesus was wrapped in swaddling clothes when he was born. These were not really clothes but cloth wrapped tightly around a baby to keep it warm and secure. It was also believed that swaddling protected a baby's body. Newborn babies today are still comforted by being swaddled in a blanket.

OF CLOAKS AND COATS

Cloaks were worn over tunics for extra warmth. Many people did not own blankets and used their cloaks for cover at night.

CAREWORN

Sackcloth was a rough material made of goat's hair. People would wear it when they were very sad or grief-stricken or to show that they were sorry for their sins.

Festive Clothes

◆ ◆ ◆

CLOTHES WORN for festivals and special occasions, such as weddings, were made much like everyday clothes, but they were more colorful and were decorated with fancy embroidery. They were usually made of linen instead of wool.

At some weddings, guests were given a special robe to wear. If they did not wear it, the host would be offended. The bride and groom both wore special robes and jewelry.

For events like this, women liked to wear their best jewelry. They also wore fancier headdresses. Isaiah described some women he thought were overdressed. He said they wore bangles, headbands, necklaces, earrings, bracelets, veils, ankle chains, sashes, perfume bottles, charms, rings, nose rings, and crowns—in addition to fine robes, capes, and cloaks.

Many people had a nicer cloak to wear for special times. Samuel's mother made him a new one each year. These were expensive, and most people had only one. Sometimes people would tear their cloaks to show they were sad. This meant their problem was more important than money.

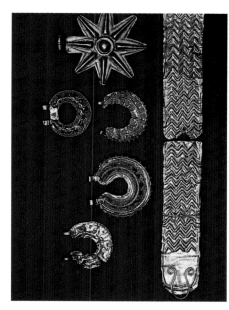

Ancient jewelry

WEDDING CHIC

Brides in biblical times wore rich and beautiful dresses. The Book of Proverbs describes one wedding dress as "woven with gold." The bride also wore jewels and a veil. The groom would be dressed in a festive robe and might have worn a garland of flowers around his neck.

For men, tassels were sometimes added to their nice clothes. These were attached to the outer garments, such as the cloak. The tassels contained a blue thread to remind them of God's commandments. Jewish men today still wear shawls with tassels attached to the corners of them when they pray.

One group of religious leaders, the Pharisees, liked to stand out in the crowd. They wore expensive linen clothes decorated with bright colors. Their tassels were longer than everyone else's. They did this to attract attention. Jesus denounced the Pharisees for this. "You look great on the outside, but you are empty on the inside," he said.

The priests wore very colorful and expensive clothes in the temple—long-sleeved linen tunics with beautiful belts made of blue, purple, and red. They wore long, loose underpants and a white linen hat. The high priest wore the same thing, but he also wore a blue robe fringed with gold bells over those. His hat was also blue. Over this he wore a short cloak, like a vest, embroidered with gold, red, blue, and purple. He wore a gold and linen pouch around his neck, called a breastplate. There were 12 jewels on the pouch, one for each of the 12 tribes of Israel.

WHITE WAS SPECIAL

A white robe, or stole, was worn for special occasions. People in heaven were said to wear pure white robes to show that Jesus had washed away their sins.

KEEP IT SIMPLE

The prophet Isaiah made a list of fine clothes that showed that people were too full of pride. Many of these were copied from other countries, like Egypt. The prophet Zephaniah also warned against wearing strange clothes. The clothes he was concerned about may have included pants like the Persians wore.

VALUABLE APPAREL

Cloaks were a valued possession in biblical times. They were used as a sack to carry things in, as something to sit on, and as a promise to pay a debt. The prophet Elijah once put his cloak on Elisha's shoulders to show that Elisha would be the next prophet. Later, when Elijah went to heaven, he left his cloak behind for Elisha.

No Shoes Inside

PEOPLE SOMETIMES went barefoot. But when they didn't, they usually wore sandals. These were made of a piece of leather or wood cut in the shape of a foot and then tied with strips of leather. There were shoes that covered the tops of the feet, too, like sandals with closed tops. Only the wealthy could afford shoes like that.

When people came inside, their feet were very dirty from walking on dusty roads. To welcome visitors, the host would bring a basin of cool water and wash and dry their feet. If the host was wealthy, a servant or slave would untie the leather strips on the visitors' sandals and wash their feet.

Because he knew Jesus was the Son of God, John the Baptist said he was not even good enough to untie Jesus' sandals. But Jesus himself was willing to serve others. The night before he died, Jesus washed the disciples' feet.

At first Peter said no, but Jesus insisted. "Unless I wash you, you have no part with me," Jesus said. "I'm setting an example for you, so you will serve each other."

The priests were barefoot when they were working in the temple. Taking off one's shoes was a way to show reverence. When God appeared to Moses in a burning bush, he told him to take off his shoes. "The place where you are standing is holy ground," he said.

SHOELESS

Shoes were part of some customs in the Old Testament. Taking your shoes off and putting them on a piece of land showed you owned it. If a man refused to marry his brother's widow, one of his sandals was taken away in court. People took off their shoes when someone close to them had died. This showed that they were sad.

Something to Lean On

◆ ◆ ◆

PEOPLE IN BIBLICAL TIMES spent a lot of time walking. They often used a staff, or walking stick. A staff was usually four to six feet long, made from a straight, peeled branch. Travelers used the staff to climb, to clear twigs or rocks from the path, to kill snakes, or to lean on when they were tired.

God helped Aaron use his staff to perform miracles. When Aaron put his staff in the Nile River, it turned to blood. Another time, he struck the dust with his staff, and the dust throughout Egypt became lice. These were ways that Moses and Aaron showed God's power to Pharaoh. Once, Moses threw his staff on the ground, and it became a snake. When he picked it up, it became a staff again.

In addition to a staff, travelers also carried a bag. This was usually made of animal skin and was carried over the shoulder like a purse. It held food or money for the journey.

Money was also often carried in their belts, a folded piece of cloth or leather that held their tunic in place. The belt could also hold a knife or sword, especially for soldiers. King Saul's son Jonathan once gave David a belt as a gift, along with his royal robe.

When working or running, people would often tuck their tunic up into their belt so they could run faster or work harder.

MORE ACCESSORIES

Both men and women wore jewelry, including rings on their fingers, toes, and noses. For women, bracelets and anklets were common. Necklaces were also very common and highly desired. The jewelry was made of colored glass or stones, jewels, and precious metals such as gold and silver.

On Guard

◆ ◆ ◆

AFTER JESUS DIED, Roman soldiers were sent to guard his tomb. They were no match for Jesus and his angels, of course. When Jesus was resurrected, the soldiers were terrified and ran away. But Roman soldiers were normally not easily frightened; they were among the best trained in the ancient world. They were professionals who had signed up to be soldiers for 25 years.

A Roman legion had about 5,000 soldiers. Each soldier was armed with a short, two-edged sword called a gladius and a heavy, six-foot spear called a javelin. The sword was used for stabbing, not cutting. The javelin was sharp on both ends. A soldier wore a jacket made of small iron rings and a helmet that covered his neck and forehead.

The Romans had two ways to conquer a walled city. First, they would build a second wall around the entire city. They would guard this to make sure no help or food entered the city. Soon the people would begin to starve and would eventually give up.

If this didn't work, or if the Romans were in a hurry, they would build a ramp up to the city's wall. Then they could move battering rams up to the wall and begin to knock it down. They also had machines called catapults to hurl burning javelins or rocks into the city itself.

AGAINST THE ODDS

The Hebrews often found themselves outnumbered, fighting against armies with better weapons. But God sometimes sent earthquakes, floods, angels, and even hornets to help them. Gideon and his army did not use normal weapons to conquer the Midianites, they used trumpets and torches to confuse their enemy. When Joshua entered and conquered the promised land, he knew God had helped him. He told the people what God said: "You did not do it with your own sword and bow."

BATTLE READY

When the Hebrews first entered the promised land, their enemies had two advantages: chariots and iron weapons. By the time of King David, however, the Hebrews also had these things. A foot soldier's main weapons were spear, sword, and slingshot. Many warriors were also skilled with bows and arrows.

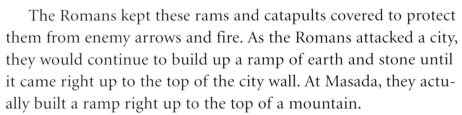

TORTOISE FORMATION

Sometimes, when marching into battle, Roman soldiers would lock their shields together to form a solid wall or roof. The soldiers' rectangular shields formed a pattern that resembled a turtle's shell, and so this became known as the tortoise formation.

WORDS AS WEAPONS

In Proverbs 25:18, the Bible says that telling lies about someone is as harmful as hitting him with an axe, or wounding him with a sword, or shooting him with a sharp arrow.

The Romans kept these rams and catapults covered to protect them from enemy arrows and fire. As the Romans attacked a city, they would continue to build up a ramp of earth and stone until it came right up to the top of the city wall. At Masada, they actually built a ramp right up to the top of a mountain.

When Jesus was alive, he said that the temple would be destroyed. The people laughed. The temple was protected by thick, high walls. But after he died, in A.D. 70, the Romans did destroy the temple. They leveled everything and burned the city.

Today, nothing is left but the temple's supporting walls. Jews still go there to pray and mourn the loss of the temple.

A Troubled Kingdom

◆ ◆ ◆

FOR A LONG TIME, the Hebrews had no king but God himself. But the nations nearby had kings, and the Hebrews wanted one, too.

The prophet Samuel warned the people that a king would only cause trouble. He would tax them and take their sons as his servants and soldiers. But the people insisted. So God told Samuel to anoint Saul as their first king.

Saul helped to free Israel from the Philistines. He was a strong and brave warrior. But he was also moody and ill tempered. He tried to kill David, a young hero. God was not pleased with Saul, and so David became the king.

David was Israel's greatest king. He loved the Lord, and he loved the people. When he did wrong, he was sorry for his sins. He was also a mighty man of war. He brought the people together as one nation, with Jerusalem as its capital.

After he died, his son Solomon became the king. Solomon built the temple in Jerusalem and built fortresses to protect the nation. He built a large palace for himself and for his many wives. Solomon began to do what Samuel had warned the people a king would do. He took their money and their land and their sons so he could build buildings and forts.

When Solomon died, the nation was divided into two parts, Judah in the south and Israel in the north. Each part had its own king. Many of these kings were wicked, and they wanted the people to worship other gods.

KINGS AT COURT

When Saul was king, he continued to work as a farmer. He held court under a tamarisk tree. By the time Solomon was king, he had a throne of gold and ivory with statues of lions on either side. He had many wives, officials, and bodyguards. Kings then had absolute power. They could have someone killed or thrown in jail without a trial.

The Good Shepherd

◆ ◆ ◆

IN THE BIBLE, sheep were used for wool, milk, and meat. Shepherds cared for and protected these valuable animals. The shepherd would lead the flock to find food and water. He would find them shelter during storms or cold nights. The sheep knew their shepherd's voice and would come when he called.

Shepherds often passed the time playing a flute or singing songs. They practiced using a slingshot or throwing a short club so they could defend the sheep from wild animals.

King David was a shepherd when he was a boy. Later, as a young man, he killed a giant with a slingshot and played music for King Saul. He was called the shepherd king, because he loved his people and took care of them like a shepherd takes care of his sheep.

David wrote many songs. In one of them he says God is also like a shepherd to his people. God told the prophet Ezekiel that this was true. "I myself will search for my sheep, and I will rescue them," God said. "I will be a shepherd to my people, and seek the lost, and bring back the strays."

Jesus described himself the same way. "I am the good shepherd," he said. "The good shepherd lays down his life for his sheep. I know my sheep and my sheep know me—and I lay down my life for the sheep."

A USEFUL TOOL

Shepherds used a slingshot for a number of purposes. If a sheep had gone astray, the shepherd would fling a rock that would land in front of the animal, startling it into going in the right direction. A slingshot was also used, along with a club, to ward off lions and bears that attacked the flock.

A Job to Do

❖ ❖ ❖

THE HEBREWS considered work a blessing from God, and it was no disgrace for them to work with their hands.

There were very few slaves in Israel, so most of the hard work was done by free men. Many of these men became very good at what they did. Some men worked dying or weaving cloth. Blacksmiths worked with metal. Others were potters or carpenters or brick makers.

One man could do many of these things well. His name was Bezalel. He was in charge of building the Tabernacle in the wilderness. The Bible says God gave him skill, ability, and knowledge in all kinds of crafts. He did beautiful work in wood, metal, and stone. He made the altar and the Ark of the Covenant—which had statues of two cherubim made from pure gold on the top.

Bezalel was helped by Oholiah, who worked with cloth and dyes. He embroidered angels in the curtains. Together these two men supervised the work of many others to make the Tabernacle just as God had directed.

Bezalel and Oholiah had learned their craft in Egypt. But the Law for-

IMPORTANT WORK

The Apostle Paul learned to make tents as a young man living in Tarsus. Later, he would sometimes work as a tentmaker during his travels. He was able to work and support himself as he preached the gospel in new places. Once he spent a year and a half in Corinth, living with Aquila and Priscilla. They were tentmakers, too.

bid the Hebrews from making any images of people or animals. God did not want them to make and worship idols. For this reason, Hebrews did little painting, carving, or making statues.

So when Solomon built the temple, few Hebrew craftsmen were capable of engraving and embroidering the designs he needed. Solomon had to hire a man from Lebanon, a half-Hebrew named Hurum. Hurum was skilled in working with both metal and cloth. He created the designs for the altars, basins, furniture, and walls of the temple.

But Hebrew stonemasons and carpenters did the basic work. Later, Jesus himself would work as a carpenter. Boys automatically learned their father's trade as they grew up. Jesus worked with his hands, helping Joseph make things like boxes and beams for the people in his village. Later, when he began to preach, the people from his village did not believe what he said. "He is just the carpenter's son," they said. They didn't realize he was also the Son of God.

HELPING THE POOR

Beggars were a common sight in biblical times. They would ask for money outside the temple or along roads near the cities. Most of them were unable to work. They were lame or blind or sick. The Law required those who could to give some money to the poor. These gifts were called alms.

HOME WORK

In larger cities, people with the same job often lived in the same neighborhood. There would be a potters' section, a bakers' section, a tanners' section, and so forth. People worked in their home and sold their products outdoors, usually near the city gate. Most people lived in small villages and worked as farmers, shepherds, or fishermen.

Crime and Punishment

❖ ❖ ❖

IN ANCIENT ISRAEL, the elders and the priests worked together to make sure everyone obeyed the Law. The elders were the leaders of the community.

There were no police, but if someone did something wrong, his neighbors would bring him to the elders of the city, who sat at the city gate. They would listen to both sides and make a decision. For someone to be found guilty, there had to be at least two witnesses who saw him do it.

The elders would decide what to do. If he was guilty, they might make him pay back money or replace a missing animal. Sometimes, they would have him beaten with a rod. The Law said he could not be beaten more than 40 times, so they would order 39 strokes—just to make sure they didn't go over.

For some crimes they ordered death. This was done by stoning. The victim was taken outside the city. Then the witnesses threw rocks at him. Then the crowd of people would throw rocks at the victim until he died. In fact, the people often kept throwing rocks until the victim was buried.

CRUEL AND UNUSUAL

Most prisoners were criminals, but many Christians were jailed, too, simply because of their religious beliefs.

TERRIFYING PLACES

Prisons in biblical times were dark, underground dungeons, usually with no windows. One famous prison mentioned in the Bible was carved out of rock. Prisoners were shackled with chains and often forced to do hard work. In ancient days, prisoners were guilty until proven innocent and rarely received a fair trial. Several books in the New Testament were written by people who were in prison.

EGYPTIAN JAILS

In ancient times, muddy pits sometimes served as prisons. A room in the inner court of the temple or a guarded room outside in the palace courtyard could be a prison, too. Joseph endured an Egyptian prison for two years. Egyptian prisoners wore heavy iron collars and painful shackles.

Sometimes an angry mob would stone someone without even going to the elders. This happened to the Apostle Paul in Lystra. The crowd dragged his body outside the city and left him for dead. His friends were amazed when he stood up and went back into the city.

The Law listed the crimes for which a person could be stoned. These included murder, worshiping idols, practicing witchcraft, and blaspheming God—speaking of him without respect. People could also be stoned for breaking the Sabbath or talking back to their parents. Another serious crime was adultery—sleeping with someone else's husband or wife.

Once, some men brought a woman to Jesus who had been caught committing adultery. They demanded that she be stoned, but they failed to mention the man. Jesus startled them with his answer. "If any one of you has not sinned, let him cast the first stone," he said.

One by one the crowd left. All of them had sinned also. Then Jesus told the grateful woman that he forgave her. "Go and sin no more," he said.

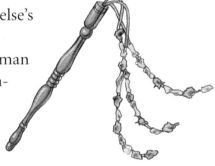

CORPORAL PUNISHMENT

Roman prisoners were sometimes beaten with a scourge, a wooden-handled instrument with three leather straps studded with small pieces of iron. After being beaten, prisoners were often placed in stocks, which were wooden frames with holes just big enough for the ankles or wrists.

THE COURAGEOUS HANANI

Hanani was a courageous prophet. In obedience to God, he delivered an unwelcome message to King Asa of Judah. The king became angry and put Hanani in chains.

Travel by Sea

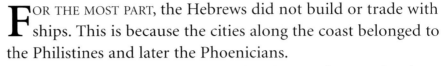

FOR THE MOST PART, the Hebrews did not build or trade with ships. This is because the cities along the coast belonged to the Philistines and later the Phoenicians.

The Phoenicians, on the other hand, were famous for their ships. Their sturdy trading vessels carried grain, spices, cloth, pottery, glass, jewelry, metal, slaves, and ivory back and forth across the Mediterranean Sea. They often towed cedar logs from Lebanon to countries where wood was scarce. The Phoenicians were so good at what they did that when they were conquered, their new rulers just collected taxes and let them go on about their business.

When Solomon became king, he made a treaty with the Phoenicians. They helped him build a fleet of ships on the tip of the Red Sea. Soon, he was sending his ships to buy and sell along the coasts of Arabia and Africa.

The Bible says Solomon's ships carried copper and iron and brought back gold, silver, ivory, apes, and peacocks. The round trip took three years. He also brought cedar and gold from the nearby Phoenician city of Tyre to help build the temple. He paid for this with wheat and oil and silver.

About 100 years later, King Jehoshaphat started building ships again, but all his ships were destroyed in a storm. Ship building in Israel ended.

GRACEFUL DESIGN

The sterns and bows of Philistine ships were carved in the shape of a bird's long neck. These ships, which were oarless, were sometimes used in battles at sea.

THE COMPANY YOU KEEP

King Jehoshaphat of Judah was a wise ruler who loved God, but he made a mistake when he joined with the wicked King Ahaziah of Israel to build trading ships. A prophet named Eliezer told Jehoshaphat that his plans would be ruined. Sure enough, the ships were later wrecked and the partnership ended.

STRANGE DISAPPEARANCE

The city of Tarshish is mentioned often in the Scriptures. It was a famous port city reported to have vast wealth, especially gold. Surprisingly, no one today knows for sure where Tarshish was located.

Seaport of Corinth

A WICKED CITY

Corinth was a famous seaport noted for its wickedness. Paul wrote two famous letters to the Christians in this city, encouraging them to live more like Christ would want them to live.

A SMALL SEA

Jesus often crossed the Sea of Galilee by boat. The Sea of Galilee is a large lake in northern Israel. The boats used in Jesus' time were small fishing boats rowed by four men. They could hold about 15 people. Sometimes Jesus spoke from a boat to a crowd on the shore.

By the time Jesus was born, the Romans ruled the seas with powerful warships over 100 feet long. These had two or more decks of rowers. The crew of a ship with two decks included 108 rowers (slaves), 25 sailors, and 80 soldiers. There was a large ram on the front of the ship for sinking other ships in battle.

Paul was taken to Rome as a prisoner in a Roman cargo ship. There were no passenger ships at that time. Travelers such as Paul would have to travel on the main deck, exposed to crashing waves and wind in a storm. His ship was wrecked in a storm off Malta. Soldiers planned to kill the prisoners to keep them from swimming away, but the captain said no. Everyone jumped overboard and swam to shore.

Paul was shipwrecked at least three different times, and he once spent a whole day and night in the sea. No wonder most Hebrews preferred to travel by land!

A Rocky Road

◆ ◆ ◆

MOST OF THE ROADS in ancient Israel were little more than paths filled with rocks and weeds. There were a few highways, but these were really just well-worn trails between Syria and Egypt. These were used by armies and by merchant caravans of camels.

Most of the time people walked, usually single file along the narrow paths. On their farms and near their villages, they used small carts pulled by oxen to move heavy loads. The roads were too rough and hilly for chariots. And no one could afford chariots anyway.

Chariots were used only by kings and mighty warriors—and they were practically useless if it rained.

ANCIENT TANKS

Chariots were like modern-day tanks. They gave the armies that used them a great advantage since they were light and fast. A chariot crew consisted of two to four men: a driver and one or more warriors with bows or spears. The archers could shoot accurately—even from a bumpy chariot. During peacetime, chariots were used for hunting and for parades.

Deborah and Barak defeated the army of Sisera when his 900 chariots got bogged down in a storm. By the time of Solomon, roads had improved, although they were still not paved. Solomon had 1,400 chariots and 12,000 horses, which he imported from Egypt and other lands.

A LONG WALK

Most people could not afford to take a ship to Rome. But they could walk. The trip was over 2,000 miles and took about four months. Even then they had to go by ship part of the way—about five days on a boat. The Apostle Paul often traveled by ship. But he walked a lot, too. He once walked from Antioch to Troas, about 600 miles through the mountains.

The Romans did build some roads paved with stone, but things were not too much better when Jesus was born. Mary and Joseph traveled from Nazareth to Bethlehem near Jerusalem. They probably traveled by foot, although they may have had a donkey. The trip was a hard one, and it took about five days. People could travel about 15 miles a day.

While Jesus was growing up, his family made the 75-mile trip to Jerusalem at least once a year for Passover. They may have gone there for other festivals, too. Jesus and his disciples made this trip several times, always by foot.

Sometimes a donkey was used to ride on or to carry baggage. Donkeys were strong, sure-footed, and friendly. Jesus once rode a donkey into Jerusalem as the people cheered and tried to make him king.

Camels cost more than donkeys, and they were less friendly. Camels were used mainly by merchants to carry cargo for long distances, especially across the desert. The magi may have traveled by camel, but they might have used horses.

Horses were very expensive. Only the wealthy could afford them for everyday use. They were also used by the army.

The Way of the Sea

INTERSTATE TRAVEL

Two highways existed in ancient Israel. The King's Highway went from Syria to Egypt by way of the Red Sea. The Way of the Sea went from Syria to Egypt along the coast. These were important trade routes. Many wars were fought in Israel as armies marched along these roads. When Solomon was king, he charged tolls to use them.

THE KING'S MULE

When King David chose his son Solomon to be king, Solomon was placed on the king's mule and taken to the Tabernacle to be anointed. Later, Jesus would ride a donkey to the temple as the people waved palm branches and shouted for him to be king. This was the Sunday before Easter. We call it Palm Sunday.

Making Music

◆ ◆ ◆

LIKE MOST PEOPLE, the ancient Hebrews loved music. They sang happy songs to celebrate military victories and sad songs when someone died. They sang at weddings and at the temple. They loved to dance and play musical instruments.

The first instrument mentioned in the Bible is the harp. It was a wooden frame shaped like a triangle with strings stretched between the wood. The number of strings varied, anywhere from 12 to 40. Simple strings could be made from twisted grass, but better strings were made from dried animal intestines. The lyre was like a harp, but smaller, with fewer strings.

David learned to play the harp while watching his father's sheep. Later, he got a job in King Saul's court, playing his harp for the king. King Saul had a violent temper, and the music would calm and soothe his spirit.

Eventually, David used his musical ability to write many of the songs in the Bible. These were used in the temple. Music in the temple was often loud and joyful. An orchestra of flutes, tambourines, trumpets, cymbals, and drums accompanied the temple singers and dancers. During the Feast of Tabernacles, people would dance until morning every night for a week. They would do this in the court of the temple, accompanied by flutes.

Jesus liked music, too. He and his disciples would often sing together. Jesus' own brother James became a leader in the early church. "Are you happy?" James asked. "Then sing a song."

A JOYFUL NOISE

Psalms 150 says people should praise the Lord with every instrument they have. According to the Apostle Paul, you don't even need an instrument. In a letter to the church at Ephesus he wrote: "Sing and make music in your heart to the Lord, always giving thanks to God the Father for everything."

A Lamp Unto My Feet

❖ ❖ ❖

THE EARLIEST LAMPS were clay saucers filled with olive oil. A wick made of flax or wool floated in the oil. Later, the corners of the saucer were pinched up to hold one or more wicks. Lamps became more like bowls, and they eventually had a lid and a spout for the wick.

The lamps were not very bright. Sometimes they would be put on a stand. This made them higher so they would brighten a bigger space. But even these lamps were small and had to be refilled often.

Jesus told a story about lamps that had to be refilled. Ten young women were waiting to go to a wedding party. Five of them had brought extra oil and five had not. The host did not come to get them until midnight. By that time, their lamps had gone out. The ones with no oil had to go and get some more. By the time they did this, the banquet had begun. They went to the party, but the host refused to let them in.

Jesus talked about lamps often. He said no one would put their lamp under a bowl. Instead, they would set it on a stand to light the whole house. "Don't hide your light," he said. "Let your good deeds shine for all to see. Then they will praise your heavenly Father."

The Psalms say that the Bible is like a lamp. It lights our path by revealing God's wishes and keeps us from stumbling in the dark.

Looking for a City

❖ ❖ ❖

NOMADS LIVED IN TENTS, moving from place to place to find food or water. Living like this is common in deserts—large open areas covered with sand and rocks and small bushes.

Most nomads were shepherds. When their sheep or cattle ate all the grass in one place, they would move to another place. Sometimes, they would raid cities or offer their services to a king who needed an army.

Nomad tents were made of black goat hair, which kept out the rain and heat. The tent was divided into two rooms, one for the women and children and one for the men and guests. Many people slept in the same room on straw or wool mats.

Nomads often traveled in groups as large as 30 or 40 families. They were friendly to strangers, and they offered them food to eat and shelter from the hot sun. Goat's milk and cheese were part of their diet, as well as stews made with meat from their herds. Their tents, clothes, sandals, and bottles

WELCOME RELIEF

Deserts are hot and dry, but sometimes springs of water create an oasis of flowers, grass, and trees. Date palms thrive around an oasis. Dates are a juicy, delicious fruit. Nomads were happy when they found an oasis because it provided them with water, fruit, and shade.

Desert oasis

AN OASIS FOR YOU

The prophet Isaiah said God's kingdom will be like an oasis. After the world is destroyed, there will be a new world where only beautiful and good things exist. There will be no sickness or death. Only people who love and obey God will live in this perfect world.

were all made from the hair and skins of their animals.

Abraham was a nomad. The Bible says he spent his whole life living in tents and looking for a city built by God. He left Ur to travel to Canaan, a land God promised to him and his children. He traveled with his nephew Lot and many servants and herdsmen.

When food became scarce, he would move his family to another spot. Once, he took them to Egypt, where he stayed for several years. He liked to stay in one spot as long as he could. For ten years, he camped in an oak grove near Hebron.

Sometimes he would get involved in local quarrels. He once rescued his nephew Lot, who had been taken prisoner by the king of Elam.

Like other nomads, Abraham welcomed visitors. One day, he saw three men standing outside his tent. "Rest under this tree and let me get you something to eat," he said. The three men turned out to be angels. One of them promised Abraham that he would have a son, even though he and his wife Sarah were too old.

A year later, Sarah did have a son named Isaac. When Isaac was grown, he did not move around as much as Abraham had. Isaac dug wells and planted crops. Isaac had a son named Jacob, and Jacob's sons became the nation of Israel.

Present-day Bedouins

NOMADS NOW

Nomads still live in and around Israel today. Called Bedouins, they live in tents and move from place to place with their sheep and goats. They live today much like Abraham did about 4,000 years ago.

OLD–TIME RELIGION

Years after the children of Israel had settled in Canaan, one group still practiced the nomadic ways of their ancestors. Jeremiah brought this group, called Rechabites, into the temple and offered them wine. They refused and said Rechab had told them not to drink wine or build houses. "You shall live in tents all your lives," he had said.

School Days

◆ ◆ ◆

IN ANCIENT ISRAEL, most children were taught by their parents. They learned to work at home, helping with the sheep or in the fields.

The most important thing they learned was the Law. They listened to their fathers talk about the Law with other men. They listened to stories about Abraham and Moses. They were taught that God had brought their people out of slavery in Egypt.

They learned a prayer called the Shema, which said they were to love God with all their heart and mind and strength. They also learned other passages of Scripture from their parents, who knew these passages by heart. Some boys, like Samuel, were sent to the scribes and priests to learn how to read. These boys were likely to become scribes or priests themselves.

After Solomon's temple was destroyed, the Hebrews who were taken to Babylon began to meet to study and pray. The places where they met were called synagogues. These synagogues were places for both

SMART WOMEN

Girls did not go to school, but they stayed home and learned to be wives and mothers. Some women, like the judge Deborah, did know a great deal about Israel's history and law. Women were more respected in Israel than they were in surrounding countries. The Book of Proverbs encourages children to listen to the instruction of their mothers.

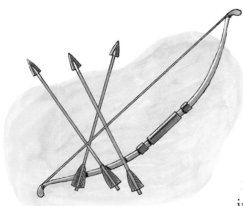

worship and instruction. Eventually, many synagogues had schools for young boys. Only boys six and older were allowed to attend, and they learned sitting on the floor around their teacher. Classes started early in the morning, followed by a break in the middle of the day when it was hot. Then there were more classes in the afternoon.

Most of the work at school was memorizing the Scriptures. There they memorized the Shema, which is a collection of three passages from Numbers and Deuteronomy. They also memorized many of the psalms. The students all met in the same room and recited the passages and prayers often and out loud.

Jesus warned his followers not to say their prayers so often that they quit thinking about what they meant. "Don't recite the same prayers over and over," he said. "God doesn't pay any more attention to you if you repeat yourselves."

Students were done with school by the time they were 13. Those who did well could go on and study the finer points of the Law. The Apostle Paul went to such a school, and he was taught by one of the greatest Hebrew teacher of his time, a man named Gamaliel.

For the Hebrews, it was a great honor to know and read God's Word.

TORAH'S MEANING

A word related to the Torah is *yarah,* meaning "to shoot an arrow." Like an arrow, the Torah aims a heart toward God.

Child reading Torah

THE HAZZAN

The responsibility for keeping the scrolls in the synagogue was considered so important that it was assigned to a kind of librarian, called a hazzan. He took out the scrolls to be read in worship and returned them afterward. In Nazareth, Jesus handed scrolls to a hazzan after reading from the Book of Isaiah.

STUDYING THE WORD OF GOD

Psalm 119, the longest of all the Bible's psalms, is a poem about the delights of studying God's Word. Its form is also unusual. It is an acrostic, which means each section starts with a different letter of the Hebrew alphabet.

Meal Time

BREAKFAST WAS seldom served in Bible times, although people may have had a piece of fruit or a snack of roasted grain. The first meal was at lunch, usually some bread with olives or fruit.

Bread was the most important food. In fact, the Hebrews often used the same word for both bread and food. Women usually had to bake bread every day. First they had to grind grain into meal. This was mixed with salt and water to make dough. Then it was baked on small outdoor ovens.

Sometimes oil was added, or dough from the day before. That would make the bread lighter and fluffier. On special occasions, they added honey or raisins. Preparing food took all day. Since most of it was boiled, the women also had to get water from the village well or a nearby spring.

After the sun went down, the family would gather by light of dim oil lamps for supper. The people worked hard all day and looked forward to this time together. As they ate, they talked and told stories and sang together.

THE STAFF OF LIFE

Bread was a necessity at every meal. It is referred to hundreds of times in the Bible. The round, flat loaves of the day were made of wheat or barley.

A THOUGHTFUL GIFT

In addition to eating food, people in the biblical era gave food as gifts to friends and family. Because food was sometimes hard to get, it was considered valuable and, therefore, a thoughtful gift.

THOU SHALT NOT!

The Law had many rules about what the Hebrews could eat and could not eat. They could eat animals that chewed grass and that had divided hoofs. That meant they could eat a goat but not a horse. They could absolutely not eat any pigs! Only certain kinds of birds and fish could be eaten. They couldn't eat lizards, but grasshoppers were alright.

They sat on the floor together for a supper of spicy stew made of lentils or beans. They ate out of the same pot, using flat loaves of bread to scoop up their food. Milk was almost always part of the meal. They had vegetables, too, including cucumbers and onions.

The Hebrews did not eat meat very often because it was expensive, and there was no way to keep it from spoiling. For most Israelites, the only meat they ever ate was part of the sacrifices during the religious festivals.

Of course, wealthy people had more to choose from. In King Solomon's court, the meat used in one day included 10 oxen, 20 cows, and 100 sheep, along with wild game such as deer. Rich people sat around low tables, reclining on cushions.

By Jesus' time, people had tables with benches or chairs. Sometimes they would sit on the floor around a low table to eat. Jesus often joined friends and strangers for dinner, sitting around and talking with them afterwards.

He knew they were hungry for more than food. "I am the bread of life," he told them.

AN IMPORTANT INGREDIENT

Olives grow on short twisted trees that do well in the dry, rocky soil of Canaan. Oil pressed from olives was a basic part of the Hebrew diet. It was mixed with flour to make bread and cakes. It was also used as a fuel for lamps, in religious ceremonies, as a medicine, and for soap.

Making Wine

❖ ❖ ❖

THE HEBREWS drank a lot of milk from sheep and goats. But they also drank a lot of wine made from grapes.

Grape vines grew well on the rocky hills of Israel. In fact, when Moses sent spies into Canaan, they returned carrying a cluster of grapes so large it took two men to carry it. When the Hebrews settled there, they continued to grow grapes. The hillsides were covered with vineyards.

Vineyards had to be carefully tended, weeded, and pruned. In July, when the grapes first appeared, watchmen were hired to keep the foxes and other creatures away. In September, the grapes were cut and collected in baskets. These were carried to a winepress, a large square pit carved in stone. There the people would stomp on them with their bare feet, singing and clapping joyfully.

The juice flowed from there into a collecting basin, where it sat for several days until it began to ferment. Then it was collected in jars and bags made of goat skins, called wineskins. After 40 days, it had turned into wine.

The wineskins were made new every year. That's because as the grape juice turned to wine, it would expand. An old wineskin was already stretched, so it would break if they put new wine into it. Jesus said his new teachings could not be obeyed in old ways, just like you could not put new wine in old wineskins.

ENOUGH IS ENOUGH

Wine was a common drink because there was no way to keep milk or juice fresh. Since drinking wine can make people drunk, the Bible warns several times against drinking too much wine. Wine was also used as medicine and as a sacrifice.

Water From a Well

❖ ❖ ❖

WATER WAS very important in the hot, dry land of Israel. Shepherds needed to know the location of any wells and springs so they could find water for their flocks. The people needed water for washing and cooking.

Towns and villages were built near springs or wells. The wells were deep pits cut through the rock. Water was drawn from the wells by ropes attached to clay jars or buckets made of animal skins.

Abraham once sent his servant to Nahor to find a wife for his son Isaac. The servant knew right where to go. He went to the well where the women came twice a day to get water. One woman gave him water and offered to water his camels, too. He knew he had found the right woman.

Abraham's son Isaac and grandson Jacob dug several wells. Jacob's well was in Samaria. One day, Jesus stopped and talked to a woman there. "Will you give me a drink?" he asked.

The woman was surprised. Jews did not usually talk to Samaritans. His disciples were surprised, too. The woman had a bad reputation. In fact, she was living with a man who was not her husband.

But Jesus cared about her and about her need for everlasting life. "Everyone who drinks this water will be thirsty again," he said. "But if you drink from the water I give you, you will never be thirsty again."

Jesus was the water that satisfied her thirst for God.

TO SAVE A CITY

In times of war, a city's supply of water could be cut off. King Hezekiah had men dig a tunnel through solid rock to bring water from a spring into the city of Jerusalem. The tunnel was 1,700 feet long. Two teams started at each end and met almost exactly in the middle.

Mourning for the Dead

❖ ❖ ❖

WHEN SOMEONE DIED, the family was very sad. The people showed how sad they were by weeping and crying out loud. This is called mourning.

Mourning usually began at the moment someone died and continued without stopping until after the burial. One day, Jarius came to Jesus and asked him to heal his daughter. By the time Jesus got to Jarius' house, the girl had died. A crowd was already there, weeping and crying loudly. Jesus raised the girl from the dead.

Part of the crowd that came to cry was hired by the family. These professional mourners would help the family show their sorrow. They would cry out loud, beat their chests, pull out their hair, throw dust on their heads, and tear their clothes. These were all ways to show grief. They would also wear a rough, uncomfortable fabric called sackcloth. The mourners would accompany the body to the tomb.

The weeping did not stop after the burial, however. It continued for at least seven days, usually 30 days.

Jesus had a friend named Lazarus who died. When Jesus got to Lazarus' tomb three days later, the people were still going to the tomb each day to cry. Jesus wept, too. Seeing the people mourn made him sad. Then he called Lazarus out of the grave. Lazarus came out, still wrapped in burial clothes. He was alive again!

MUSIC FOR MOURNING

Mourners followed the body to the burial site accompanied by flute players. According to Jewish rules, even a poor person had to be accompanied by two flute players and at least one weeping woman.

Ancient Burials

❖ ❖ ❖

WHEN SOMEONE DIED in ancient Israel, the burial took place almost immediately—usually within eight hours. That's because the body would begin to decay rapidly in the hot weather.

Not being buried well was a terrible disgrace. Being buried well meant that the body was washed and anointed with perfume. Then it was wrapped it new, white linen cloths. These were layered with many pounds of spices, such as myrrh and aloe.

Then the men in the family carried the body to the burial place, with the women walking in front, crying and tearing their clothes. Other mourners followed behind, along with flute players.

All people were buried outside the city in tombs cut out of rock. These were underground rooms with shelves for the bodies. The tomb was sealed and the body was left to decay. A stone might be rolled in front of the tomb as a door. Years later, the bones were placed in a small box. That way the tomb could be used again.

Jesus once told some of the religious leaders that they were like a white-washed tomb filled with dead men's bones. He meant they looked alright on the outside, but on the inside they were filled with selfish thoughts.

ANCIENT COFFINS

The Egyptians and Philistines often buried their dead in large clay coffinlike boxes. The top third or half of the box was cut away so the body could be inserted. After the body was in place, the top was replaced. On the front of the coffin, a likeness of the deceased person's face was molded in clay.

Party Time

◆ ◆ ◆

THE HEBREWS loved to celebrate, and weddings were the biggest and best parties in any town or village. The only thing that could be better was going to the temple in Jerusalem for one of the festivals.

According to later Jewish traditions, the night before the wedding, the young man and some of his friends went to get the bride. She was wearing a veil, waiting for him with her friends. The bride was carried to his house under a white canopy trimmed in gold. All the friends came along, laughing and singing and dancing in the street.

The party continued at his house, where a room was ready for the bride to spend the night with her friends. The next morning, the whole village turned out for games and more singing and dancing.

That night there was a great dinner. The bride, dressed in finery with lots of jewelry, had the seat of honor under the canopy. She still wore her veil.

Then the bridegroom joined her under the canopy. Seeds were thrown at their feet, or a

Modern Jewish wedding under a canopy

WEDDING GOBLET

During a Jewish wedding ceremony, the bride and groom drink from the same goblet before smashing it to the floor. This is a sign of their wedding vows.

A MARRIAGE SUPPER

The Bible compares Jesus to a bridegroom and the church to a bride. Jesus said he would come back some day and take the church to his father's house in heaven. Then there will be a great celebration in heaven called the Marriage Supper of the Lamb.

PRICE OF A BRIDE

It was customary for the groom to pay the father a bride price. In most cases, money was paid, but the bride price could be a gift or service. King Saul ordered David to kill 100 Philistines for marrying his daughter Michal. Saul figured David would be killed instead, but David did what the king asked.

pomegranate was crushed, or a bottle of perfume was broken. The party continued as the bride and bridegroom left and spent the night together. Only then was the veil removed.

The veil was part of a trick Laban once played on Jacob. Jacob worked seven years so he could marry Laban's daughter Rachel. But the morning after the wedding, he found he had married her sister Leah instead.

After the couple spent the night together, they returned to the party and joined their family and friends. The party went on for at least a week, sometimes longer.

Jesus once went to a wedding party with his disciples. It was there that he performed the first miracle the Bible tells about. So many people had come to the party that they had run out of wine. Jesus told the servant to fill some large jugs with water. Then, when they took the water to the host of the party, it had become wine. And it was very good wine. The party could continue.

RULES OF ENGAGEMENT

The parents decided who their children should marry, usually by the time they were 12. The couple was betrothed (engaged) for a year or so, until the boy was about 16 to 18. During this time, they got to know one another better. In Old Testament times, a young man did not have to serve in the army while he was engaged.

A Happy Day

◆ ◆ ◆

CHILDREN WERE BORN at home, with the help of family members or a midwife. It was a happy, exciting time. The Hebrews believed babies were a blessing.

After birth, the cord between the baby and its mother was cut and tied. Then the midwife washed the baby and rubbed salt, water, and oil on the baby's skin. She wrapped it tightly in a blanket and gave the baby to the father, who named it. After this, the baby was given back to the mother, who began nursing it.

The baby was regularly unwrapped and washed in salt, water, and oil. Then it was wrapped in a blanket again. On the eighth day, boy babies were circumcised. All boys were circumcised to show that they were Hebrews.

The mother could not go to the temple for 40 days if she had a boy and 66 days if she had a girl. Then she would take a lamb and a dove or pigeon to the temple as a sacrifice. (If she was poor, she could take two birds.)

While they were at the temple, the parents would also "buy" the baby back from God if it were a firstborn son. The

NAMING BABIES

Naming a baby was very important. A child was given a first name, but not a last name. A father's name was used to show what family the child was from. For example, Joshua was called Joshua, son of Nun. Sometimes, one of God's names was used as part of the name. Other names were just common words. Caleb means "dog" and Leah means "wild cow" in Hebrew.

A SECOND CHANCE

It was important to have at least one boy baby. For the most part, only males could inherit land or property. They could also make the money needed to care for parents in their old age. If a man died without having any sons, the law required that his father or brothers try to have a baby with the widow. This way she would not be left with nothing.

Hebrews believed the firstborn son belonged to God.

When Moses led the Hebrews out of Egypt where they were slaves, God sent many plagues to convince Pharaoh to let the Hebrews go free. One of these plagues was the death of the firstborn. But he spared the Hebrew children. Because of this, the Hebrews would make an offering on the 40th day after the first son was born.

The offering was usually five pieces of silver. Jesus' parents followed this custom, too. They brought the baby Jesus to the temple and presented him to the Lord. That same day, God told an old priest named Simeon to go into the temple. Simeon held the baby in his arms and praised God. He had waited all his life to see the Son of God.

The mother would usually nurse her baby until it was two years old. When the baby was weaned (stopped getting milk from its mother), it was a reason to have a big family party. Babies were important to the Hebrews.

AN OLD BELIEF

An old superstition claimed that mandrake roots had magical qualities, including the power of fertility. Leah received mandrakes from her son, Reuben, and she and her husband, Jacob, soon had another child.

MIDWIVES

Midwives helped a woman who was having a baby. A midwife was like a nurse. She had helped deliver other babies and knew what to do. Two Egyptian midwives helped save Hebrew babies when Pharaoh ordered that all male babies be killed. They lied to Pharaoh and said they couldn't get to the mothers in time.

A Separate Society

◆ ◆ ◆

WHEN THE HEBREWS entered the promised land, God commanded them not to marry Canaanites or worship their gods. The Hebrews were God's people, and they were supposed to be different. They had different laws, different food, different clothes, and different customs.

But quite often the people would forget the Lord and worship other gods. They would adopt the customs of the people around them. Then God would send a prophet to call the people back to God. Sometimes, the prophets scolded them for dressing or acting like people from other nations.

Finally, God judged Judea for its sins. Jerusalem was destroyed and many of the Hebrews were carried away to Babylon. They were homesick there. They studied the Law together, and they tried to obey God. When they returned home, they rebuilt the temple and tried to worship God again.

The people who had not gone away had married Canaanites and forgotten God. A priest named Ezra came back from Babylon and tore his own hair out he was so sad. He fasted and prayed for many days.

GREAT FAITH

Although some Jews in his day would not talk to a non-Jew, Jesus was not like this. He healed Hebrews and Gentiles alike. Once, a Roman officer came to him because his servant was sick. "If you just say the word, he will be healed," the officer said. Jesus said he had not seen so much faith in all of Israel.

SUPPER WITH SINNERS

One group of Jews who were very careful not to associate with non-Jews was the Pharisees. These religious leaders were very strict about keeping the Law. They would only eat food prepared in a certain way off plates cleaned in a certain way. They often criticized Jesus because he ate with sinners.

Then he commanded the men to leave their foreign wives and worship only God. They did so, eager to please God.

From that time on, the Hebrews were more and more aware of being different. When the Greeks later conquered Judea, most of them refused to sacrifice to the Greek gods or adopt Greek ways. They were very aware of who was a Hebrew and who was not a Hebrew.

By the time Jesus was born, some very religious Jews would not even speak to a Gentile. They called them dogs and refused to associate with them in any way. This caused a problem in the early church. The first Christians were Jews, and they did not like to be around Gentiles. They weren't even sure God had included the Gentiles in his plan.

One day, the Apostle Peter had a dream. A sheet was lowered from heaven filled with animals Jews were not allowed to eat, such as pigs. "Get up and eat," an angel said. But Peter refused. "I have never eaten anything unclean," he said. "Do not call anything God has made unclean," the angel said. This happened three times.

Later Peter understood what the dream meant. "I should not call any person unclean either," he said. Then he began to preach to the Gentiles. Salvation is for everyone.

POINT OF VIEW

There were many ways in which Jews were different from non-Jews. They did not eat pork. They did not work on Saturday. Men wore tassels on their cloaks and did not trim the corners of their beards. They did not paint or draw. Boys were circumcised. The Gentiles thought the Jews were very strange.

NO LONGER STRANGERS

In Ephesians, the Apostle Paul told Gentiles that Christ had broken down the wall between Jews and non-Jews. "You are no longer foreigners, but fellow citizens with God's people and members of God's family," he said.

Home Sweet Home

◈ ◈ ◈

THE HEBREWS lived in houses with flat roofs. Sometimes, it seemed like they lived on their roofs. They spent so much time there that they were required to put fences around their roofs so no one would fall off.

People used their roof for drying plants and fruit. They washed their clothes there. On hot nights, they slept there. Sometimes they went there to pray. During the Feast of Tabernacles, many people would build a small shelter on their roof and stay there for a week.

They got to the roof by an outside staircase or a ladder propped against the wall. In the city, the houses were so close together someone could run from rooftop to rooftop without much trouble or danger.

When Joshua sent two spies into the city of Jericho, a woman named Rahab hid them on her roof under some stalks of flax. Later she let them down by a rope from her window, since her house was next to the city wall.

WHERE DO I SIT?

Furniture was rare during Old Testament times. Poor people had no furniture at all, and wealthier people might have only a couple of chairs or benches and a table in their whole house. People usually slept on a rug or straw mat, covered with the cloak they wore during the day.

Windows were small and usually very high up, with no glass. Most cities were walled, with houses crowded together. Streets were narrow. There was a large open area near the gate called the market.

Most people with more money had homes made of limestone. These homes usually had four rooms built around a courtyard with a garden. Of course, rich people and kings lived in much nicer homes. They even had bathtubs! Some poorer people lived in caves. Some even lived in tents.

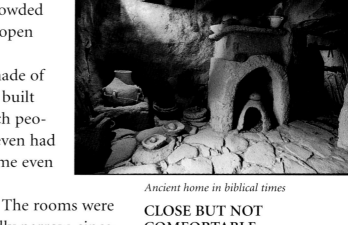

Ancient home in biblical times

The rooms were usually narrow, since lumber was expensive and long beams to stretch from wall to wall were difficult to get.

The roof was made with layers of brush and mud or clay—and often leaked. Four men once easily tore a roof apart to let a lame man down into a crowded room where Jesus was teaching. Floors were usually hardened mud, covered with straw mats.

DID JESUS HAVE A HOME?

Nicer homes were more common by Jesus' time. They often had two stories, with tile floors and balconies facing the courtyard. Jesus ate the Last Supper with his disciples upstairs in such a home. Jesus often ate or stayed with friends. The Bible says foxes had holes and birds had nests, but Jesus had no home of his own.

CLOSE BUT NOT COMFORTABLE

In very ancient Israel, large families lived, worked, ate, and slept together in one room. In the winter, it was dark and smoky—there was no chimney for the fire. In the summer, there were many insects. In some houses, people slept on a low platform while their animals slept on the ground.

FOLLOW INSTRUCTIONS!

Jesus once told a story about a wise man who followed directions and built his house on solid rock. But a foolish man built his house on the sand. When a storm came with rain and wind, the foolish man's house came crashing down, while the wise man's house was left standing. Jesus said it was important to follow his directions.

The City of the Great King

JOHN'S VISION

The Apostle John had a vision of a new Jerusalem. The city would be made of gold as clear as glass, with walls made of jewels and gates made of pearl. A river of life will flow through the city. There will be no crying or death or pain. God will bring this city to earth some day, and those who believe in his Son will get to live there.

WHEN DAVID BECAME KING, he needed a city for his capital. He chose a walled city near a spring at the base of several hills. He captured the city from the Jebusites by crawling up a water shaft with a small band of men.

He named the city Jerusalem, which means "city of peace." It is also called the City of David, or the City of Zion. Zion was one of the hills in the city. Both David and his son Solomon filled in some of the areas between the hills, enlarging the city and its walls. Both built palaces there, and Solomon built the temple.

Later kings would also improve the city. They added gates and extended the walls. Hezekiah had a tunnel built to bring water from the spring. In 586 B.C., the city was destroyed by Babylon, and the people were taken prisoner. When they returned, Nehemiah rebuilt the walls and Zerubbabel rebuilt the temple. Later, King Herod would build a new temple and new walls. This was the temple Jesus went to. It was a massive, magnificent structure. "What wonderful stones!" one of the disciples said.

From David's time until now, the Jewish people have loved Jerusalem. They would try to go there three times a year for the great religious festivals. The psalms are filled with references to Zion and to the Holy City, the City of the King.

A HOLY CITY

Jerusalem is holy to three different religions. Jews honor it because it is the City of David and the site of the temple. Christians honor it because Jesus died there and was resurrected there. Muslims say their greatest prophet, Mohammed, was transported to heaven from Jerusalem.

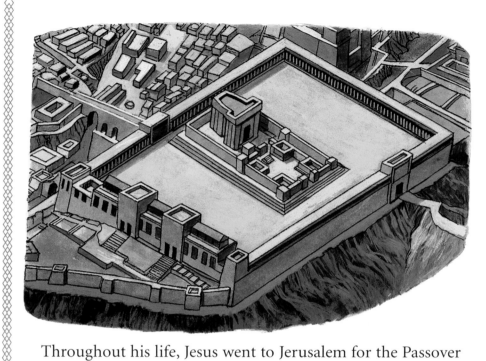

Throughout his life, Jesus went to Jerusalem for the Passover and other festivals. He joined thousands of other pilgrims, singing and praying. As they climbed the mountains toward the city, they would recite certain psalms, called the Psalms of Ascent.

It was a breathtaking sight—shining in the distance—that the pilgrims would see as they topped the mountains surrounding the city. Just before he died, Jesus came over the hill from Bethany and saw the beautiful city. He was so sad that he wept. "The day will come when your enemies will surround you and dash you to the ground," he said.

A few years later this came true. In A.D. 70, the Romans put down a revolt by the Jews, completely destroying the temple and burning the city. Even though the city was rebuilt, only part of the temple wall remains today. Jews still go there to pray for the peace of Jerusalem.

DOME OF THE ROCK

A Muslim mosque is now located on the site of the temple. The mosque is called the Dome of the Rock because it covers a huge rock almost 60 feet long where the Muslims say Mohammed ascended to heaven. Many Jews and Christians believe this is the rock where Abraham almost sacrificed Isaac to God.

THE CITY DUMP

There was no trash pick-up in ancient Jerusalem. A valley running down the center of the city was completely filled with rubble from each time the city was destroyed. The people took their trash to another valley outside the city and burned it. This was the Hinnom Valley, which came to remind some people of hell.

Questions & Answers

◆ ◆ ◆

Q: What's a talent?

A: Jesus talked about a master who gave his servant several talents. But that doesn't mean the man could play the violin! A talent was a unit of money—a lot of money. One talent was 88 pounds of silver, worth 15 years' wages for a laborer.

Q: How did they measure things in Bible times?

A: Lengths were measured in cubits, the length from a man's elbow to the tip of his finger. It's about 18 inches. Other measurements were a span (half a cubit), a fathom (six feet), a reed (six fathoms), and a furlong (about 200 yards).

Q: What's a bath?

A: Liquids were measured by the bath—almost 6 gallons. The same amount of something solid, like grain, was called an ephah. Other measurements of volume included a hin (one sixth of a bath) and a homer (10 baths).

Q: What did they use for money?

A: In earliest times, people traded for things they wanted. But eventually they used gold or silver, weighed by the shekel (less than half an ounce). Eventually, a silver coin that weighed a shekel was called a shekel. Other coins included the drachma (half a shekel) and the denarius, which was a day's wage.

Units of money in Jesus' day included the talent, the drachma, and the shekel.

Q: What's a dowry?

A: When a woman got married, she brought a dowry to the marriage. This included any jewelry she owned, plus gifts from her father, such as cattle or land. One dowry in the Bible was a spring of water. When Solomon married Pharaoh's daughter, she brought an entire city as her dowry.

Q: How did people catch fish?

A: They used nets, mostly. They used a small net that was cast by hand or a large net that was several hundred yards long. This large net had to be pulled in by at least two people. The Bible also mentions catching fish with a hook or spear.

Q: Can salt lose its flavor?

A: Jesus talked about salt losing its flavor. Strictly speaking, that doesn't happen with salt we buy in the store today, but in Jesus' day they used mineral salt from the Dead Sea. This salt had other minerals and sand mixed with it. This could dissolve, leaving a useless, tasteless substance that no longer could be used for seasoning food or cooking.

Q: How did people season their food?

A: Honey was used as a sweetener. The Hebrews liked to use garlic and onions as flavor in their soups and stews. Jesus also mentions mint, dill, and cumin, which are green herbs. He said some people gave part of their hoard of herbs to God, but they failed to give him what he really wanted: justice, mercy, and faithfulness.

Q: Did the law respect people?

A: God's law was sensitive to people and their needs. If a man used his cloak as a promise to pay a debt but he could not pay, the lender could not come inside his house to get the cloak. He had to wait outside. And if the borrower was poor, the lender had to bring the cloak back at night because people used their cloaks as blankets.

Q: When's the best time to fight a war?

A: Samuel talks about this. He said David sent his general Joab off to fight "in the spring of the year, the time when kings go forth to battle." They did this because the rainy season was over. David should have gone, too; he would have stayed out of trouble if he had. He stayed home, he fell in love with a married woman, and he had her husband killed so he could marry her.

Q: Why did children ask "What does this mean"?

A: Children would ask this questions about certain symbols, like the 12 stones Joshua set up so the people would remember when they crossed the Jordan River.

Israelite families ate their meals sitting on the ground.

They asked the same question about the Law and the Passover feast. Jewish children still ask this question today at the Passover seder celebration.

Q: What is a cistern?

A: The opposite of a brethren? Nope. It was a huge hole cut into the rocky ground to store water. Joshua and Jeremiah were both imprisoned in empty cisterns, although Jeremiah's was nearly filled with muck. Ucck!

Q: Where there other ways to get water?

A: Yes. The Romans constructed aqueducts across their empire. These were bridges that carried water from sources outside the city into it. Jerusalem's aqueducts, for example, brought water from as far away as 25 miles. Some of these aqueducts were still in use almost 2,000 years later.

Q: Where did people sleep?

A: Only wealthy people had beds like we have today. Most people slept on a mat made of straw that they rolled up in the morning and put away. They used their cloaks as blankets. When Jesus healed a man and told him to take up his bed and walk, it wasn't hard for the man to do.

Family Life

◆ ◆ ◆ ◆

THE BIBLE is a book about families much like yours. They laughed together, cried together, and worked together. Sometimes they were sad, like when someone died. At weddings they danced all night, happy for the chance to be with their friends and neighbors. They talked about God and how much he loved them. That's still an important thing to talk about with your family and with your friends.

Husband and Wife

❖ ❖ ❖

MOSES MET his wife by being kind and helpful. He had fled from Pharaoh after killing an Egyptian soldier who was beating a Hebrew slave. The only safe place for him was in the desert, in Midian. Moses had stopped by a well for a drink of water, when seven young women came along to water their sheep.

While he was there, some other shepherds came by. Several men tried to drive the women away to make more room for their own flocks. But Moses stood up for the women. He made the men stop bothering them. He even watered the women's flocks himself.

That afternoon, the young women returned home early. "Why are you home so early," their father Jethro asked. They told him about the Hebrew who had protected them. "Where is he? Why didn't you invite him to dinner?" Jethro asked. So the women found Moses and invited him to dinner. Later, Jethro would give his daughter Zipporah to Moses as a wife.

Moses and Zipporah had a son named Gershom. His name means "I am a stranger here." Soon, Moses was not a stranger

MORE OF EVERYTHING

Some Old Testament men had more than one wife, but it was unusual and did not follow God's plan. The wives were sometimes jealous of each other, and the children had arguments. Jacob had four wives, and they were jealous of each other. Solomon had 700 wives who came from other countries and led him away from God.

BAD ADVICE

Like Job, his wife was very sad about losing her children and her home. But unlike Job, she did not trust in God's goodness. She told Job to curse God and die. Job refused. He did not believe he should accept only the good things in life and not the bad.

any more. His wife and his father-in-law taught him how to survive in the desert. He stayed there for 40 years, learning the things he would need to know to lead the children of Israel through the wilderness.

Later, Zipporah saved Moses' life. Other biblical women helped their husbands, too. Sarah trusted Abraham and followed him to Canaan. Rachel helped Jacob secure his inheritance.

A hard-working wife was a great blessing. Proverbs describes such a woman. It says her husband and her children will stand up when she enters

BATHSHEBA

Bathsheba was married to someone else when King David first saw her. Because David sinned when he had Bathsheba's husband killed, their first child died. They did have another child, Solomon, who later became king.

the room and bless her. Many Hebrews believed a man could not be a leader if he did not have a sensible and talented wife.

Jesus surprised everyone by saying these relationships would not be as important in heaven as they are now. A group of rich and powerful leaders, called Sadducees, tried to trick him. "Suppose a woman's husband dies. Then she marries his six brothers, one after the other. All of them die, too. Whose wife will she be in heaven?" Jesus said there will be no marriage in heaven. But people will still be kind and helpful, like Moses in the desert.

Corinth

THE GOOD NEWS TEAM

Priscilla and Aquila, a wife and husband, met the Apostle Paul in the city of Corinth. They were Jewish Christians who had been forced to leave the city of Rome. They were also evangelists. This means that they worked to spread the news about Jesus' resurrection, and they tried to persuade others to become Christians.

DIVORCE? JUST SAY NO!

Jesus taught that marriage was intended to be permanent. But divorce, in certain circumstances, was allowed in biblical times. In Deuteronomy, Moses lists reasons for divorce.

A Baby Was a Blessing

❖ ❖ ❖

ONE DAY, an old priest named Zechariah went into the temple to burn incense before the Lord. Suddenly, the angel Gabriel appeared, standing by the altar. Zechariah was startled. "Don't be afraid," the angel said. "Your prayer has been heard. Your wife Elizabeth will have a son and you are to name him John. He will be a joy and a delight to you and a blessing to others, because he will turn the hearts of fathers toward their children."

Zechariah couldn't believe his ears. Children were considered a blessing in ancient Israel, but he had prayed for many years and now he and his wife were old. "How can I be sure?" he asked. "Because you do not believe me, you will not be able to speak again until after the baby is born," the angel said. Immediately, Zechariah lost his voice.

Sure enough, Elizabeth became pregnant. "The Lord has done this," she said. "He has taken away my disgrace." In those days, a woman felt shame if she could not have children.

Shortly after that, Gabriel appeared to Mary. She was a young, unmarried girl.

WHERE DO BABIES COME FROM?

Psalm 139 has a beautiful passage about how life is created. David, who wrote the psalm, praises God for making his life and says, "For it was you who formed my inward parts; you knit me together in my mother's womb. I praise you, for I am fearfully and wonderfully made."

"The Lord is with you," he said. "His Spirit will come upon you and you will have a son. Name him Jesus. He will be the Son of God. Your cousin Elizabeth will have a son, too, even though she is old. Nothing is impossible with God."

"May it be to me as you have said," answered Mary. Then Mary became miraculously pregnant. She hurried to Judea to see Elizabeth. As soon as Elizabeth saw Mary, the baby inside Elizabeth leaped for joy. "You are blessed, and your baby is blessed, too," Elizabeth said.

"My soul rejoices in what God has done," said Mary. Both women were excited. It was a great honor to have a child, especially one that honored God.

Later, when Elizabeth had her son, her husband, Zechariah, began to speak again. "Praise the Lord," he said. A child had been born. That was a blessing in Israel.

BOYS AND GIRLS

Every child was welcome in Israel, but sons were especially important. They were stronger, and they could work in the fields and help grow crops to sell. Sons could own property and give their parents money when they were old. Girls helped in the house. Sometimes they watched sheep or helped in the fields, especially if there were no sons.

A BLESSING AND RESPONSIBILITY

The Bible says that children are a gift from God. The Hebrews believed this, even though some of the people around them did not. The Canaanites even sacrificed humans on their altars. In Israel, people thought a man with many children had been blessed by God. Every father was expected to teach his children to love God and to keep his commandments.

CHILDREN OF THE KINGDOM

Jesus thought children were a blessing, too. His disciples once tried to send some children away so they would not bother Jesus. But Jesus stopped them. He took the children and blessed them. "To enter the kingdom of God, you have to be like a little child," he said.

Playing With Fire

◆ ◆ ◆

NADAB AND ABIHUM were sons of Aaron, the first high priest. They were learning to be priests, too. Nadab was the oldest. He should have been a high priest like his father. But neither of the sons followed strict instructions about how to burn incense at the altar inside the Tabernacle. God had said how this was to be done. The priests were only to use coals from the bronze altar outside the Tabernacle. And they were only to offer incense at certain times.

On the very first day of worship in the new Tabernacle, Nadab and Abihum took other coals to the altar of incense. Immediately, holy fire came out from the presence of the Lord and destroyed them both—although their bodies and tunics were not even burned. "I will be honored by those who approach my presence," God said.

Three other young men were also engulfed in fire without getting burned. But they didn't die. Shadrach, Meshach, and Abednego were carried away to Babylon as servants to the king. They were commanded to eat food that God had said Hebrews were not to eat. The young men asked if they could eat vegetables instead. Ten days

ABEL'S OFFERING

Abel was the first child to please God by obeying him. He gave God a lamb as an offering, exactly as God had asked him to do.

SORRY SONS

Sometimes, priests and prophets were so busy they failed to instruct and discipline their own children. Both Eli and Samuel had sons who grew up and were sinful. Eli's sons kept the best part of the sacrifices for themselves. Samuel's sons took bribes and cheated the people.

later, they were healthier and stronger than all the other servants who had eaten the king's food.

Later, the king built a statue of himself. "When the music begins to play, everyone should bow down and worship my statue," the king said. If anyone refused, they would be thrown into a blazing furnace. But when the music started, the Hebrews refused to bow. The king was furious. "I will have you thrown into the fire," he said. "Then what god will rescue you?"

The Hebrew children still refused to worship the idol. "Our God can save us, but if he doesn't, we still will not bow." So the king had the fire made even hotter. It was so hot the soldiers who carried the Hebrews to the door of the furnace died.

But then the king leaped to his feet in amazement. The young men were walking around in the fire, completely unharmed. "Servants of the Most High God, come out here" the king shouted. Shadrach, Meshach, and Abednego came out of the furnace, and their robes were not scorched. They didn't even smell like smoke!

Unlike Nadab and Abihum, they had honored God and obeyed him.

TIMOTHY

Timothy was a young pastor in the early church. His mother, Eunice, and grandmother Lois taught him the word of God from the time he was a very small child. The Apostle Paul wrote two letters to Timothy that are now part of the New Testament. He said the instruction Timothy had received made him wise. Paul and Timothy became so close that Timothy became almost like Paul's own son.

GOOD KID, BAD KID

A disrespectful or disobedient son was a disgrace to the family. The Law promises a long and happy life to children who honor their parents. The Book of Proverbs says a son who obeys his parents is a delight to them.

A Great Treasure

❖ ❖ ❖

WOMEN HAD a hard life in Bible times. Each day, they would grind wheat or barley and make bread. They had to go to the spring or well and get water, too, carrying heavy pots or jars on their heads. Then there were clothes to make and wash. When it was time to harvest, they worked in the fields along with the men.

But a woman had little legal or political power. Before she was married, her father made all the decisions—including who she would marry. After she was married, her husband made the decisions. Her husband could divorce her, but she could not divorce him or leave him. If she made a contract, he could decide not to keep it.

But in everyday life, Hebrew women had it much better than women in other countries at that time. In many cases, the Law treated both men and women the same. The penalties for crimes were the same. The Law required children to honor them both. A wife was not treated like a slave or unpaid servant. Instead, she was honored as the mother of sons.

CHILDLESSNESS

In biblical times, being childless was a woman's greatest misfortune. Childless women mentioned in the Bible are Sarah, Rebekah, Rachel, Hannah, and Elizabeth. The Lord eventually blessed each of these women with a child. Psalm 113:9 states, "He gives the barren woman a home, making her the joyous mother of children."

Although women could not be priests, they could enjoy all the religious festivals and bring sacrifices to the temple. Women singers were part of the temple choir. Sometimes, God used women to speak to the people, including at least three prophetesses: Miriam, Deborah, and Huldah.

God once used Queen Esther to save the entire nation. Evil Haman had gotten King Xerxes to sign a law requiring all the Jews to be killed. At the urging of her uncle Mordecai, Esther went to the king—even though she risked her life by going to the king without being invited. Other women were part of God's plan, too, like Rebekah who helped secure Isaac's blessing for her son Jacob.

The Bible taught that a wife was a treasure and said men should love them and delight in them. In Proverbs, King Lemuel described the woman who was honored by her husband and children. She prepares food, spins cloth, buys land, plants crops, gives to the needy, and sells cloth to the merchants. "She is worth far more than rubies," he says. "Give her the reward she has earned, and let her works bring her praise at the city gate."

A woman who worked hard was respected by all those who knew her.

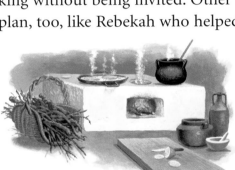

FRESH BREAD, BAKED DAILY

Baking bread was a daily chore for women in ancient days. Bread was made of wheat, rye, barley, or millet, and usually baked on flat stones that had been heated. In later times, some families used ovens. One kind was an earthenware dish that was placed upside down over a fire. The bread cakes were baked on the curved surface. Another kind was shaped like a cone. Bread cakes were placed on the inside of the cone and baked.

NO TIME FOR DOLLS

Girls were supposed to help their mothers with chores around the house. A girl might gather wood for a fire, press dough into cakes, or sew clothing.

TRUE BEAUTY

Proverbs says not to praise a woman because of her beauty, but because of her love for God. This idea is repeated in the New Testament. The Apostle Paul said a woman's beauty does not depend on her jewelry or clothes, but on her quiet and gentle spirit. True beauty is on the inside, not the outside.

A Perfect Match

◆ ◆ ◆

ABRAHAM DID not want his son Isaac to marry a woman from Canaan. The Canaanites worshiped idols, and he wanted his grandchildren to worship the true God. So Abraham sent his chief servant to a different land to find a wife for his son. The servant traveled to Nahor looking for a wife for Isaac. He decided to sit by the well and wait for the women to come by. He prayed and asked God for help. "If any of them offers to water my camels, let her be the one," he prayed. He had ten camels, so that would be a lot of work.

Before he even finished praying, a beautiful young woman named Rebekah came to get water. He hurried to meet her. "May I have a drink from your jar?" he asked. "Certainly, sir," she said. "I'll draw water for your camels, too."

Then the servant gave her a nose ring and two expensive gold bracelets. "Whose daughter are you?" he asked. She told him that her father was Laban. Then the servant knew that she was a distant relative of Abraham, and that her family worshiped God. "Is there room for me to

MADE IN HEAVEN

The Bible says God made marriage so people would not be alone and could work together to make a safe place for children. Jesus said if a man and woman got married, they should stay together and love each other for the rest of their lives.

DO I HAVE A CHOICE?

Arranged marriages did not always mean men and women had no say about whom they would marry. Shechem and Samson both asked their parents to arrange a marriage with a particular girl. Sometimes, young men married women against their parents' wishes. Esau married two foreign women who were a source of grief to his parents.

Modern Jewish wedding

WEDDING PARTNERS

It was generally forbidden for Hebrews to marry foreigners. It was feared that a spouse might lead God's people to worship other gods.

stay at your father's house?" he asked. "Yes," she said. Then she ran home to tell her family. Her brother came to the well to invite the servant to stay at their home. They set out dinner for the servant, but he was so excited he couldn't eat.

"I will not eat until I tell you what I have to say," he said. Then he told Rebekah's father and brother about his master, Abraham, and about his prayer that afternoon at the well. "This must be from the Lord," they said. "Here is Rebekah. Take her and go, and let her become the wife of your master's son." The servant then gave her more gifts—along with gifts for her family.

Her father wanted her to stay a few days, but Abraham's servant was eager to return. "I will go with him," Rebekah said. So Rebekah traveled over 500 miles to marry a man she had never seen.

They got to Canaan in the evening, and Isaac saw the caravan coming from across the field. Rebekah saw him and got down off her camel. She took her veil and covered herself. Then she came to Isaac. The servant told Isaac everything that had happened. Isaac took Rebekah and married her. He loved her, even though someone else had chosen her for him.

HEAVENLY MARRIAGE

Jesus told several stories about weddings to show the joy of life in heaven. The Apostle Paul said the church was the bride of Christ and Jesus was the bridegroom. The Apostle John had a vision of a great celebration in heaven. He called it the Marriage of the Lamb.

Respected Elders

◆ ◆ ◆

WHEN MOSES LED the Hebrews out of Egypt, he acted as the judge for all the people, sitting and listening to their problems all day long. His father-in-law suggested that he appoint good and godly men to help him judge. These men were called elders.

Later, each village or town had their own elders. These were older, wiser men who could give good advice. They were well respected. They knew the Law and knew what to do when there was a problem.

The elders sat at the threshing floor of the village or the gate of the city, listening to the people and solving their arguments. They also enforced the Law, much like judges today. They decided who was guilty and what the punishment should be. It was an honor to be one who "sat at the gate."

Even when there was a king, the towns and villages still had elders. After the exiles returned from Babylon, the elders joined with the priests and scribes to run the government. By Jesus'

OUCH!

Towns had a different number of elders, depending on the size of the city. Succoth had 77. Once, they refused to give Gideon and his army food as they went out to war. After he won the battle, Gideon returned and had all 77 men beaten with thorns and briars.

time, there was a Jewish court made up of elders, scribes, and priests. It was called the Sanhedrin. They had the final say in religious matters, in collecting taxes for the temple, and regarding punishment for certain crimes. They were also responsible for the relationship between the Jews and the Romans.

Jesus was brought before the Sanhedrin and condemned to die. They thought he was breaking the Law by claiming to be God. They were also afraid the people would make him king. Then the Romans would be angry, and come and attack their nation.

Later, the idea of elders was used in the early church. The elders in Jerusalem helped decide which Jewish laws would apply to Christians. The Apostle Paul appointed elders in the churches he started. These were people who knew the Scriptures and could lead the local church.

Paul said an elder should be hardworking, thoughtful, orderly, gentle, and full of good deeds. Elders were supposed to have well-behaved children. They could not drink too much or argue or be greedy. Like the elders of ancient Israel, people would look to them for advice. It would still be an honor to be an elder.

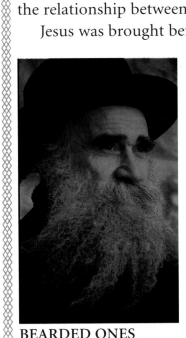

BEARDED ONES

The Hebrew word elder comes from another word that meant "beard." So an elder had to be old enough to have a beard. Respect for the elderly was required, since they had learned many things and had become wise. Proverbs says "Gray hair is a crown of splendor; it is attained through a righteous life."

HEAVENLY ELDERS

John saw elders in his vision of heaven. This is described in the Book of Revelation. Twenty four elders sit around the throne of God. They wear white robes and crowns of gold and sing songs of praise to the Lamb.

GOOD SEATS

Elders were given the best seats in the synagogue. Later, elders in the church also got special seats. But James said someone should not get a good seat because he was rich or had nice clothes. "Don't show favoritism," he said.

A Room of Their Own

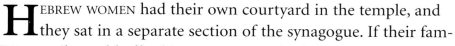

HEBREW WOMEN had their own courtyard in the temple, and they sat in a separate section of the synagogue. If their family could afford it, women even had their own room or their own tent.

There were two reasons for this. One reason women were kept separate from men was for privacy. Separate rooms or seats allowed them to go to the bathroom or nurse a baby without someone seeing them. Bathing was even part of some worship ceremonies—but the women needed a place of their own.

The other reason is that the Hebrews thought it was shameful to be naked. Nakedness was a part of worship among the Canaanites. But the Law said Hebrews should not let others see their body. It was a disgrace to do so, even a sin. When Hanun cut the clothes off some of David's servants, the men were terribly embarrassed. When Noah's son saw his father naked, the son was cursed.

When he was on his rooftop, David was not being careful about these important rules when he spied Bathsheba bathing. Later, he slept with her and had her husband killed.

That's the second reason women were kept separate—to protect them from men who might hurt them or take advantage of them. This was not

HELPING THE POOR

Poor people often had only one item of clothing. At night, some had no cloak or mantle to protect themselves from the cold. Several times, the Bible says to give clothes to the poor. That was one way to help them.

uncommon. One day, David and his men returned to camp and found that all the women had been captured and taken away. The Bible says David and his men wept so long and so hard they had no strength left to weep.

Then some of the men wanted to stone David because he had not been careful enough about protecting the women. But David took 400 men and went after the raiding party. They brought back all the women, including David's own two wives.

A king often had many wives—and a separate palace where they could be protected from other men. Other men tried to protect their wives, too. This is why women wore veils.

It's also why women seldom went out alone, except to the well or spring twice a day. Moses and Jacob both met their wives at a spring or well, and that's where Abraham's servant found a wife for Isaac.

The Hebrews tried to give women their own separate, private space. This helped protect them.

WIDOW'S MITE

In Jesus' day, if a man died, his widow was to be taken care of by his brothers or uncles. But if a widow had no male in-laws, she usually ended up very poor. So when Jesus saw the widow giving a mite (a very small amount of money) at one temple, he was impressed with her generosity. It may have been a little amount, but it was a great amount for her to give—since she had very little.

NOT ASHAMED

The Bible says that Adam and Eve were naked and were not ashamed. But once they sinned, they began to see things—and each other—differently. They tried to cover themselves with leaves but that was not enough. God made them clothes from animals skins.

BLESSINGS FOR EVERYONE

God was careful to include women in his blessings on Israel. The prophet Joel said that God would pour out his Spirit on both men and women. The Apostle Paul said the same thing about the church. When it comes to the Holy Spirit and his gifts, there is no difference in God's sight between men and women, Jews and Gentiles, or free people and slaves.

The Law of the Land

◆ ◆ ◆

WHEN THE 12 TRIBES of Israel entered the Promised Land, each tribe was given a certain amount of land. Then each family within the tribe was given a plot of their own. Families held on to their land for generation after generation.

The father gave the land to his sons—and his first son got twice as much as his brothers. But what if a man had no sons?

Zelophehad, for example, had five daughters. After he died, his daughters came to Moses. This was before the land was divided. "Our father died in the wilderness, but he left no sons," they said. "Why should his name disappear because he had no sons? Give us his share of the land."

God told Moses that the daughters were right. "If a man dies and leaves no son, give his inheritance to his daughters," God said. The daughters had to marry someone from their own tribe, however. That way the land would stay in the same tribe.

If a man had no daughters either, his land went to his brothers or his uncles. It was important that a family have and keep their land. God once judged a king

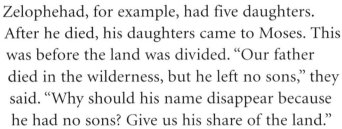

THE ROOT OF ALL EVIL

A man who wanted his brother to divide a family inheritance with him asked for Jesus' help. Instead, Jesus warned the man how greed and possessions can ruin a soul.

who did not honor this important rule.

King Ahab asked Naboth to sell him a vineyard near his palace. Naboth refused. "The Lord will not allow me to give you the land of my fathers," he said. Ahab was furious. He wanted the land for a vegetable garden. Ahab went back to his palace, and lay on his bed, sulking. He told his wife, Jezebel, what had happened. "Cheer up," she said. "I will get you the land."

She sent letters to the elders of Naboth's village, asking them to accuse Naboth of cursing God and the king. The elders did this, because they were afraid of Jezebel. So Naboth was falsely accused, and he and his sons were stoned to death. Then the king took the land.

But the prophet Elijah went to Ahab and said God was angry with him because he had stolen the land. Both Ahab and Jezebel were punished by God because of their sins. Ahab and Jezebel had broken the law of the land.

THE OWNER OF EVERYTHING

The Bible teaches that God owns everything. People only take care of things for him. They act as his stewards, servants responsible for managing their master's affairs. As his stewards, we are to treat animals kindly, give to people in need, and try to do what is right.

THE LEVITES

The tribe of Levites received no land when they entered the promised land. They lived as priests in cities and depended on the gifts that other tribes were supposed to provide.

SPECIAL RULES

Some men had more than one wife, so rules and customs helped decide what to do with the land. The first son of the first wife usually got the biggest share. But every son got something, even if his mother was a slave.

A Time for Fun

◆ ◆ ◆

THE ANCIENT HEBREWS had to work hard, but they took some time to play, too. Many toys from that time have been discovered, including rattles, dolls, dollhouses, target games, and board games. Many board games were simple; they were carved or scratched on a flat piece of stone. But wealthy people had quite elaborate games made of ivory and even gold.

Some of these games were like chess and checkers. One game, the Royal Game of Ur, has been played for over 4,000 years. It involves moving pieces of colored stone around a series of pits using dice. It was probably first played in the dirt, but a very fancy game board has been found.

Kids played outside, of course, with marbles and balls as well as sticks and stones. Pictures carved in stone from nearby Egypt show boys playing tug-of-war and girls playing a singing or chanting game. The prophet Zechariah talked about children playing and singing in the streets. Jesus mentioned this, too. He said

RUN THE RACE

In New Testament times, Greek games were popular, although most Jews refused to participate. The Greeks began the Olympics, and their games included boxing, racing, and throwing the discus or javelin. The Apostle Paul often referred to these games. He said Christians should "run the race" of faith and win a prize.

Ancient lots

boys and girls played make-believe games, like weddings and funerals.

Weddings were a chance to have a party. In fact, many things were a chance to have a party—having a guest, weaning a baby, picking grapes, or going to a festival in Jerusalem. At these events, adults had fun, too. There was drinking and dancing and lots of music. (Although men and women did not dance together.)

MAKING DECISIONS

Casting lots was a way of deciding what God wanted. This was done by putting colored or marked stones in a container and shaking it until one fell out. Each stone represented a different choice. Lots were used to decide if someone was guilty. Lots were used to decide which job in the temple a priest had.

Contests were held at these parties. These included wrestling, running, and shooting a slingshot or bow and arrow. Riddles were a great party game. At his wedding, Samson asked his guests a riddle—and bet them 30 sets of clothes that they couldn't solve it. The men threatened Samson's wife and made her tell them the answer. He was so mad he went out and killed 30 men to get the clothes to pay off his debt.

Ancient game

Gambling was not allowed. But dice games were common, even if they were against the rules. Soldiers even cast dice to decide who would get Jesus' cloak when he was crucified.

Part of God's will was for people to have fun. The writer of Ecclesiastes said there is a time for weeping and for laughing. He wrote: "There is nothing better than for a man to be happy and do good."

ACCEPTING YOUR LOT

Casting lots was the way the land was divided between different families when the 12 tribes entered the promised land. After that, a man's piece of land was his lot, a term we still use today. Eventually a man's lot meant everything he received from God, including his family or job. Solomon said each man should accept his lot in life as a gift from God.

Fishers of People

◆ ◆ ◆

T HE ANCIENT HEBREWS were not great fishermen. (By Jesus' day, fishing had become popular.) The Hebrews did not live along the coast, and the one large lake, the Sea of Galilee, was on the northern edge of the country. This was far from Jerusalem and most of the people. In fact, they knew so little about fishing that they only had one word for fish, regardless of the size or kind.

They did fish some, but more for food than for sport. They caught fish in three different ways. The prophet Habakkuk mentions all three. One way was to use a hook and line—but no pole. They also used a small round net that they could toss from shore. It had weights along the bottom so it would fall on top of the fish, surprising them and wrapping around them. The third way was to use a different kind of net that was dragged between boats and made into a circle, from which the fish could not escape.

Mussels

FISH FOOD

The Law did not allow the Hebrews to eat catfish. Eels, sharks, and rays were also off limits, along with clams and mussels. The rule was they could eat no fish or seafood without scales and fins.

TWO BY TWO

Peter and Andrew worked together, as did James and John. Both of these pairs were brothers. Fishing was often a family business. Matthew listed all the disciples as pairs, which may have been the way they sat together in the boat.

Even though most people did not catch fish, they did eat fish. There was a Fish Gate in the wall of Jerusalem where dried and salted fish were brought to market. By Jesus' time, this had become an important trade, with whole cities built near the Sea of Galilee for catching and drying fish to sell.

Large nets several hundred yards long were hauled up on shore after each fishing trip. Fishermen spent many hours making, washing, drying, and mending these nets. The boats were small, with room for two or four men. Fishermen often worked in pairs, with one steering and one tending the net.

Jesus called several of the disciples in pairs, since that's how they worked together. One day, he asked Peter and Andrew if he could sit in their boat to teach the people who crowded around him. When he was through teaching, he asked Peter to take the boat out into deeper water and let down his nets. "Lord," said Peter, "we have already fished all night and caught nothing. But I will do it because you asked me to." When he did what Jesus asked, he caught so many fish his nets began to break. They had to call their partners James and John to help.

From that time on, all four men followed Jesus. They fished for people.

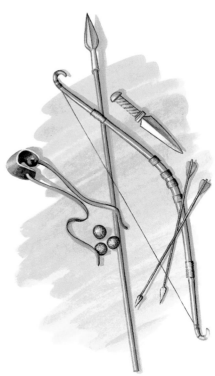

HUNTING SEASON

Hunting was not a popular sport in Israel like it was in Assyria. It was just a way to get food or protect the flocks. Large animals, like lions and bears, were caught in pits camouflaged with nets and mats. Deer and other animals were hunted with bows and slings. Partridge and quail were usually trapped with snares and nets.

FRESH FISH

There are no fish in the Dead Sea, a very salty lake southeast of Jerusalem. Ezekiel had a vision that one day the Dead Sea would be alive, filled with fresh water and teaming with fish. He wrote: "Fishermen will stand on the shore, and there will be a place for spreading nets."

The Family Farm

◆ ◆ ◆

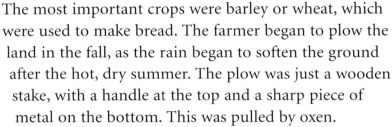

EVERY FAMILY in ancient Israel had a farm. When the Hebrews entered Canaan, each family was given a plot of land. Even if they lived in the city, they would farm their land or have someone else do it.

The most important crops were barley or wheat, which were used to make bread. The farmer began to plow the land in the fall, as the rain began to soften the ground after the hot, dry summer. The plow was just a wooden stake, with a handle at the top and a sharp piece of metal on the bottom. This was pulled by oxen.

Throughout the fall and winter, the farmer would sow the seeds, scattering them by hand. Then the land was plowed or raked again to work the seeds into the soil and protect them from pests. This was all done during the rainy season, as the family prayed their crop would not be destroyed by thunderstorm and hail or eaten by caterpillars or locusts.

Everyone was happy in the spring, as the barley was harvested in April or May. The wheat was ready a month later.

THE CUSTOM OF GLEANING

Moses taught that the harvest should be for everyone, including the poor and outsiders. When the harvest was gathered, much food was left behind in the fields. After the harvesters left, the poor were allowed to collect, or glean, what had been dropped or left on the stem.

EVEN RAVENS GET FED

To remind his listeners of God's love for them, Jesus talked about ravens. They did not plant or harvest, yet God fed them. Thus God feeds us because he loves us.

The farmer grasped the grain with one hand and lopped it off with the other hand, using a short, sharp sickle. The wheat was collected in bundles and taken by cart or donkey to the village threshing floor.

The threshing floor was a circular patch of ground, drained and stamped down hard. It was usually on a hill, where the wind was strong. It belonged to the whole village. Throughout the year, it was used as a meeting place, but at harvest time it was a busy place where every family came to separate the grain from the straw.

SOWING SEEDS

A sower in biblical times carried his seed in a large shoulder bag. The seed was not planted in the field in straight rows as it is today. Instead, the farmer would take handfuls of seed from his bag and toss it on the ground as he walked along.

This was often done by having an ox walk on it, going around and around in circles. The ox pulled a heavy wooden sled. This broke up the straw, which was then carried away and stored to feed the animals. It was also mixed with manure to make fuel for the fire.

The grain was left on the threshing floor, where it was tossed into the air so the wind would blow the light husks—called chaff—away. The grain fell to the ground in a heap, where it was sifted and stored, either in deep holes carved in stone or in huge clay jars.

THE FIRST FRUITS

The harvest was a time of celebration in ancient Israel. But God did not want his people to forget that he was responsible for the abundant crops. Therefore, the people had to bring the first fruits of the season to their priest as an offering. The Israelites were not allowed to eat any of the harvest until this ceremony was performed.

HOW FAITH GROWS

The Apostle Paul once compared the job of gaining new believers to sowing seeds. One Christian would plant a seed, another would water it, and God would bring about growth.

Living in Tents

◆ ◆ ◆

THE FIRST HEBREW, Abraham, lived in a tent. Living in a tent was not an easy life. Most of the people who lived in them longed for something better, something more secure. The Bible says Abraham spent his whole life looking for a city built by God. Instead, he lived in a tent made of goat hair sewn together and stretched over poles. The material was fastened to the ground with ropes attached to stones or pegs made of wood. One of these pegs made a Kenite woman named Jael famous. The Kenites were nomads whose ancestor Hobab was a scout for the Hebrews while they crossed the desert on the way to Canaan.

An evil Canaanite general named Sisera had oppressed Israel for 20 years. Finally, he attacked them but was defeated by Deborah and Barak. He escaped, and asked Jael if he could hide in her tent. "Come right in," she said. "Don't be afraid."

He was exhausted. She covered him with a blanket and gave him some warm milk to drink. He fell right to sleep, exhausted from the battle. Then Jael took a tent peg and a hammer and drove it through his skull. He died instantly, and Israel was free of a bitter enemy. Later, the prophetess Deborah sang a song about Israel's victory and called Jael the "most blessed of tent-dwelling women."

As the Hebrews settled down in Canaan, most of them had houses. But one group who lived in

REMEMBERING THE TENTS

At Jewish weddings today, the bride and groom are married under a tent, a canopy of cloth stretched over four poles. This is because a tent was put up for the new couple in the family camp after a wedding in ancient Israel. Even after the Hebrews lived in houses, they still used the Hebrew word for tent to refer to their homes.

tents was the Rechabites, descendants of Jonadab. He had said they should never drink wine or live in houses. They lived in tents for over 200 years and only settled in Jerusalem when the country was threatened by an invading army. The prophet Jeremiah offered them wine, but they refused to drink it. God said he wanted his people to obey him just like the tent dwelling Rechabites obeyed their father.

In the New Testament, very few people lived in tents. But enough people needed tents that the Apostle Paul could earn a living making and selling them. He told Christians that their bodies were like tents. Just like Abraham, we long for something better. In heaven, Christians will have new bodies, a house that will not get sick or grow old.

Modern nomad baking bread

THE ISHMAELITES

Ishmael was the son of Abraham and Hagar, Sarah's servant. Ishmael became the father of the Ishmaelites, a tribe of fierce nomads who lived in tents in the Sinai wilderness.

FATHER OF TENT DWELLERS

Tent dwellers have been in biblical lands from the earliest days. Genesis names Jabal, a descendant of Cain, as the father of all who live in tents.

TENTMAKERS

The Apostle Paul was a tentmaker. In Paul's time, tentmakers worked with leather as well as goat hair and made things like harnesses, mattresses, and cushions.

A Love Story

❖ ❖ ❖

LIFE WAS NOT always easy for families in Bible times, but love could hold them together just like it does today. The Book of Ruth tells a story about love like this.

It began when Elimelech left his home in Bethlehem and traveled to Moab because there was a famine in Israel. He took his wife, Naomi, and his two sons, who ended up marrying Moabite women, Orpah and Ruth.

Eventually, the man and both sons died. Naomi decided to return to Israel. She kissed Orpah and Ruth good-bye and wept, because she loved them. "Return to your own homes," she said. "May the Lord take care of you."

So Orpah went home, but Ruth would not. "Where you go, I will go," she said. "Your God will be my God, and your people will be my people." The two women went to Israel, but they had no money and no food. One day, Ruth went to a field to pick up the barley the reapers had dropped.

Boaz, the owner of the field, noticed her and asked his workers who she was. They told him that she was Naomi's daughter-in-law, and she had come from

A NEW BABY

Boaz and Ruth had a son named Obed, who became the grandfather of King David. The Bible says the baby was a comfort to Naomi in her old age, and she was his nurse.

Moab to take care of her. Boaz was a relative of Naomi and was glad someone was helping her. He told his workers to leave extra grain behind and to give Ruth water and lunch.

That night, Ruth took more grain home than Naomi expected. "Blessed is the man who noticed you," Naomi said. "What is his name?" When she heard it was Boaz, she told Ruth to only glean in his fields until the end of harvest. When the harvest was over, she told Ruth what to do.

"There is a law here that says if a man dies, one of his relatives should marry the widow and take care of her. Tonight, Boaz is sleeping in the field, guarding his grain. Take a bath and put on your best clothes. Then go and uncover his feet, and lie down." So Ruth did what Naomi said. Boaz woke up in the middle of the night, startled. "Who are you?" he asked. "I am Ruth," she said. "Protect me, sir, for you are our nearest relative."

"You are very kind," Boaz said. "You have not gone after younger men, rich or poor. Don't be afraid. I will marry you." So he did. And he loved Ruth and Naomi, and took care of them both.

A BEAUTIFUL PROMISE

Ruth's promise to stay with Naomi is often used in weddings today. This is the complete promise: "Where you go, I will go; Where you lodge, I will lodge; your people shall be my people, and your God my God. Where you die, I will die— there will I be buried."

A CUSTOM OF COVERING

Ruth uncovered Boaz' feet so he would wake up and notice her. It was a custom that Boaz understood. It meant she wanted him to protect her. She also asked him to spread his garment over her, which he did. That meant he would marry her.

SIGNED WITH A SANDAL

Before Boaz could marry Ruth, he had to get permission from a man who was a closer relative than he was. He did this at the city gate, in front of ten witnesses. The man took off his sandal and gave it to Boaz—a sign that the deal was final.

Questions & Answers

◆ ◆ ◆

Q: Did Jesus have a wife?

A: No, but women were important to Jesus. He often stayed with his good friends Martha and Mary and their brother. Several women followed him and listened to his teachings. These women came to the tomb after he died, and they were the first ones to know that he was alive again.

Q: Did he have brothers and sisters?

A: Yes. Jesus had at least four younger brothers and two or more younger sisters. After he died, one of his brothers, James, became a leader in the early church. He was probably the author of the New Testament Book of James, one of the first New Testament books written. Another brother wrote the Book of Jude.

Q: Do babies go to heaven when they die?

A: Yes. King David and Bathsheba had a baby that became very sick. David wept and lay on the ground and prayed for several nights. He wouldn't eat. But when the baby died, David washed and ate and went to the temple to worship God. He knew he would see his son in heaven. "Someday I will go to him," he said.

Q: When does a boy become a man?

A: During New Testament times, a boy became a man when he was 13. There was a special ceremony called a bar mitzvah, which means "son of the law." After

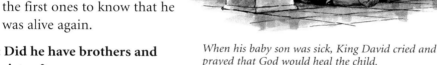

When his baby son was sick, King David cried and prayed that God would heal the child.

that, he was regarded as an adult and took his place in the synagogue and the community. Jewish boys today have a bar mitzvah—but they still have to wait until they're at least 16 to drive.

Q: Did kids have fun?

A: Yes. They played games and had simple toys. But children had to work hard, helping around the house and in the fields. Because of all this responsibility, they grew up quickly. There was no such thing as being a "teenager" with lots of time to hang out with friends. Most people in Bible times were married between 16 to 18 years old.

Q: Did families worship together?

A: Fathers were responsible for the religious training of their families, and they taught the Scriptures in their own homes. They also led their families in singing and praying, often several times a day. If possible, they took their family to Jerusalem for the religious festivals at the temple.

Q: What's the first family in the Bible?

A: Adam and Eve had many sons and daughters. We know the names of at least three of their sons: Cain, Abel, and Seth. Cain was jealous of his brother Abel, and he killed him. Later, Eve had another son, Seth. The Bible says his birth comforted her. "God has granted me another child in place of Abel," she said.

Q: Is it okay for a man to cry?

A: Not only did King David cry when his baby died, he cried for his older sons as well. When his son Absalom tried to take over the kingdom, David's soldiers defeated his army and killed Absalom. David cried when he heard the news. "I wish I had died instead of you," he said.

Q: What's the most famous family in the Bible?

A: For Christians, the answer is probably the holy family—Jesus, Mary, and Joseph. But the Bible tells more about Abraham and his wife Sarah than it does about any other family. Two important groups besides Christians, both the Jews and the Muslims, share a high regard for this couple and their immediate descendants.

Q: Did men have more than one wife?

A: Jacob had two wives and two slaves—called concubines. Solomon had hundreds of wives. But having just one wife was expected and preferred. Divorce was discouraged, too. Healthy, happy marriages were the foundation for healthy, happy homes—just like today.

Q: Were there blended families like there are today?

A: When men had more than one wife, there was often friction between the children of one wife and the chil-

Absalom was killed by soldiers after his head got stuck in a tree's branches.

dren of another wife. A good example is Jacob and his 12 sons. One son, Joseph, was sold into slavery by the other brothers. But many of these families worked their problems out and pleased God.

Q: Were there families without fathers?

A: Sure, but God promised to be a father to the fatherless. And the Bible is careful to insist that everyone should help care for both widows and orphans. One famous pastor, Timothy, may not have had a dad around. He was taught the Scripture by his mother and grandmother.

Q: Could you be adopted?

A: Adoption was common under Roman law. An adopted son had the same rights and responsibilities as any natural-born children. The Apostle Paul said this is what happens to people who trust Christ for salvation—they are adopted into God's family as his own children, and Jesus becomes their brother.

Q: Did everybody have to join the army?

A: In war time, most men were drafted to help fight. But there were exceptions. If a man had built a house but hadn't dedicated it, or if he had planted a new vineyard but hadn't harvested it, he did not have to go to war. He was excused from service for a year after he was married. Land and family were important.

Parables

❖　❖　❖　❖

ESUS WAS a great storyteller! He used stories so people could remember and understand what he had to say. The stories were about ordinary things, like trees, or bread, or lamps, or seeds. But his ideas weren't ordinary at all. He used these simple stories, called parables, to show people how to treat each other and to love God. These stories will also help you remember and understand what Jesus taught.

Nathan's Parable

◆ ◆ ◆

KING DAVID had sinned with Bathsheba. Perhaps he thought no one knew the depth of his sin. Perhaps he had forgotten for a while that God always knows when we sin, and he will never ignore sin or let it go unpunished. God spoke to his prophet Nathan and told him to confront David about this sin. Nathan used this parable.

There were two men who lived in the same city. One man was rich and the other was poor. The rich man had many large flocks of sheep and herds of cattle. The poor man had nothing except one little lamb. The lamb was a pet that the man and his family loved.

One day, a traveler came to see the rich man, who decided to prepare a nice meal for his visitor. Rather than use one of his own sheep for the meal, he took the poor man's lamb and prepared it for his company's dinner.

King David was very angry to hear about this man's mean actions. He asked Nathan who the rich man was. He planned to punish him harshly. Nathan told David, "You are the rich man!" David understood what Nathan was telling him. He remembered that God knew all about his sin and that he would not let David go unpunished. David asked God to forgive his sin, and he faced his punishment. God forgave David.

DAVID'S TROUBLES

Nathan predicted that David's family life would always be troubled. His words came true. First, the child he had with Bathsheba died. Then David's sons fought: Amnon was killed by his half-brother Absalom, after Amnon had attacked Absalom's sister Tamar. For years, Absalom and David did not speak to each other. Then Absalom led a bloody rebellion against his father that ended in Absalom's death. At the end of his life, David watched his sons Solomon and Adonijah fight over the throne.

Song of the Vineyard

❖ ❖ ❖

IN THE OLD TESTAMENT, the prophet Isaiah used a parable to warn the Jewish people that God was not pleased with their sinfulness. Here is the parable Isaiah told.

There was a man who owned a vineyard. It was on a hillside with very rich soil. The owner had taken out all the rocks so the vines could grow easily. He carefully chose and planted only the best vines in his vineyard. The owner built a wall and tower to protect the plants and grapes from animals that might come in and to keep out anyone who might try to damage or rob the vines. The vineyard owner expected his vines to be so fruitful he even built a winepress. He had done everything that could be done to make his vineyard the best it could be, but after all his hard work it turned out to be a disappointing failure. Even choosing and planting the best vines had not helped because only sour, useless, wild grapes grew. They took over the vineyard, spoiling it and keeping it from producing any good harvest. Isaiah then said, "This vineyard is the nation of Israel."

Isaiah loved his people and wanted them to follow God. He hoped this parable would make his nation turn from their sinful ways and return to serving God, but the people would not listen. Not many years later, their nation was conquered and lived under the rule of foreign kings for hundreds of years.

ISAIAH AND JESUS

The prophet Isaiah is quoted in the New Testament more than any other Old Testament prophet. Isaiah loved his people and told the parable about the vineyard to warn them about sin. In Matthew, the first book of the New Testament, Jesus also tells a parable about a vineyard. Jesus loved the people, too. He also told a parable about a vineyard to warn them about sin.

The Sower

◆ ◆ ◆

JESUS OFTEN used parables when he was teaching the people. A large crowd came to hear Jesus. This is one of the parables he told.

A farmer was in his field sowing seeds. Some of the seeds fell on the hard unplowed ground at the edge of the field. The birds soon came and ate those seeds. Some of the seeds fell where there were many rocks and only a thin layer of soil. These seeds began to sprout in just a few days, but because the ground was so rocky, the plants did not have deep roots. The plants felt the scorching heat of the sun and soon withered and died.

Other seeds fell where there were thorns and thistles growing. The seeds grew, but the thorns and thistles grew faster and were larger. They choked the sun and water from the good seeds so they died quickly, too. But the rest of the seeds fell on good ground, and those seeds grew and made a crop a hundred times larger than the number of seeds the farmer had planted.

Jesus explained that the seeds that did not grow represent people who hear God's Word but do not believe and follow it. The seeds that fell on good soil and grew represent people who hear and believe God's Word and love him.

SOWING SEEDS

A sower in biblical times carried his seed in a large shoulder bag. The seed was not planted in the field in straight rows as it is today. Instead, the farmer would take handfuls of seed from his bag and toss it on the ground as he walked along. He plowed the ground after he sowed the seed.

Weeds Among the Wheat

❖ ❖ ❖

JESUS TOLD the people another parable about seeds to teach a different lesson. A farmer had his workers plant good seed in his fields. When the men finished their planting, they went home. During the night, while everyone on the farm was asleep, the farmer's enemy came. He sowed the seeds of weeds where the good seed had already been planted. The enemy planned to ruin the farmer's harvest by doing this. No one knew the bad seeds had been planted until all the seeds began to grow.

When the seeds came up and the workers saw weeds growing in the field, they were very upset. They knew they had only planted good seed. They realized the farmer's enemy had tried to destroy their hard work and the farmer's good crop by sowing weeds. The workers went to the farmer and told him what they had found in the field. They asked if they should pull up the weeds so the crop could be saved. The farmer told them to leave the weeds because good plants might be pulled up along with the bad. He told the workers that when the harvest time came, the weeds could then be separated from the good plants. He also told the workers that at harvest time they were to burn the weeds and put the good crop in his barn.

Jesus was telling the people that one day God would separate those who love and obey him from those who do not.

GETTING THE POINT ACROSS

Most people in Jesus' day were farmers. Thus, the parable about planting seed would have had special meaning to his listeners. By speaking to them about a task most of them knew well, he was able to get across his message.

The Fig Tree

◆ ◆ ◆

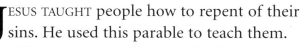

JESUS TAUGHT people how to repent of their sins. He used this parable to teach them.

There was a man who had a fig tree. He could hardly wait to taste the wonderful figs he knew this tree would produce. For three years, he faithfully checked on the tree, watching its growth. The tree was large enough and old enough to bear fruit, but no fruit ever grew on it. The man finally ran out of patience. He told his gardener he had waited patiently for fruit for three years but none had grown. He told the gardener to chop the tree down so the ground wouldn't be wasted.

The gardener was more patient than the man. He asked him to please wait one more year. He said he would give the tree special care, fertilize it, and even dig around its roots. He said if the tree didn't give the man fruit after that then it could be chopped down.

Jesus is like this caring gardener. He waits patiently for us to grow and bear fruit. We bear fruit when we live godly lives and tell others about Jesus and his love for us. To help the tree grow, the gardener used fertilizer and special care. What helps us grow in our hearts is reading God's Word, praying, helping others, and telling others about God's love. Like the gardener in the story, God is eager for us to "bear fruit."

COMMON FOOD

After a fig tree is first planted, it must grow for three years before it will produce any fruit. Figs were an important part of the diet of the people in Bible days. Probably most people had fig trees growing in their yards. Jesus knew they would understand that a tree that did not bear fruit in three years would be destroyed. He knew they would understand the parable about the unfruitful fig tree.

A Vine and Its Branches

❖ ❖ ❖

ONE DAY, Jesus was teaching his disciples more about how they should live. He wanted them to be wise and strong in their faith and understand how God wanted them to grow. He wanted them to understand what it meant to live fruitful lives for God. Vineyards, fields where grapes are grown, were very common in that part of the world. He knew the disciples would understand what he was saying if he compared himself to the vine and the disciples to the branches of a grapevine. He reminded them that just as the branch of a grapevine would dry up and no longer grow fruit, their hearts would not grow unless they continued to follow God.

A grapevine is a very useful plant, and from one plant many grapes will grow. Jesus reminded the disciples that if a branch of a grapevine does not grow and produce fruit, the vineyard keeper must prune it, cutting away the bad part. He does this not to harm the plant, but to help it grow stronger and healthier. This cutting back will help the grapevine produce more and better fruit.

God is like a gardener who must sometimes prune, or discipline, his people. God is very patient, kind, and loving. He wants only what is best for us and what will help us grow to be stronger and wiser in following him. When he disciplines us, it is because of his great love for us.

VINEYARDS

Vineyards were usually located on a hillside and were protected by a wall. There were also high watchtowers with booths at the top. At harvest time, families sometimes lived in these booths.

The Mustard Seed

◆　◆　◆

THE PEOPLE were very curious about heaven. Jesus used the tiny mustard seed to teach them. The mustard seed was one of the tiniest seeds used by farmers in Jesus' day. Many of the people had their own gardens and probably planted mustard seeds, so they understood what Jesus was saying.

Jesus reminded the people that if a mustard seed was carefully cultivated and given the right care, it could grow to be as much as ten feet tall. He also reminded them that as tiny as the seed was, the mustard plant could grow to be strong enough for the birds to land in. He was showing them that even though the kingdom of heaven had started with only one person believing in God, it could grow and grow just like the tiny mustard seed does. He wanted them to know that they were like a gardener or farmer when they tell others about their faith and trust in God.

Jesus was teaching how little things can become big things when God is behind them. Little seeds often become big trees.

In the same way, God's kingdom on earth grows mysteriously. It started with Jesus and his followers. And today, it includes millions and millions of people all around the world.

JESUS' HILLSIDE SERMON

Matthew 5–7 is called the Sermon on the Mount because Jesus sat on a mountain and spoke words of wisdom to the crowds of people that followed him.

The Treasure in a Field

❖ ❖ ❖

IN JESUS' DAY there were banks, but they did not have strong vaults with thick walls to keep the money safe from thieves. Some people did not trust someone else with their money. They wanted to find their own safe hiding place. Many people did not live in cities, so they did not have banks where they could keep their money. They had to be responsible for their own treasures. Sometimes people would put their money and other valuables in jars or strongboxes and bury them in their fields. The field would look like a common ordinary field, but only the landowner would know there was a treasure buried deep in the dirt.

Jesus knew that some people learn from one kind of illustration and others learn from another, so he used more than one kind of parable to teach the people about the same thing. He used this parable to teach about heaven.

He told the people the kingdom of heaven was like a treasure hidden in a field. When a man found the treasure, he was overjoyed. He buried the treasure again, went and sold everything he owned, took the money and bought the field, knowing the hidden treasure would now be his.

Jesus wants us to understand that discovering God's love is a wonderful surprise—it's like finding a treasure when you least expect it. And when you find it, you will treasure it above everything else.

STASHING IT AWAY

Why was treasure buried in the middle of a field? The answer is simple. There were bankers in ancient times, but no banks as we know them today. Thus, it was quite common for the wealthy to hide valuables in their fields.

The Pearl of Great Price

◆ ◆ ◆

PEOPLE TODAY are very much like the people in Jesus' day. We like to own things that are very valuable, just like the people did in Jesus' day. Jesus wanted the people of his day to know that there is nothing that has more value than the kingdom of God. He wants us to realize that, too. He used this parable to teach that truth.

There was a merchant who must have known a lot about pearls and been able to recognize the different values of the pearls he saw. One day, he was sorting through a collection of pearls when he found one that was especially lovely. Immediately, he realized that this one pearl was more valuable than all the other pearls he had ever seen in his whole life. There were many valuable pearls there, but he wanted this special one. The merchant valued and wanted this one pearl so much he was willing to do anything to make it his. He decided to sell everything he owned so he would have enough money to buy this one pearl.

The meaning of the parable is that the kingdom of heaven is like the pearl of great price. When we find God for the first time, we are surprised. He is so precious to us that we are willing to give up anything for him.

PEARLS BEFORE SWINE

Jesus said that trying to teach holy things to people who did not want to hear them was like giving expensive pearls to pigs.

218

The Great Catch of Fish

❖ ❖ ❖

MANY MEN in Jesus' day made their living as fishermen. Several of Jesus' disciples had been fishermen before they began following him. When Jesus taught this parable, he was talking to his disciples. In this story, the fishermen threw their net into the water. When they gathered the edges of it together, the net was filled with all kinds of fish. The fishermen took their full nets to the shore. They spread them out and began sorting the fish. The good fish that could be eaten were put in a pile and the bad ones were thrown away.

This story illustrates that one day God will gather all the people together so that the godly people can be separated from the wicked people. Jesus taught that God will have the angels separate the evil people from the godly people.

Jesus asked the disciples if they understood what he was telling them. They said they did. This parable must have made some who were listening to Jesus feel uncomfortable. They knew they were not following God as they should.

In the final separating of the faithful from the unfaithful, there will be much sadness. It will be a final and complete judgment that will not be changed.

FISHING WITH NETS

Fishing is often mentioned in connection with the Sea of Galilee. One popular method involved the use of a circular casting net, which was thrown either from a boat or while standing in shallow water. At the end of each workday, the nets had to be washed, mended, and hung to dry.

The Lost Sheep

◆ ◆ ◆

SOME OF the most hated people in the land often came to hear Jesus teach. They were known to be cheaters, people who lived openly in sin, or lying tax collectors. Sometimes, Jesus would even eat with these people. The religious leaders thought this was awful and were very angry about it. They thought he should stay away from such terrible people. Once they asked Jesus why he was often seen in the company of such wicked people. Jesus told this parable.

There was a shepherd who had 100 sheep. One day, one of the sheep wandered away and got lost. The shepherd immediately left the 99 sheep behind in the fold and went to look for the sheep that was lost. When he found it, the man placed it on his shoulders and carried it home to put it with the rest of the flock in the safety of the fold. He then invited his neighbors to come have a feast to help him celebrate the lost sheep being found. The man was happier over finding the one lost sheep than he was over the 99 who had not strayed.

Jesus wanted the scribes and Pharisees to know that there is greater rejoicing in heaven when one lost soul comes to God than there is over the many faithful people who have never strayed from him.

THE LORD IS MY SHEPHERD

The deep concern of the shepherd for his lost sheep reminds us of the care provided by the shepherd in Psalm 23. The psalm, written by King David, compares God to a protecting shepherd who leads and comforts his flock.

The Lost Coin

❖ ❖ ❖

MOST EVERYONE has lost money at some time in their life. Jesus used that as a way to illustrate this parable.

A woman had ten silver coins. Somehow she lost one of them. When she realized one of the coins was gone, she began to look all over her house for it. First, she lit a lamp so she could see better. Perhaps she hoped the rays of the lamp would reflect off the coin and catch her eye. Then she began to sweep her house, making sure to get under every piece of furniture. She may have even moved the furniture to be sure she did not miss a single inch of where the coin might have fallen or rolled and been hidden. She looked high and low. Finally her careful patient searching paid off. The woman found the lost coin. She was overjoyed and called on all her friends and neighbors and invited them to come to her house to celebrate. She said, "Come rejoice with me because I have found the coin that was lost."

The coin the woman lost was worth a whole day's wage. It is easy to see why she would search so hard for one lost coin. A soul is worth even more to God. In this parable of the lost coin, it is also easy to see why heaven rejoices when one sinner turns back to God.

A DAY'S PAY

The ten silver coins mentioned in the parable of the lost coin were drachmas, Greek coins worth about a day's wages each. Thus, a lost coin really was worth searching for!

Estimating the Cost

◆ ◆ ◆

JESUS WANTED the crowd to think about what their actions and choices would cost them. More and more people were following Jesus from place to place to hear him preach. He wanted them to think about what it would cost them to follow him. Jesus wanted his listeners to know that following him would not always be easy.

This is the parable he told. When someone wants to build a tower, he first figures out how much money it will take. If he doesn't have enough money to finish building the tower, he won't even begin. No one would begin a building they couldn't finish. They wouldn't want people to see their unfinished work and make fun of them for not thinking ahead and counting the cost.

Jesus also said that a king doesn't go to war against another king without considering whether his 10,000 soldiers would be able to conquer another king with 20,000 soldiers. If he sees he can't win a war, he should send out a peace delegation rather than look foolish for not counting the cost of fighting a stronger army.

Jesus told the people that anyone who was not willing to put him above everyone and everything else could not be his disciple. Just like long ago, he still wants us to count the cost of following him.

PLANNING FOR THE FUTURE

When David was king of Israel, he wanted to build a beautiful new temple. But God said David's son Solomon was to build it. David obeyed God and did not begin the building, but he did have his builders plan the temple and figure out how much it would cost to build. For years, he collected material and money so Solomon would have enough to finish the temple. David was a wise king.

The Rich Fool

◆ ◆ ◆

JESUS KNEW that many people would have trouble with greed. He also knew how greed could cloud a person's thinking so they might make wrong or unwise choices. He used the parable of the rich fool to teach that.

There was a farmer who planted his crop for the year. When harvest time came, the man's fields gave such a large yield he didn't have enough room to store the crops. He decided to tear down his old barns and build new barns that were much bigger. He also became so proud of his ability as a farmer, he decided he had enough harvest to last for years. He thought he would never have to work again. He was so proud of his crop he thought he didn't need God. He thought he had all he could ever need. The rich man told himself that since he had all he would ever need, he could relax and eat and drink and have a good time.

God was very displeased with this man's attitude. The man thought that things on this earth were more important than things in heaven. God told the man that his thinking was very wrong and that very night he would die. All the man's big plans would amount to nothing.

That is the way it is with people whose hearts are not rich with the love of God. Putting money before God is very dangerous. We never know when our life will be over, and when God will ask us about it.

TRUSTING IN GOD

It was not wrong that the man had a good crop. It was not wrong for him to tear down his old barns or to build new barns. What was wrong, or foolish, was for the rich man to think that his plans for his life were better than God's plan for his life. He trusted in money or things rather than in God. That is why the Bible called this man the rich fool.

The Wedding Banquet

❖ ❖ ❖

THE PARABLE of the wedding banquet tells about a king whose son was getting married. The king sent a servant to invite the important people of the land to the wedding.

When everything was prepared, the king sent a servant out again telling the guests the celebration was ready. Each person the servant saw gave an excuse why they would not be able to attend the wedding feast. One man said he had bought land and had to go inspect it. Another said he would not be able to come because he had just bought five oxen and had to see how well they would work. A third invited guest said he had just been married so he couldn't get to the wedding.

When the servant returned to say that no one would be coming to the wedding feast, the king was very angry. He sent the servant out again, but this time he told him to go into the city and invite everyone he saw. He told him to even include the beggars in the street. All these people came, and soon the king's banquet hall was filled and the celebration began.

The lesson this parable teaches is that we should not make excuses when God invites us to follow him. He wants us to accept his invitation, and he is eager for us to join him. But like the king in the parable, God will never force anyone to follow him.

TWO INVITATIONS

It was the custom in Jesus' day to send two invitations when parties were given. The first invited the guests, while the second indicated that all was in readiness.

The Watchful Porter

◆ ◆ ◆

WHEN JESUS told a parable, it was usually to a large group of people. The parable of the watchful porter was told to just his disciples. Jesus had been talking with them about what would happen in the future.

Peter, James, John, and Andrew asked Jesus when all the things he had been talking about would happen. Jesus told them to be careful and watch out for people who would tell them lies, saying they know the day and the hour when he would return. He said some would even come saying Jesus had sent them. He told them that no one, not even the angels, know when he will come back. Only God the Father knows the day and time he plans for Jesus to return. Then Jesus told them this parable.

There was a man who was going to a far away country. He gave each of his servants authority over a particular area of his property. He assigned special work for each to do while he was away. He also told the doorkeeper to watch faithfully. Then he told them all to work faithfully and watch for his return. He said it could be in the evening or at midnight. It could be at daybreak when the rooster was crowing or in the middle of the morning. When the parable was finished, Jesus told the disciples, "This is what I am telling you to do. Watch!"

BE ON WATCH!

When Jesus told the parable of the watchful porter, the land of Israel was ruled by the Romans. The four times Jesus mentioned to watch for the master's return were evening, midnight, cockcrowing, and morning. Those were what the Roman army called the four watches of a day. Jesus was saying we should be watchful for his return every minute of every day.

The Sheep and the Goats

❖ ❖ ❖

ANOTHER INTERESTING parable is the story of the sheep and the goats. In this parable, Jesus calls himself the Son of Man and is pictured like a shepherd who brings his flock of sheep and goats in from the pasture. He then separates them into two herds, only sheep in one group and only goats in the other.

The parable is teaching about the final judgment, and that like a shepherd, Jesus will separate those who truly are his followers—the sheep—from those who say they are his followers but really are not—the goats.

Jesus said the sheep, or true followers, were those who helped feed the hungry, gave water to the thirsty, clothed the poor, and took in strangers. They also visited those who were in prison. He said every time his followers showed kindness or were helpful to others, it was the same as if they had done those things to him.

The goats, or false followers, did not reach out to others. Jesus said when they turned their back on the poor and needy and refused to help them it was the same as turning their back on him.

Many people say they follow God, but in their hearts they do not. They might be able to fool other people, but no one can fool God. Jesus will know his true followers, and they will be rewarded forever in heaven. But those who have never followed God and lived obediently will be very surprised at their punishment.

HEAR MY VOICE!

Sheep are interesting animals. They will only respond to the voice of their own shepherd and recognize it from any other shepherd's call. If several flocks are together, only the sheep that belong to a shepherd will come when he calls. The other sheep wait for their shepherd's call. Jesus is often called the Good Shepherd. Those who love and follow him should always be listening with their heart to obey his call.

Forgive and Forgive

◆ ◆ ◆

THIS PARABLE about forgiving tells about a servant who owed the king a large amount of money. The servant's debt was so large that he would probably never be able to repay it. The king asked the servant to pay his debt, but the servant said he could not. So the king ordered that the man, his wife, his children, and everything they owned be sold to pay off the debt.

The servant fell down before the king and begged him to have mercy on him and his family. He begged for more time to pay off what he owed. The king was filled with pity for the man, and he decided not to have him or his family sold. He even forgave the debt—the servant no longer owed the king money.

A little later, the servant saw a man who owed him some money. The servant demanded that the man pay his debt to him. He said he would have the man thrown into jail until the debt was paid. The man begged for mercy, but the servant had him put in jail anyway.

Someone saw what happened and told the king. The king was so angry that he had the servant put in prison because he had been forgiven but was unwilling to forgive another.

Jesus told his listeners that this is how God would treat us if we are unwilling to forgive each other.

HOW MUCH WAS THAT?

The amount of money the servant owed the king was about the same as 10,000,000 dollars. The king forgave his whole debt. The other man only owed the servant about 17 dollars. No wonder the king was angry that the servant was unwilling to forgive such a small debt when he had owed so much. We need to be generous to others, after all, Jesus is very generous to us!

The Prodigal Son

◆ ◆ ◆

IN THE PARABLE of the prodigal son, Jesus told about a man who had two sons. The younger son decided he wanted his inheritance before his father died. The father gave him the money, and the son took it and went to live in the city. Soon, he had spent all of his money on wild parties and sinful living. The son was hungry and begged a farmer to give him a job. The farmer hired him to feed the pigs. The young man was so hungry that even the pig's food looked good to him. He finally realized he had been terribly wrong to dishonor his father by demanding his inheritance. He knew he was also wrong to waste the money on wild and sinful living. He wanted to go home. He thought about how his father's servants weren't hungry like he was. He felt he could no longer be treated like a son, but he decided to ask his father for a job. At least that way he wouldn't be hungry.

The young man began walking home. He didn't know his father had watched every day for his return. When the boy was a long way away, his father saw him and began running toward him. The father kissed his son and welcomed him home.

This is the way it is with God. When someone is truly sorry for their wrongs and wants to leave their sinful life behind, God fully forgives them and welcomes them back to him.

ESPECIALLY FAVORED

In ancient Israel, the firstborn son received special preference. According to the Book of Deuteronomy, a father dividing his estate was to give the eldest son twice the amount of property as his other sons.

The Good Samaritan

◆ ◆ ◆

THIS STORY that Jesus told was especially upsetting to the Jews of Jesus' day. There was a man who was traveling from Jerusalem to Jericho. Before he could reach the safety of Jericho, he was robbed, beaten, and left at the side of the road. He was too badly hurt to do anything to help himself. He lay on the side of the road for hours before he heard anyone coming who might help him.

A religious leader came by. When he saw the hurt man, he crossed to the other side of the road and continued walking as if he hadn't even seen him.

Later, another religious leader, a Levite, came along. The Levite looked at the poor hurt man, but he, too, crossed the road and did not help him.

Much later, the man heard footsteps again. This time a Samaritan was coming by. When he saw the poor man, he felt sorry for him. He bandaged the man's wounds, put him on his own donkey, and took him to an inn. The next day, when the Samaritan had to continue his journey, he paid the innkeeper to take care of the injured man until he returned.

This story was told to encourage the people to love their neighbors. It must have been surprising to some of Jesus' Jewish listeners who thought they only had to love people whom they knew. Jesus was showing them that our neighbors also include people who are different from us.

SAMARITANS

Samaritans were people who lived in Samaria, a region north of Jerusalem or Judea. They accepted only the first five books of the Bible as Scripture. The Samaritans were descendants of Jews who had married people from other nations. The Jews living in Palestine looked down on Samaritans as unrighteous people. When Jesus showed love for the Samaritans, it made many people angry.

The Workers in the Vineyard

❖　❖　❖

AMAN WHO owned a vineyard needed help. He went to town early one morning to hire workers. The men agreed to work for the wages, so the landowner sent them to the fields.

In the middle of the morning, the landowner went back to town and found more men who were willing to work. He sent them to the fields also. At noon and then again in the middle of the afternoon, the man hired more men.

In the late afternoon, when the work day was almost over, the man saw several men standing around. He asked why they were not working. They said no one had hired them. The man said, "I will hire you. Help harvest grapes and at the end of the day I will pay you." The men agreed and went to work.

At the end of the day, the man paid the workers in the order from those who worked the least to those who had worked all day. The men who had worked all day thought they would be paid the most since they had worked the longest. They were angry when they were paid the same amount as the men who had worked the least. When they asked about it, the man reminded them that they had agreed to work for the amount they were paid.

The lesson of this parable is that God's grace is the same for everyone, whether they accept it early in their life or late.

A DENARIUS SAVED...

A denarius was a Roman coin, and the drachma was a Greek coin. Both were equal to a typical day's pay in New Testament times.

Parable of the Talents

❖ ❖ ❖

THE PARABLE of the talents is about a man who was going away on a trip. Before he left, the master gave one servant five measures of gold, called talents. Another servant received two talents, and a third servant was given one talent.

The servants knew their master expected them to be careful with the money, using it as wisely as possible. The first servant used his five talents to buy things he could sell again in the market-place. Soon he had made five more talents of gold for a total of ten.

The servant who had two talents had been wise also. He had made a total of four talents.

The third servant, however, was very foolish. He was so afraid of losing the one talent and making his master angry that he buried it in the ground.

When the master returned, he called his servants to him. He was very pleased with the first and second servant, and he rewarded them for their faithfulness. When he heard what the third servant had done, the master was angry. He told the man he was foolish and lazy. He said the least he could have done was put the money in a bank and let it earn interest.

In this parable, Jesus was teaching his listeners that God expects us to be wise in the use of our money, time, and abilities. One day, we will have to answer to him for what we do and do not accomplish with our lives.

WHAT IS A TALENT?

A talent was not a coin. It was a unit of measure that refers to a weight of about 30 kilograms. In the parable of the talents, it would mean a large amount of money and represent several years' wages.

The Widow and the Judge

Jesus was talking with his disciples about prayer. He told them this story. There was a woman who needed help. Someone owed her money, but because she was a widow and had no husband who could help her get it, the person would not pay her. She knew the only person who could help her was a judge. The judge listened to the woman's story, but he had a hard heart and did not really care whether justice was done or not. He did not do anything to collect the money for her. The woman may have been discouraged, but she did not give up. She went back to the judge day after day and asked again and again for his help in collecting the debt. The judge began to wear down, and finally he got tired of hearing the woman's case over and over. At last, he agreed to help her.

Jesus told the disciples, "If an evil judge could be worn down by being asked over and over for help, don't you think God will hear the prayers of his people who pray day and night?" Jesus wanted them to continue to pray and ask God for help until he answered their prayers. He wants us to be faithful in the same way when we pray.

LIMITED JUDGMENT

The judges who lived in Jerusalem in Jesus' day had the power to settle their cases without interference from Rome. However, they could not have a person executed. That was left to a Roman official called a procurator. The punishment a procurator might hand down included crucifixion, public whipping, or a lifetime at hard labor in the mines. The council that tried Jesus turned him over to Pontius Pilate so that he could be crucified.

God Will Be There for You

◆ ◆ ◆

IN THIS PARABLE, Jesus was again teaching about prayer. There was a man who heard a knock on his door in the middle of the night. It was friends who had traveled far and were hungry and tired. The man welcomed them to his home, but when he went to get food ready he discovered he was out of bread. What could he do? His guests were hungry, and he wanted to be a good host. Then he thought of his neighbor. Surely they would let him have some bread until he could make some more tomorrow and repay them.

He went to his neighbors. It was late, and the lights were out. He knew he would be waking them, but he knocked anyway. Soon he heard a voice asking who was at the door and what they wanted. The man told his neighbor what had happened and asked for the bread. The man didn't want to

send his guests to bed hungry so he asked again and again for help until finally the neighbor gave him the bread.

Jesus wanted his listeners to be faithful in prayer—to continue asking even when a prayer isn't answered quickly. He wants us to be faithful in prayer, too. He said, "Ask and it shall be given to you."

FOOD FOR THOUGHT

There are other parables about bread. One talks about the yeast that makes bread rise and uses it to illustrate how a little sin can affect many people. In another parable, Jesus says yeast is like the kingdom of heaven. It shows how when we share our faith the kingdom of heaven grows. The Bible also says we cannot live by bread alone. We also need God's Word to know how to live right.

Lamp Under a Bushel

❖　❖　❖

A GREAT CROWD had gathered to hear Jesus teach. They were eager to hear what he had to say, and they were not disappointed. The sermon Jesus preached was called the Sermon on the Mount. He told the people what to do when others treated them badly because of what they believed. He taught about the reward God has for those who faithfully obey him. He told the people how to live their life in a way that pleases God. He told them how to go to heaven. He also told them that just like salt brings flavor to food and makes it taste better, they bring flavor to the world and make it a better place when they obey God's Word. Then he used this parable to encourage them to share their faith.

Jesus said no one would light a lamp and cover it to keep the light from shining out. He said no one would light a candle and hide its light under a bushel baket. Jesus told them that anyone who lights a candle puts it on a lampstand so that everyone who comes into the room can benefit from the light.

In this parable Jesus was telling the people that they knew the truth of how to live in a way that pleases God. They knew what to do to go to heaven. Knowing God is like shining light—it is our responsibility to share what we believe, not hide it.

LET YOUR LIGHT SO SHINE

There were no electric lights in Jesus' day, so the people he was teaching understood how much light just one candle or small oil lamp could give on a dark night. Jesus wanted the people to understand that one person speaking the truth can be as powerful as one candle in the dark. Electricity may make a candle seem dim, but the power of speaking the truth has not faded one bit since Jesus' day.

Camel Through the Eye of a Needle

◆ ◆ ◆

A RICH YOUNG MAN came to ask Jesus what he needed to do to go to heaven. Jesus told him to keep the commandments. The young man asked which commandments he needed to keep. Jesus said, "You shall not murder. You shall not commit adultery. You shall not steal. You shall not bear false witness. Honor your father and your mother and love your neighbor as yourself."

The young man said he had kept all of those commandments since he was a boy. Jesus told him that if he wanted to go to heaven, he needed to sell everything he owned and give his money to the poor. When he had done that the young man should come and follow Jesus.

The young man listened to what Jesus told him, but he loved his money too much. He could not bear the thought of giving it all away. He sadly shook his head and left.

Jesus was sad, too, by the young man's choice. He told his disciples this parable, "It is hard for a rich man to give up his money to enter the kingdom of heaven. It would be easier for a camel to go through the eye of a needle than for a rich man to enter the kingdom of God."

Jesus meant that some people would rather trust in money than in God. Trusting God is the only way to go to heaven.

USEFUL ANIMALS
Camels were domesticated (tamed) in 3000 B.C., but were not commonly used until the twelfth century B.C. They are ideal for use in deserts, because they can go for a long time without water. We get our word "camel" from the Hebrew word *gamel*.

Two Sons and the Vineyard

❖ ❖ ❖

JESUS TOLD a story about a man and his two sons. A man had two sons. One day, he went to his first son and said, "Son, I want you to go and work in the vineyard today." The son said, "No! I do not want to work today."

Later, after the father had gone away, the son felt badly that he had refused to work for his father. He got up, went to the vineyard, and he worked.

The father went to his second son and said, "Son, I want you to go and work in the vineyard today." That son said, "Yes, sir, I will go." The father left thinking the son would keep his word. But the second son did not go to work in the vineyard.

Jesus asked the Pharisees, "Which son did what his father asked?" They answered, "The first son."

Jesus told them they were right. He told them that tax collectors and harlots who turn to God and obey him would be in heaven before they would. The Pharisees said they followed God, but Jesus knew that though their actions made it seem as if they were obeying God, in their hearts they were not. Jesus wanted them to know that God is not fooled by outward appearances. He sees into our hearts.

JUST FOR SHOW

The Pharisees would fast (not eat) to show how holy they were, then they would moan and groan about it. When they put money in the offering, they made sure they were metal coins so they made a lot of noise when they hit the bottom of the offering box. The Pharisees would pray loudly on street corners and beat on their chests, but they only did this for attention. They could not hide their wicked hearts from God.

Sign of the Fig Tree

◆ ◆ ◆

WHEN JESUS told his disciples the parable of the fig tree, he knew he would soon die and rise again. He also knew that shortly after he arose from the grave, he would ascend into heaven. He had also told them that he would return one day with no warning and take all believers to heaven with him. There would be no announcement that he was coming, but things would happen in the world that would let the believers know that the time of his return was close. He wanted them to be careful to remain faithful and to be always watching for his return. Jesus used a budding fig tree as a picture to remind them to always be watchful.

Jesus told the disciples to look at the fig tree. He reminded them that like the other trees, it puts out buds in the spring. He told them that when they saw that happening, they would be seeing a sure sign that summer was coming soon. He told them that just as the fig tree's flowering is a sign that summer is near, when believers see the signs he has spoken about, his return would be near also.

Jesus knew that something they saw every day would be a good and constant reminder for them to be ready for his return. He wants us to remember and be watching for his return also.

COMMON THINGS, UNCOMMON LESSONS

Jesus often used everyday things to remind us of his teachings. When he was trying to teach people about faith, he talked about a mustard seed. He often talked about vineyards, sheep and shepherds, lamps, and bread. These common things made the teachings of Jesus more understandable to people.

Questions & Answers

◆ ◆ ◆

Q: How is the Bible like a mirror?

A: When we look into the Scriptures, we can see what we truly are. James says if we know what God's Word says but don't do it, it's like looking in a mirror but then walking away and forgetting what we look like.

Q: Why did Jesus use parables?

A: The disciples asked Jesus that same question. He said he used these stories so those who were wise could see and understand. He seldom taught without using these wonderful little stories. But not everyone understood them. Not everyone was wise.

Q: Why did Jesus say not to put new wine into old wineskins?

A: Wineskins were bags made out of goat skin. Jesus said you couldn't—and shouldn't—put grape juice in old wineskins. The juice would expand and break the old wineskin, which had already been stretched. His new ideas would not fit into old ways of doing things either.

Q: Where did weddings take place?

A: The groom came to the bride's house and took her back to his home for the wedding. Friends joined in a parade from the one house to the other. Jesus tells a story about five bridesmaids who didn't have oil for

Jesus said to take the worst seat at a banquet, not the best.

their lamp when the groom arrived—so they missed the party!

Q: Where should you sit at a party?

A: Jesus said not to take the best seat, because the person giving the party might ask you to move. That would be embarrassing. Instead, take the worst seat. Then if the host or hostess asks you to sit in a better seat, you will be honored, not shamed.

Q: What will happen to people who reject God's Son?

A: Jesus told about a man who rented his vineyard. He was supposed to get part of the crop. When he sent his servants to get his portion, the renters beat them and killed them. So the landowner sent his son—and they killed him, too. Then the owner came and destroyed the renters, giving the land to someone else. We should be careful not to be like the people who rented the vineyards.

Q: Who is a faithful servant?

A: A servant who expects his master to return and so does the right things will be rewarded. A servant who misbehaves, and so is surprised when the master returns, will be punished. Jesus said we should be like the servant who watches and waits, serving the master with eagerness and joy.

Q: Can someone choose to be a slave?

A: A slave was set free after he served his master for seven years. But if he loved his master and wanted to keep serving him, his ear was pierced with an awl driven into the doorpost. This showed everyone he served his master because he wanted to, not because he had to.

Q: Where did people keep their money?

A: There were no banks. Sometimes people buried their money to keep it safe. And sometimes they even forgot where they buried it. Jesus told about a man who found a lot of money buried in a field—so he went and bought the whole field so the money would be his.

Q: What happens when we die?

A: When a poor man named Lazarus died, Jesus said angels carried him to "Abraham's Bosom," a place of comfort and honor. Another man—who had not believed God or obeyed him—was carried to a place of torment and flame. These two places are separated by a "great gulf."

Q: What language did Jesus speak?

A: Jesus read from the Scriptures at the synagogue in Hebrew. But he told the parables and taught the peo-ple in Aramaic, a related language spoken by most people in the Middle East at that time. Some people think he may have also spoken *Koine* (everyday) Greek, the language widely used for trading.

Jesus said to build your house on solid ground, not on sand.

Q: Did Jesus only use parables in teaching?

A: Jesus used parables most of the time. But he also asked a lot of questions, trying to find out what other people were thinking. Sometimes he exaggerated, to get his listeners' attention.

Q: How do we get lousy leaders?

A: Jotham told a parable about the trees of the forest gathering to choose a king. The olive tree, the fig tree, and the grapevine all turned down the job. So the trees chose the bushes to rule over them, because the most qualified trees refused the responsibility.

Q: Where should people build their houses?

A: Jesus said that people should build their houses on stone, so that when the rains and winds come, the houses will not wash away. People who build houses on sand will watch them be washed away when the rains fall. Jesus also wants us to build our lives on solid ground, which means we should live our lives the way Jesus taught.

Animals and Plants in the Bible

❖ ❖ ❖ ❖

EOPLE IN BIBLE TIMES used animals for clothing, food, and transportation. Most people worked as farmers and shepherds. Because they depended so much on plants and animals, they knew how amazing God's creation was. For example, they knew a camel could drink lots of water—25 gallons in just a few minutes. As you read about some of the many plants and animals mentioned in the Bible, you will be amazed, too.

The Making of a King

◆ ◆ ◆

DONKEYS ONCE played an important role in a king's life. Saul was the son of a rich man who owned many donkeys. Nearly every family in biblical times, even the poorest, owned a donkey, but to have many donkeys was a sign of wealth. One day, the rich man's donkeys wandered off. Saul and a servant were sent to

find them. They searched everywhere without success. Finally, the servant suggested that they ask the prophet Samuel, who lived in a nearby town. When they entered the city, they met Samuel coming toward them. He told Saul that the donkeys had been found and then puzzled him by saying, "You own all the wealth of Israel now!" What Saul didn't know was that God had told Samuel to make Saul the new king. Samuel took Saul to a banquet, anointed him, and told him the surprising news.

BALAAM'S STRANGE ENCOUNTER

Balaam was a prophet who worked for the king of Moab. He had been ordered to curse the Israelites. On a journey, Balaam began beating his donkey because it stopped in the road. The donkey turned and spoke to him! Only then did Balaam realize that an angel had been blocking the path. Balaam quickly agreed to do what the angel said.

PALM SUNDAY

The final week of Jesus' life began when he rode a donkey into Jerusalem. Along the way, people placed palm branches and their cloaks in the road—a sign of respect—and shouted, "Hosanna!" Today, many churches remember this event as Palm Sunday.

The Four Horsemen

❖ ❖ ❖

IN THE BOOK of Revelation, God told the author, John, to give a description of what will happen in the last times before Jesus returns to earth. The first part of the book talks about the four horsemen of the Apocalypse. Each horse is a different color and represents a different part of God's judgment.

Some Bible scholars believe that the white horse represents Christ the conqueror. The rider of this horse has a bow and wears a crown. He rides forth conquering the enemies of God. Later on, the white horse is mentioned again. This time Christ is named as the victorious conquerer.

The red horse represents war. The Bible says that before Jesus returns, there will be wars and rumors of wars. The third horse is black; it represents famine and death. The last horse is called the pale horse. It represents disease, famine, and wild animals. Anyone who trusts God and follows his Word does not need to be afraid of the future or what these horses represent.

DIRECTIONAL GUIDES

In Psalm 32:9 the writer warns, "Do not be like a horse or a mule, without understanding, whose temper must be curbed with bit and bridle, else it will not stay near you." God wants believers to willingly let him guide them.

Passing the Mantle

◆ ◆ ◆

THERE WAS a farmer named Elisha. One day, something very unusual happened as he finished plowing a field. He looked up and saw a man walking toward him. It was Elijah, the prophet of God. He walked up to Elisha and placed his cloak on Elisha's shoulders. Then he turned and walked away.

Neither of them had said a word, but Elisha understood Elijah's strange actions. He knew that it meant God was calling him to be a prophet, too. Elijah was growing very old and soon God would take him to heaven. He needed someone who could help him. God wanted someone to continue preaching the truth after Elijah was gone. Elisha was to be that replacement. Elisha did not hesitate to accept God's calling for his life.

BEAST OF BURDEN

A Hebrew farmer would prize an ox more than a modern farmer might prize a tractor. An ox could plow fields, thresh and grind grain, pull heavy wagons, and drive a water wheel.

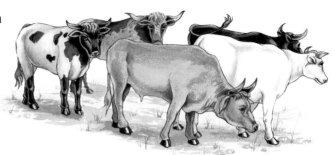

CRIME AND PUNISHMENT

The Old Testament had many laws that set punishment and fines for owners of animals that injured people. An ox that killed a person was supposed to be stoned to death. If the animal had a history of hurting people and if the owner ignored the problem, then the owner could be fined—or even executed.

He ran and caught up with Elijah. He said he would stop farming and follow God. First, he went to his parents and told them he would not be a farmer any longer. After telling them good-bye, Elisha returned to the oxen. He killed them and used the wood from the plow to build a fire and cook their meat.

Elisha and the other plowmen sat down and had a big feast. By getting rid of the oxen, Elisha was showing that he was serious about serving God. Without oxen or a yoke, he could not return to farming. That part of his life was gone forever. He then went to Elijah to begin his work for God.

HIGHLY PRIZED

Oxen in the Middle East varied greatly in size and shape. Some had long horns, others had short horns, and a few breeds had none. They could be all white, white with black patches, or entirely red. All the breeds supplied milk, which was made into butter and cheese. Because oxen were so valuable, laws protected them. For instance, a person could not watch a neighbor's ox wander off without helping. The neighbor had to report what he had seen so the animal could be brought back. In the Ten Commandments, God said that we shouldn't covet our neighbor's oxen.

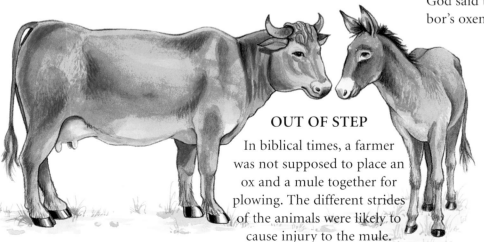

OUT OF STEP

In biblical times, a farmer was not supposed to place an ox and a mule together for plowing. The different strides of the animals were likely to cause injury to the mule.

EXCEPTION TO THE RULE

Wells that were dug into the earth often became a hazard for animals. Because God wanted all animals to be treated with kindness, an ox that fell into a well was to be rescued at once, even if it was the Sabbath, a day of rest. As Jesus pointed out, even the strict Pharisees rescued their animals on the Sabbath.

The Ship of the Desert

❖ ❖ ❖

CAMELS ARE very unusual looking animals, but they were very important and useful in Bible times. God designed these creatures so they could endure the hardships of the desert. Sometimes camels are called "ships of the desert." This is because they are used to transport merchandise across the desert's hot sand.

A camel can carry as much as 600 pounds. They are not fast travelers, but they can walk 60 to 75 miles a day. They have a reputation for being ill tempered. They can go without water for several days, but when camels drink, they drink a lot.

The camels mentioned in the Bible were the one-hump camels from Arabia. They are especially accustomed to the hot, dry climate of the Middle East. Some people think camels store water in their humps, but this is not true. Their hump is made of fat. When a camel has to go without food, it lives on the fat stored in its hump.

Camels can go without water for so long because God designed their stomachs with special tissue that absorbs water. Camels shed their hair, and it is

A TEDIOUS CHORE

Giving water to camels was no easy job. A thirsty camel can drink more than 25 gallons of water in ten minutes. When Abraham's servant asked God to show him the ideal wife for Isaac, he wanted a sign. That sign would be the woman who offered to water his camels. Rebekah displayed that kindness. When she offered to water the camels, she showed herself to be kind and thoughtful—and hardworking.

WALKING ON NAILS

Camels' feet appear to be encased in divided hooves, but they really have toenails. The camel was forbidden food for Israelites because it does not have divided hooves.

saved and woven into cloth. There was one man in the New Testament who was known for wearing camel-hair clothing. This man's name was John the Baptist. He was a prophet of God. The job God had given him was to warn the people that the promised Messiah was coming very soon.

ADAPTED TO THE DESERT

The camel is amazingly well suited to work in the desert. Its long eyelashes and efficient eyelids keep the blowing sand from blinding it. It can go for days without water and can digest the toughest desert plants. When food is not available, the camel can live off the fat stored in its hump.

ONE HUMP OR TWO

Camels were just as important as sheep, cows, and donkeys in the Old Testament. Camels have been described as unintelligent and quarrelsome, but they were a necessity for people living in desert areas. They were used to transport both goods and people. The camels mentioned in the Bible were from Arabia and were accustomed to the hot, dry climate of the Middle East. They were easy to tell from other breeds because they had only one hump. The more familiar two-humped camels are the Bactrian variety. This species is bigger, heavier, and has more hair than the one-humped camel. These camels are native to Asia and are usually found in colder climates.

A DIFFERENT TYPE OF TRAIN

A caravan is a long train of camels that travels through the desert from city to city. Merchants usually traveled this way, because it was safer and better for business to travel in groups. Many caravan routes went through Israel; it was on the main route between Egypt, Arabia, and Mesopotamia. Joseph was sold by his brothers to a caravan of Ishmaelites. Also, the Queen of Sheba once assembled a huge caravan to take costly gifts to King Solomon.

Beware of Bears!

◆ ◆ ◆

AMONG THE MANY animals included in the Bible, bears are mentioned several times. One of these stories tells about a day in Old Testament times.

The prophet Elisha was well known throughout the land as a man of God who would tell the people exactly what God told him to say. One day, he was on his way to the town of Bethel. As he was walking down the road, some young men came along from the city. They recognized Elisha and began making fun of him. Perhaps they did not want to hear the truth of God's Word. Perhaps they were involved in a particular sin and Elisha was confronting them about it. Perhaps they were just troublemakers.

The Bible doesn't tell us why they were taunting and jeering at him, but it does say they were being very disrespectful to him. In Bible times, just like today, children were expected to respect adults. These young men said, "Go on you bald-headed old man! Go on with

NOT A PICKY EATER

The Syrian bear is probably the one described in the Bible, standing six feet tall and weighing more than 500 pounds. Its diet included plants and animal flesh, although most of the time it lived on fruits and berries. When food ran low—usually in winter—the bear was more likely than at other times to threaten a farmer's livestock. The Syrian bear has disappeared from Israel, but it still lives in other parts of the Middle East.

PEACEABLE KINGDOM

What will the kingdom of God look like? The prophet Isaiah painted a picture of the peace that will reign on earth. In the book that bears his name, he says that the bear and the cow will graze together. The fierce lion will eat straw like the ox, and the wolf will live with the lamb. Even a child will be able to play near a nest of poisonous snakes without being harmed.

STAR GAZING

The constellations Ursa Major (Big Bear) and Ursa Minor (Little Bear) have been watched for thousands of years. Job describes the God who made the constellations known as the Bear and Orion.

BOY VERSUS BEAR

Shepherds often had to defend their flock from wild animals, including bears. To persuade Saul that he could fight Goliath, David told him that he struck down bears that had caught his sheep. If one came after him, he would grab it by the jaw and kill it!

your old baldhead!" By their actions Elisha knew their hearts. When anyone does wrong, sooner or later they have to pay the price for their sin.

UNBEARABLE FOOL

The Book of Proverbs says that it is better to meet a she-bear robbed of her cubs than to catch a fool in the middle of something he shouldn't be doing.

Suddenly, two she-bears came out of the woods and killed 42 of the young men. Perhaps the bears that came after the young men were only protecting their young cubs. Perhaps the boys shouting at Elisha had startled or frightened them, but most likely the bears were sent by God as judgment.

Stronger Than a Lion

❖ ❖ ❖

IN BIBLE TIMES, lions roamed about and were a threat to other animals, and to humans as well. Whether people traveled from one city to another or were just out in their fields, they always had to be on the lookout for lions. Proverbs 30:30 describes the lion as the king of the animals who would not be frightened by any other animal. When King David was a shepherd taking care of his father's sheep, he once had to face a fierce lion and kill it.

There was another man who also had to fight a lion. In fact, he proved that he was stronger than a lion, and very brave as well. This man was named Samson. One day, as Samson and his parents were on their way to the city of Timnah, a lion

PERSIAN LIONS

Persian lions were about five feet long. They had heavy manes and tails about 30 inches long. They could not climb and were active at night.

REGAL SPLENDOR

King Solomon's throne must have been an impressive sight. It was made of ivory and overlaid with gold. On the side of the seat were armrests and two lions of gold. Twelve more lions stood on the sides of the six steps that led to the throne. It was said that nothing like it had ever been constructed in any kingdom.

HUNTING BIG GAME

King Darius of Media and Persia, who lived about 550 B.C., kept a large collection of captured lions in his park. This is probably the lion's den that the prophet Daniel was thrown into. Other kings stalked lions for sport. Assyrian rulers hunted from chariots while footmen prodded the cats into the kings' range.

A lion stamp used to seal letters with wax.

KINGS AND LIONS

Lions were a favorite of kings. Lions were used in hunting, and Ramses II was said to have kept a tame lion that went with him into battle.

APPEASING THE HEBREWS' GOD

When Israel was conquered by Assyria, most of the Israelites were moved to other lands. Assyria sent settlers to take the land and build homes. But soon after the settlers arrived, many were killed by lions. A messenger told the king of Assyria that they had upset Israel's God, so they sent a Hebrew priest back to Israel to instruct the settlers on how to properly worship God.

attacked him. Samson did not have a weapon, but the Lord gave him great power and amazing strength. Samson grabbed the lion by its jaws and ripped it apart with his bare hands.

When he had finished his business in Timnah and was on his way back home, he passed the carcass of the lion still lying by the side of the road. Samson noticed that a swarm of bees had built their honeycomb in the lion's skin. He took some of the honey and ate it on his way home. Later, he gave his parents some of the honey, but he did not tell them where he had gotten it.

The Graceful Deer

❖ ❖ ❖

IN THE SONG of Solomon there is a conversation between a young man and the woman he loves. The woman describes her husband as a young deer. This is a compliment because a deer is thought of as graceful, gentle, and loyal. It is also pictured as being always on the watch for danger, always on alert for an enemy that is waiting to attack it or its fawn.

Like the deer, we should have a gentle, quiet spirit, but at the same time we should be alert to the sin our enemy, Satan, would try to make us fall into.

In Psalms 42:1 the deer is mentioned. This verse says that our hearts should long to know God the same way a deer longs for water. The two times a deer most wants water is when it flees from danger or when it has been in battle with an opponent. We should thirst for God's Word, the living water, when we are in danger of sin. His Word alone quenches the heart that is thirsty for God.

FLEET OF FOOT

The red, the fallow, and the roe were types of deer in biblical times. The red deer was most common and was served on King Solomon's table daily.

DEER ANTLERS

The antlers of the fallow deer are large and flattened out. They resemble an open hand, palm up, with its fingers spread out.

252

The Gadarene Swine

◆ ◆ ◆

WHEN JESUS came to the country of the Gadarenes, he met a man who had been possessed for a long time by demons. The man wore no clothes and lived chained in a cemetery among the tombstones. The demons were so strong that the man often broke his chains and ran through the hills screaming and cutting himself. Jesus commanded the demons to leave the man. The demons begged to be sent into a herd of pigs on a nearby hill. Jesus agreed, and the demons rushed into the animals, which then plunged over a cliff and drowned in the sea below. Every person in the city came to see what had happened. They found the man who had been possessed fully clothed and sitting calmly at Jesus' feet. Sadly, this frightened the Gadarenes, and even though they had witnessed a miracle, they told Jesus to go away and leave them alone.

A BIT OF A BOAR

A wild boar ruined crops by eating or trampling them. The boar, which is like a large hairy pig, could be brown, gray, or black. It had only four teeth that continued to grow throughout the animal's life.

A WASTE OF TIME

Jesus told his followers not to cast their pearls before swine. Pigs could not appreciate the beauty of pearls and would only trample them. So it is with people who have no interest in God's message. It is useless to try to persuade them, because their minds are closed.

Sheep and Lambs

❖ ❖ ❖

IN THE BIBLE, people are often compared to sheep. This is because, like sheep, we wander away from God and put ourselves in danger. Like a shepherd, God is patient with us. When we wander away from God, he lets us suffer the consequence for our sin. Like the shepherd, God is always there to help us. The prophet Isaiah said, "We, like sheep, have all gone astray."

Jesus told a parable about a lost sheep. The story was to let everyone know that God rejoices greatly when we return to him after we have strayed.

Jesus is often called the Lamb that takes away the sins of the world. He is also called the Passover Lamb that was sacrificed for the sins of the people. This is because Jesus died for our sins; we no longer have to sacrifice animals in a temple.

The Book of Revelation talks about the Lamb at least 37 times. Revelation also talked about the lamb with seven horns who lifts the scroll with the seven seals from the hand of God.

AN ESSENTIAL ANIMAL

Sheep were vital to the Israelite's way of life. They provided wool for clothing (about two pounds per sheep each year), as well as food for meals and for sacrifice. The most common breed was the broadtail sheep. Its edible tail can weigh as much as 15 pounds.

RAM'S HORNS

Ram's horns are two to three inches in diameter and were used as sharp weapons by the animal. Once removed, they were used as trumpets or as oil containers.

The Wings of an Eagle

SEVERAL TYPES of large birds of prey are mentioned in the Bible, including vultures and eagles. Since the two birds were usually observed from a distance, it was hard to tell the difference. The Hebrew word for eagle means "to tear with the beak." The eagle is the largest flying bird in Israel today, and its wingspan can exceed eight feet. The Bible often speaks of the eagle's power and beauty. Isaiah 40:31 says, "Those who wait for the Lord shall renew their strength, they shall mount up with wings like eagles."

In Proverbs, Solomon marvels that one of the things too wonderful for him to understand is how an eagle glides through the sky. The eagle was also known for the care it took of its young. In the Book of Deuteronomy, God's protection of the Israelites is compared to a soaring eagle that has spread its wings, carrying its young eaglets on its back.

A CLEAN HOUSE

For protection, the eagle builds its nest in a tall tree or in the crevice of a high cliff. A pair of eagles must collect hundreds of large branches before their nest is complete. They are also good housekeepers. When their nest becomes too dirty, the eagles will make a new floor by adding a layer of clean branches.

EAGLE PARENTS

A baby eagle is called an eaglet. Eagle parents help their young learn to fly by flying along beside the young birds. Each beat of the adult bird's strong wings creates a whirlpool of air that gives the eaglet additional lift, helping it gain strength and confidence in its new skill. Soon the eaglet will fly more than 10,000 feet in the air and glide more than 100 miles per hour, just as its parents do.

Let Them Eat Quail

◆ ◆ ◆

QUAIL, which are small game birds (related to turkeys and pheasants), are only mentioned a few times in the Bible. In one account, Moses and Aaron were leading the Hebrew nation through the western portion of the Sinai Desert, when the people became very hungry. They complained that Moses and Aaron brought them out to the desert to starve to death. They even said they wanted to go back to Egypt where they had been enslaved, but at least there they would have meat and bread to eat. The Lord heard their complaints, and he appeared to Moses in a bright cloud. He told Moses that as a sign that he was their God, each evening they would have enough meat and each morning they would have enough bread. That same evening, God sent so many quail that they were all over the camp—and in the morning there was enough bread for all.

BLESSING OR CURSE?

Huge flocks of quail migrate over the Sinai region after spending the winter in Africa. Exhausted from the flight, the quail can be easily caught.

THE HOOPOE BIRD

The hoopoe bird appears only twice in the Bible, where it is listed among the birds forbidden as food. The hoopoe is beautiful, but it smells bad and has filthy eating and nesting habits. Hoopoes are still common in Israel today. They nest in holes found in houses and buildings.

In the Form of a Dove

❖ ❖ ❖

DOVES WERE plentiful in Bible times, and they were often brought to the temple as a sacrifice. The dove has a gentle, timid nature and a soothing, restful call. The Holy Spirit is often pictured as a dove. The New Testament tells that John the Baptist had been preaching in the wilderness, telling the people to repent of their sin because the kingdom of God was close at hand. The people did not understand what John meant, but many did repent of their sins and were baptized.

One day, as John was preaching, Jesus came and asked to be baptized. John said, "Lord, I'm not even worthy to tie your shoes. I need to be baptized by you, and you are coming to me." Jesus said, "John, do this, because it is what my Father wants."

John obeyed. When Jesus came out of the water, the Holy Spirit in the form of a dove came and rested on Jesus. A voice from heaven said, "This is my beloved Son in whom I am well pleased."

MANY MEANINGS

Doves are mentioned more than any other bird in the Bible. Actually, the Hebrew word for dove is used to describe several species of pigeons. The prophet Jeremiah noted that the bird's arrival was a sign of spring and that the dove would often build its nest in a high place. Because of its faithfulness to its mate, the turtledove was also a symbol of love. In the Song of Solomon, dove is used as an affectionate name for the beloved.

Sea Creatures

◆ ◆ ◆

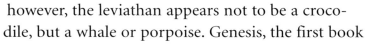

IN DIFFERENT BOOKS of the Bible the word leviathan is used. It refers to a variety of large sea creatures. The prophet Ezekiel called the crocodile a "mighty dragon lying in the middle of the river." In other parts of the Bible, however, the leviathan appears not to be a crocodile, but a whale or porpoise. Genesis, the first book of the Old Testament, tells us that when God created the earth some of the first living creatures he made were whales, or "great sea animals."

One man had a really close encounter with a sea creature when he chose to disobey God. God told Jonah to go to Ninevah to tell the people their city would be destroyed if they did not turn away from their

EZEKIEL'S VISION

In an amazing vision, the prophet Ezekiel saw a river of healing, swarming with fish and sea creatures. Similar to rivers mentioned in the books of Genesis (in the Garden of Eden) and Revelation, this special river symbolizes the blessings that flow when a person's life becomes one with God.

A WHALE OF A FISH STORY

What sort of fish swallowed Jonah? It may have been a toothed whale, which has a stomach large enough to hold a person. Others believe that God created a large fish specifically to swallow Jonah. Still others believe that the story is symbolic of something else (such as the capture of the kingdom of Judah). The important thing to remember is that the experience changed Jonah. After his experience, he went to Ninevah, the capital of Assyria, and fulfilled the command God gave him.

OPEN WIDE

The leviathan mentioned in the Book of Job was probably a crocodile. Crocodiles usually move at a slow pace, but warming on the river bank heats their body enough to make them able to move at faster speeds to catch prey. Sometimes, while a crocodile is sunning, it will lay with its jaws open wide, letting birds hop in and out of its mouth unharmed to pick leeches out of its mouth.

sin. Jonah did not want to go, so he got on a ship going to a city that was in the opposite direction. A terrible storm came, and the ship seemed about to sink in the high waves. Jonah knew the storm was because of his sin. He told the sailors to throw him overboard and the storm would stop. The sailors did not want to do that, but the storm grew so much worse they finally threw him into the sea. God sent a great sea creature, possibly a whale, to swallow Jonah. For three days and nights, Jonah was in the whale's stomach praying. Finally, God told the whale to swim toward land and spit Jonah out on the shore.

BEHEMOTH

Another baffling creature mentioned in the Bible is the behemoth. It, too, appears in the Book of Job. However, experts are fairly certain that it is a hippopotamus. Job says this creature eats grass like the ox, has bones that are like tubes of bronze, and wades in rivers.

SYMBOL OF THE FISH

The earliest Christians used the symbol of a fish as a secret sign to identify other believers. It was not yet safe to follow The Way (the teachings of Jesus), so believers could simply trace a fish in the sand or dirt and watch for acknowledgment. The Greek word for fish is *ichthus.* It is an acrostic for "Jesus Christ, God's son, savior," words that sum up Christian beliefs. The fish symbol (⤜) has been found in early Christian catacombs (underground passages and tombs) of ancient cities of the Roman Empire.

Reptiles and Other Fearsome Creatures

◆ ◆ ◆

Egyptian cobra

REPTILES OR SNAKES are mentioned several times in the Bible. When the children of Israel were in the wilderness, they complained against God over and over again. They were not satisfied with the way he was providing for their needs. The Lord had punished them before because of their complaining, but they had not learned their lesson. This time, when they complained once again, God sent serpents among the people as punishment. The snakes were described as "fiery" because their poison was so strong anyone bitten died quickly. Many of the Israelite people were bitten and died. The people came and begged Moses to ask God to save them from the deadly snake bites. When Moses prayed, God told him to make a bronze serpent, put it on a pole, and

FEARSOME STING

Scorpions are fearsome creatures varying from two inches to around nine inches in length. Their tails have stingers that can poison and paralyze. Several Bible passages—particularly in the Book of Revelation—refer to the painful sting of the scorpion. When Rehoboam became king of Israel, he wanted the people to know that he would be even more severe than his father, Solomon, and he promised to give out discipline "with scorpions."

VARIETY OF SNAKES

The ancient Hebrews were familiar with a number of venomous snakes, among them the horned sand snake (adder), the horned viper, the puff adder, and the Egyptian cobra. Most Middle Eastern snakes live on a diet of frogs and small animals. Some vipers differ from snakes in that they bear their young live rather than hatch them from eggs.

LOOKS CAN DECEIVE

When curled up tight, a scorpion can look like an egg. Thus, the passage in the Book of Luke that speaks of God's goodness to those who seek him: "What father among you, if his son...asks for an egg, will give him a scorpion?"

SWARMING HORNETS

In the Old Testament, armies sent by God into battle were sometimes described as hornets. The vast armies would "swarm" in and drive out their enemies.

raise it high above the camp so everyone could see it. If a person was bitten, he or she only had to look at the bronze snake in order to live. It was not the bronze snake that healed the people. It was their obedience in following God's direction and their belief that God could heal them.

Later in the Bible, the children of Israel turned away from God again, and this same bronze serpent had to be destroyed because the people started to worship it. Jesus compared himself to the bronze serpent. His sacrifice on the cross for the sins of the world would provide the way for others to live if they would only look to him.

Cedars of Lebanon

◆ ◆ ◆

KING DAVID wanted to build a beautiful temple where the people of Israel could go to worship the Lord. During David's reign, there had been many wars and much blood had been shed. Because of this, God told David he couldn't build the temple. David's son Solomon would be a man of peace, so he was the one who would be able to build the temple.

But David began collecting materials and making arrangements for the building process. When Solomon became king, he continued the work his father had started. He wanted the best building materials available. He knew the best wood to use was the cedar from Lebanon. Solomon made a treaty with Hiram, king of Tyre. The agreement stated that Solomon could have cedar, cyprus, and stone from the forests of Lebanon. So he sent workers in to select and prepare the building supplies for shipment. In return for this, Solomon sent wheat, oil, and wine to the king of Tyre.

It took Solomon's workmen about seven and a half years to complete the beautiful temple. In addition, Solomon also used the cedar of Lebanon wood to build his own house. It took workers 13 years to build his house.

CEDARS OF SINAI

In the Bible, many references are made to cedar trees, and most of those references are about the cedars of Lebanon. In early Old Testament times, before the cedars of Lebanon were readily available to the people in Israel, the wood from other cedar trees was used for special things. These cedar trees came from the Sinai Desert. The wood from these cedars was used in ceremonies of purification along with hyssop and scarlet.

KING OF TREES

The cedar tree grows very slowly, and that gives its wood great strength. Because of its strength compared to other wood in Bible lands, the cedar is called the king of trees. It is a very desirable wood for building homes and fancy buildings, but it is often used for roofs, too. Cedar trees have wide spreading branches. The trunk of a cedar tree can be as much as 40 inches around.

Sycamore Trees

◆ ◆ ◆

AMOS WAS a hardworking man. He had two jobs. One of his jobs was as a shepherd and sheep breeder. His second job was as a tender of sycamore trees, growing the trees and harvesting their fruit. Amos considered himself to be just an ordinary man, but God saw him as a man who would be obedient in speaking God's words of warning to the people of the nation. One day, as Amos was telling what would happen in the land of Bethel, King Amaziah became angry. He told Amos to leave Bethel and never prophesy there again because it was the king's sanctuary and the royal residence.

Amos told the king, "I am not a prophet. I am not even the son of a prophet. I am just a shepherd and the tender of sycamore trees, but God called me to prophesy to the people of Israel." King Amaziah did not want to hear about the coming judgment of God, but this did not stop Amos from speaking the truth. The words of Amos, humble keeper of sycamore trees and prophet of God, came true. As he had said, the king's family was destroyed, and Israel was conquered.

A TRAVELER'S FRIEND

The sycamore tree's strong branches spread out and are low enough to the ground to make it easy to climb. It is also a fast growing tree. Sycamore trees by the roadside gave a traveler an easy way to climb up and get a view far down the road. The sycamore tree also grows fruit that is similar to a fig.

COME DOWN RIGHT NOW!

When Jesus was going into the city of Jericho, there was a large crowd around him. Zacchaeus wanted to know what was going on, but he couldn't see because he was very short. He climbed a sycamore tree so he could see what was happening. When Jesus came to the tree, he spoke to Zacchaeus. He told him to come down because he was going home with him. Zacchaeus obeyed, and his life was changed forever.

Almond Trees

❖ ❖ ❖

WHEN THE CHILDREN of Israel left Egypt, God protected and guided them. He gave them everything they would need. He knew they would need laws to govern them, so he called Moses to Mount Sinai. There he gave Moses the Ten Commandments. In addition, he told Moses how the tabernacle was to be built. He gave instructions about what each piece of furniture in the tabernacle was to be made of and exactly how it was to look.

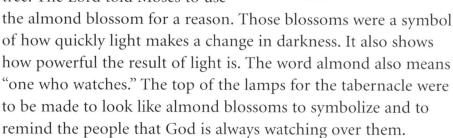

In Exodus 25:31–40, the Lord told Moses the lampstand was to have a center branch with three branches on each side of it. He said each branch was to have a bowl on it that looked like the blossoms of the almond tree. The Lord told Moses to use the almond blossom for a reason. Those blossoms were a symbol of how quickly light makes a change in darkness. It also shows how powerful the result of light is. The word almond also means "one who watches." The top of the lamps for the tabernacle were to be made to look like almond blossoms to symbolize and to remind the people that God is always watching over them.

SPRING IS NEAR

The almond tree grows in many parts of the world, but it grows best in the land where Jesus grew up. The almond tree is the first to blossom in spring. It puts out its buds when the weather is still cold in January or February and there are no leaves on the trees yet. Its early blossoming is a reminder to watch for spring. In the Bible, the almond tree is a symbol of watching or watchfulness.

Jesus' Thorny Crown

WHEN JESUS was arrested and brought before the court, the only thing he was guilty of was being God's son. He had never sinned in his life, but many people did not understand how that could be true. The religious leaders were jealous of Jesus. They did not like it that he was popular and the people wanted to hear what he had to say. They brought Jesus before Pilate.

Pilate believed Jesus was innocent of all the charges against him. As he was deciding what to do, soldiers were guarding Jesus. While the soldiers were waiting for more orders, they decided to make a cruel game of their job and make fun of Jesus. They twisted thorns and put them on Jesus' head like a crown. Then they put a purple robe on his back. They laughed and jeered and called out "Hail, King of the Jews!" Finally they blindfolded Jesus, hit him, and asked him to tell who it was that had hit him.

They were very mean and cruel to Jesus, but he loved them and was still willing to die for their sins. Before the day was over, the soldiers realized they had made a terrible mistake.

ANCIENT BARBED WIRE

In Bible times, shepherds did everything they could to protect their sheep. They would sometimes place a thick cluster of sharp thorns on the top of the sheepfold wall (where the sheep were kept) to keep wild animals out. This was a very clever way to give the sheep protection. The thorns were like the very first kind of barbed wire ever used.

Spices for Burial and Anointing

❖ ❖ ❖

WHEN JESUS was born, a star shone so brightly in the night that three men who studied the stars were curious to find out about it. They studied the prophet Isaiah and found that he had told about a wonderful Messiah that God had promised to send to the world. They believed that star was a wonderful sign of his birth, and they were determined to find him. They followed the star, and it led them to Jerusalem. They stopped at the palace to ask about the new baby that was born king of the Jews. They did not find him there. No one knew about the birth of a new king. They traveled to Bethlehem and found Jesus there.

They selected the finest gifts they could think of and brought them to the new king. The gifts they choose were gold, frankincense, and myrrh. Frankincense and myrrh are spices that have a special use.

Frankincense is made from the resin of the Boswellia tree. It is used as a perfume; it has a sweet fragrance when it is warmed or burned. Myrrh is another sweet smelling perfume. It is placed on bodies that are being prepared for burial.

Cinnamon

FORBIDDEN PERFUME

Many different spices were used in Bible times. They were used to make perfumes or were ground to a powder and mixed with olive oil and used for anointing. The most often used spices were calamus, cinnamon, myrrh, and cassia. The spiced perfumes were made by a special apothecary, and these were used only for worship. The prophet Samuel warned the girls and women that is was unlawful for them to use the perfumes for themselves.

Olives and Olive Oil

◆ ◆ ◆

OLIVES AND OLIVE OIL are two of the greatest blessings God gave to Israel. They are mentioned at least 58 times in the Bible. The olive tree can grow in very poor soil and still give an abundant crop. The fine grained olive wood was used for the doors, doorposts, and the cherubim in Solomon's temple. The wood is a lovely amber color.

The olive fruit can be eaten for food or pressed to make olive oil. Olive oil is used for cooking and in place of butter today, even as it was in Bible times. The oil can also be refined and used as oil for lamps. This refined oil was what was used in the temple lamps before the altar. The disciples used the oil to anoint people who needed healing. The oil can be processed in different ways and then be used to make fine soaps or perfumes. The olive tree usually produces two crops every year, and one tree can give enough fruit to make as much as 20 gallons of olive oil.

OLIVE BRANCH OF PEACE

Have you ever taken a really close look at a dollar bill? You'll find a universal sign for peace, a plant from the Bible, pictured on it. In one of the talons of the eagle are branches of the olive tree. Since Bible times, an offered olive branch has been a sign of peace. Olives and olive oil have also been used as money. Solomon paid for the cedar of Lebanon trees with olive oil.

LAND AHOY!

Did you ever think a leaf could tell the news of the world? It happened with the olive tree! After 40 days, Noah wanted to know what was going on outside the ark. He sent out a dove, but it soon flew back. A week later, he sent the dove out again. It returned that night with an olive leaf. The leaf told Noah the water was going down and things were growing once again.

Wormwood

◆ ◆ ◆

THE WORD wormwood means undrinkable. When it is used in the Bible, it is always warning about or describing something sad, unpleasant, or cruel that will happen or has happened.

Wormwood is mentioned nine times in the Bible. Seven of those times are in the Old Testament; the other two are in the same verse in the New Testament Book of Revelation. When John, the author of Revelation, uses wormwood he is describing some of the things that will happen on the earth when God sends his final judgment. Revelation 8:11 says, "The name of the star is Wormwood. A third of the waters became wormwood, and many died from the water, because it was made bitter." This verse tells about a star that will fall from the sky into the water on earth and make it bitter and undrinkable. If we trust God, we do not need to be afraid of the coming judgment John speaks about.

BITTER BUT HELPFUL

Wormwood is a very interesting plant. It has a yellow flower and blooms in August. Wormwood has an awful, bitter taste so people do not eat it, but strangely enough the leaves and tops can be used to make some kinds of medicine. Most often, it is used by women who put it in among their clothes to keep moths away. Evidently moths, like people, do not like the taste of wormwood.

Hyssop

❖ ❖ ❖

THE FIRST TIME the hyssop plant is mentioned in the Bible is when the children of Israel were preparing to leave Egypt. God had told Moses exactly how the people were to prepare for their journey. The pharaoh would not let the Jewish people leave to worship God, so God had sent ten plagues. The tenth and worst plague was to come that night. The death angel was going to come to every home in the land and kill the firstborn son. For the death angel to pass over the Jewish homes without killing anyone, the fathers had to do exactly as Moses instructed them. They were to take a lamb without spot or blemish and kill it. They were then to take a branch of hyssop, dip it in the blood of the lamb, and paint it on their doorposts.

In every home where the father had obeyed Moses' instructions and used the special hyssop paintbrush, there was no sadness because of death that night. The Jewish children were saved.

TO JESUS' LIPS

Hyssop was used when Jesus was crucified. After he had been hanging on the cross for several hours, Jesus said he was thirsty. The soldiers took a sponge and dipped it in vinegar. They then placed the sponge on a long branch of hyssop and raised it to Jesus' lips so he could drink. The psalmist David, the prophet Isaiah, and other authors in Scripture use hyssop as a picture of the forgiveness of sins.

Vines

AFTER BEING inside a whale for three days and nights, it's hard to believe Jonah could be upset about a vine dying, but he was. When the whale spit Jonah on the shore, he was very willing to preach in Ninevah as God had asked. Jonah warned, "In forty days your city will be destroyed if you do not turn from your sin." The people believed and repented of their sins. To show how sorry they were, the king and all the people in the land wore sackcloth and sat in ashes. They did not eat or drink. God saw how changed their hearts were and decided not to destroy the city. Jonah was angry.

As he sat outside the city to see what God would do, he made a shelter and sat in its shade. God made a vine to grow and give Jonah more relief from the hot sun. Jonah was grateful, but the next day a worm ate a hole in the vine. Jonah told God how angry he was that the plant had died. God asked Jonah how he could be sad over a dead plant but not sad over the death of everyone in Ninevah.

THREE VINE BRANCHES

A servant made the king very angry, so the king put him in prison. While he was there, the servant had a strange dream about a vine. The vine in the dream had three branches. God told Joseph what the dream meant. Joseph told the servant that the three branches on the vine meant he would be released from prison in three days and would again serve the king. In three days, the dream came true.

A TREE FOR SHADE

Vines are mentioned in the Bible at least 500 times. Most everyone in Israel had their own garden, and every garden had a fig tree and a vine. During a very hard time for Israel, the prophet Micah used the vine and fig tree to encourage the people. He told them that one day they would again live in peace. Everyone would have a tree for shade and a vine for food; this was very comforting to the people. You can read this in the Book of Micah.

Grapevines, Vineyards

❖ ❖ ❖

A VINEYARD REQUIRES great care. A vinedresser will not leave a dead plant in his vineyard. It would give no fruit and would only take up valuable ground. A wise vinedresser will cultivate the ground around his plants. He also cuts the vines back each year, because pruning will make the plants healthier and allow them to produce even more fruit. If a vine is not pruned, it will eventually stop producing fruit and have no real value.

In John 15:1–2, Jesus says, "I am the true vine, and my Father is the vinegrower. He removes every branch in me that bears no fruit. Every branch that bears fruit he prunes to make it bear more fruit."

FRUITFUL LAND

When God delivered the children of Israel from slavery in Egypt, they were looking forward to living in the land God had promised them. Near its border, Moses sent spies into the country. These 12 men returned with reports and evidence of how fruitful this new land was. One of the things they brought back with them was a huge cluster of grapes. They brought this fruit to show the richness of the promised land.

In this passage, Jesus was telling us that just like an actual vinedresser, God will remove those people who are not fruitful. Those who are fruitful, he will prune so they will bear more fruit. God's pruning means he sometimes disciplines us to help us trust him more. When that happens, we should also be more fruitful disciples.

Questions & Answers

◆ ◆ ◆

Q: How hard is it to get into heaven?

A: Jesus said it would be easier for a camel to go through the eye of a needle than for a rich man to go to heaven. The "eye of the needle" may have been a small gate in the city wall for people to go through.

Q: Did Bible characters ride horses?

A: Probably not. Horses were used to pull chariots and sometimes carts. But only the rich could afford a horse, and people seldom rode them. Jesus once entered Jerusalem on a donkey—but he borrowed it.

Q: Why do snakes have such a bad reputation?

A: Satan appeared to Adam and Eve as a snake, and ever since then snakes have been considered bad news. Satan is called a serpent several times after that. And both Jesus and John the Baptist called hypocrites (religious phonies) snakes because their words and attitudes were like poison.

Q: What was the dirtiest animal?

A: Definitely a pig. Someone who kept a herd of pigs was not even allowed to enter the temple. And if you had to get rid of a dead pig, you had to wash all your clothes afterward. Jews once started a civil war when a

The snake tempts Eve into taking the forbidden fruit.

Greek ruler sacrificed a pig on the altar of the temple.

Q: Why is the olive branch a symbol of peace?

A: When it stopped raining, Noah released a dove from the ark to see if it could find dry land. When it brought back an olive leaf, Noah knew that the raging flood was over and that the earth had been cleansed of evil and violence.

Q: Did people have parties in Bible times?

A: The people in Bible times had many festivals that had to do with planting and harvesting. But one of the most exciting times of the year was at the end of the grazing season, when the sheep were sheared. Friends and neighbors were invited to a big feast—one of the few times there was meat to eat.

Q: When is a promise like an almond?

A: God asked the prophet Jeremiah to look at an almond tree. Then God said he would keep his promise to judge Israel—and he would do it very quickly. He was playing with words—the word "almond" and the word "hasten" have the same root in Hebrew.

Q: How much did it cost to have a baby?

A: Babies were born at home, with the help of a neighbor. The real expense was a sacrifice to dedicate the baby at the temple. If the baby was a boy, the sacrifice was a lamb and a dove or pigeon. Poor people could bring two doves or two pigeons instead, which is what Jesus' mother, Mary, did.

Q: What's the most ferocious beast in the Bible?

A: The most fearsome creature may be the false prophet in the Book of Revelation. He looks like a leopard, but has the feet of a bear and the mouth of a lion. Called the "beast," he has ten horns and seven heads. Revelation also talks about swarms of giant locusts—with a sting like a scorpion.

Q: What's a thorn good for?

A: Jesus was crowned with thorns. There are many different kinds of sharp and dangerous thorns in the Holy Land. One of them, the camel thorn, was used to make perfume and even medicine. It has a very sweet smell, much like cinnamon.

Q: What did Noah plant when he came out of the ark?

A: When he came out of the ark, he planted grapevines. Grapevines were very valuable in Bible times. Owners of vineyards often put a wall around them. Sometimes they even built towers so their workers could keep watch and guard the valuable crop.

The unicorns mentioned in the Bible were probably the oryx.

Q: How many animals are mentioned in the Bible?

A: About 180 different animals are mentioned in the Old Testament and about 50 are mentioned in the New Testament. We aren't even sure what they all are, because some have become extinct. In some other cases, we aren't sure what the word means so we don't know what animal is being mentioned.

Q: Does the Bible mention unicorns?

A: Yes, but they probably weren't what you think. The unicorn is mentioned nine times in the Bible. It was probably an oryx, a white, horselike creature with two long horns. It was almost hunted to extinction over a hundred years ago, but it is slowly being restored in Israel today.

Q: Did Hebrew children have pets?

A: They may have considered lambs pets, but they definitely did not keep cats or dogs in their homes as we do today. Dogs ran wild and were considered unclean. They ate garbage, and they had a reputation something like a buzzard has today. Cats aren't even mentioned in the Bible, although the Egyptians seem to have worshiped them and used them to catch rats.

The Land of the Bible

NCIENT ISRAEL was a small country God had promised to Abraham and his descendants. That's why it was called the promised land. But it had many different features. There were river valleys and coastal plains. There were rugged mountains and rolling hills. There were dry deserts and fertile fields. It helps to understand Bible stories if you know where they happened. It even helps to understand the news from Israel today.

By Way of the Wilderness

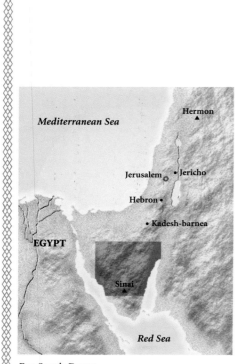

Far South Desert

NO SAND DUNES

The deserts in Bible lands do not have the great shifting sand dunes that are found in some other deserts. Instead, the land is dry and rocky. Hot winds blow fine dust and sand across flat plains and rocky hills.

To the south and east of Israel are deserts—dry and lonely wastelands made up of salt flats and rocky hills rising from a sea of sand. There is little rain there, just a shower or two each year. Sometimes it doesn't rain at all.

The Hebrews passed through this wilderness on their way from Egypt to the promised land. Thousands of them traveled with the Tabernacle and the Ark of the Covenant, camping along the way. They only moved when God would go before them as a pillar of fire, leading them to the land he had promised Abraham.

It was hot and dry, and the people complained to Moses all the time. They wanted water. They wanted food. They wanted meat. Each time they complained, God gave them what they wanted. But at Kadesh-barnea, God finally had enough of their complaining.

While the people camped at this desert oasis, Moses sent 12 spies to check out the land God had promised Abraham. He said: "See what the land is like

ZERO PERCENT HUMIDITY

The Sinai Desert is very dry, and some parts receive less than two inches of rain a year. Several months can pass without a drop of water falling.

and whether the people who live there are strong or weak, few or many. What kind of land is it? What kind of cities do they live in?"

So the spies explored the land. It took them 40 days. When they came back, they brought some figs and pomegranates. And they brought a cluster of grapes so big two men had to carry it on a pole between them.

"It is a land flowing with milk and honey," they said. "But the people there are powerful and live in large, walled cities." "We should go on and take the land, for we can certainly do it," Moses said.

But ten of the spies said it was impossible. "The people there are giants, and we are like grasshoppers," they said. Only two spies, Joshua and Caleb, were willing to go on. "Do not be afraid, for the Lord is with us," they said.

But the people complained again, and they refused to go ahead. "It would be better if we had died in the wilderness," they said. And so they did. Because they would not obey him, God said they would not enter the promised land. They would wander in the wilderness for 40 years until all the grown men and women had died. Only Joshua and Caleb and the children lived to see the promised land.

THE LONG WAY HOME

The shortest route from Egypt to Canaan was northeast along the coast of the Mediterranean Sea. There was a highway there, but the Egyptians had many forts along this route, and it went through the land of the Philistines, a nation of fierce warriors. So the Hebrews traveled south and east through the desert before they went north, camping at different oases along the way.

WONDER OF THE WORLD

When pharaohs died, they were often buried in stone pyramids. It is amazing that these elaborate and monumental tombs were built by hand using simple axes, chisels, and saws.

East of the Jordan

◆ ◆ ◆

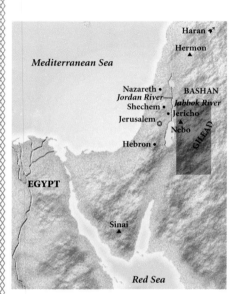

Plateau of Jordan

EAST OF THE JORDAN RIVER there is a high, rocky plateau, a flat ridge that stretches from Mount Hermon to the Red Sea. Wheat and barley grow on the western edge of the plateau; the rain falls there as clouds blow in from the sea. But olives and grapes do not do well because the desert winds are cold at night.

This is the place where Jacob went after he stole his brother Esau's birthright. With his mother's help, Jacob tricked his blind and dying father, Isaac, into thinking he was Esau, the oldest son. So Isaac gave Jacob his brother's blessing—and Esau was so angry Jacob had to leave home.

He traveled north to Haran, and he lived there for 14 years. He married Leah and Rachel, and he had children. He finally decided to return home, traveling south along the plateau. He sent a messenger to his brother. The messenger returned and said: "Your brother Esau is

NEEDED: STRONG BULLS

The northern end of the plateau east of the Jordan River is made of rich, volcanic soil. This area was called Bashan, the land of the farmer. The Bible talks about the "strong bulls of Bashan," which were needed to plow the heavy soil. Today this area is called the Golan Heights.

THE BALM OF GILEAD

On either side of the Jabbok River, the eastern plateau is broken up by a series of hills and mountains. This area is called Gilead. Rich forests were there during the time of King David, but they have been cut down. A medicine came from the forest called the "balm of Gilead."

JUST A PEEK

The Hebrews got their first look at the promised land from the plateau east of the Jordan. Moses himself did not get to enter the land because he had sinned. But God allowed him to see it from the top of Mount Nebo. Then Moses died, but no one knows where he was buried.

coming to meet you with 400 men."

Jacob was afraid, so he divided his family and servants and cattle into two groups. He thought, "If he attacks one group, maybe the other group can escape." Then he prayed to the Lord: "I had only a staff when I crossed the Jordan, and now I have a family. Save me, for I am afraid my brother will attack me and the mothers and their children."

Then he sent gifts ahead, goats and sheep and camels and cows and donkeys. He crossed the Jabbok River and met his brother. He bowed seven times, as though his brother were a king. To his great surprise, Esau ran to him and threw his arms around his neck and kissed him. They both began to cry. "Who are all these people?" Esau asked. So Jacob introduced his family.

Esau refused the gifts that Jacob had sent, but Jacob insisted that he take them. Esau offered to travel with Jacob or send some of his men along to protect him. But Jacob decided to stay where he was on the high, windy land east of the Jordan.

He stayed there about ten years before he took down his tents and crossed the Jordan River to pitch camp at Shechem. He was home at last, in the land of his father, Isaac.

WRESTLING WITH AN ANGEL

The night before he met Esau, Jacob wrestled with an angel of the Lord. "I will not let you go until you bless me," he said. So the angel changed his name from Jacob, which means "one who plays tricks," to Israel, which means "one who struggles with God."

Crossing the Jordan

◆ ◆ ◆

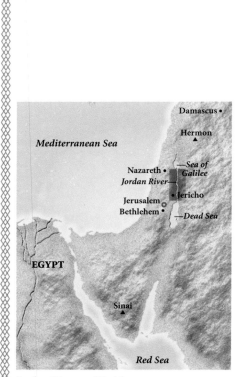

Jordan River and Jericho

JORDAN'S STORMY BANKS

"Crossing the Jordan" has come to mean the same thing as going to heaven. Just as the children of Israel crossed the Jordan to enter the promised land, Christians believe they will one day cross the river of death and enter God's heavenly kingdom.

MOST OF THE TIME, the Jordan is a slow, lazy river that flows through the Sea of Galilee to the Dead Sea. It is bordered on both sides by rocky hills and mountains. During the rainy season, the water rushes down the slopes and swells the Jordan into an angry, rushing torrent.

It was to this raging river that Joshua led the people of Israel as they marched toward the promised land. The people camped there three days, waiting for the river to subside. But the water kept coming. Then Joshua told the people to get ready to cross. "Tomorrow the Lord will do amazing things among you."

So the next morning, the priests picked up the Ark of the Covenant, a wooden box covered with gold that contained the Ten Commandments, Aaron's rod, and a jar of manna. "Tell the priests to go ahead of the people and stand in the middle of the Jordan," God said.

So Joshua told the priests what to do. They marched toward the river and then they marched straight into it. As their feet

A DEAD END

The Jordan River empties into the Dead Sea, the lowest place on the earth. There is no place for the water to go so it evaporates in the hot desert sun. Over the years, the water that evaporated has left salt and minerals behind, making the water that remains thick and bitter. The water is so salty that no fish can live there.

touched the water's edge, the water stopped flowing and backed up to Adam, a city about 18 miles away.

The people marched across on dry land, and their soldiers prepared themselves in case of battle. Then Joshua told the people to choose one man from each tribe to get a rock from the middle of the Jordan. They set these on top of 12 pillars of stone. "When your children ask you what these stones mean, tell them that the flow of the Jordan River was cut off before the Ark of the Covenant," he said.

Then Joshua told the priests to come up out of the river. As soon as they did, the river began to run again, as full as it was before. Joshua told the people: "God did this so all the people of the world will know that the Lord is powerful, and so you will always fear the Lord."

Then the Hebrews celebrated the Passover and remembered how God had led them out of Egypt and parted the Red Sea just like he had parted the Jordan River. They ate their first food from the promised land, and then they marched on Jericho. It was the first city that would fall before the armies of the Lord.

MUDDY WATER
Near where the Hebrews crossed the Jordan River, the valley widens into a flood plain. The river becomes narrow and muddy. A Syrian general named Naaman once refused to wash there because the water was not clean enough. This is where Jesus was baptized by John the Baptist.

A HIDING PLACE
The Jordan River is fed by springs and melting snow from mountains at the very northern edge of Israel. This area was lush and green, filled with thick forests and waterfalls. In Bible times, lions were plentiful. And so were bandits who hid in the forests and attacked travelers on the ancient coastal highway from Damascus to Egypt.

Between the Mountains

◆ ◆ ◆

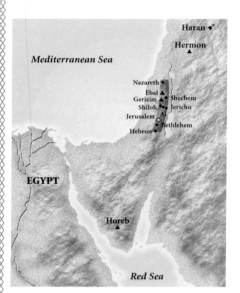

The Central Mountains

I WANT THAT MOUNTAIN

Moses sent 12 spies into the promised land, but only two came back with a good report—Joshua and Caleb. Forty years later, Joshua became the commander of the armies of Israel. As a reward for his faithfulness, Caleb received the hill country around Hebron that he had seen and claimed when he was a young spy.

A RANGE OF LOW MOUNTAINS runs up the center of Israel. In Bible times, there were many vineyards along the western slopes, where the rains fell as the wind blew clouds east from the sea. The eastern slopes were rocky and dry, a wilderness where Jesus went and was tempted by the Devil.

Many important and ancient cities are nestled in these mountains, including Hebron in the south, the burial ground of Abraham, Isaac, and Jacob. Jerusalem lies further north on Mount Zion. This is the City of David, the city where Solomon built the temple.

But when the Hebrews first entered the promised land, they worshiped farther north in Shechem, a city that guarded the entrance to a valley between two high mountains. Shechem is the city where Jacob finally settled when he returned from Haran. He buried their family idols beneath an oak tree there. Later, his son Judah killed all the men in the city because one of them had hurt his sister Dinah.

At Shechem, Joshua built the first altar to the Lord after the children of Israel entered the promised land. He built it on the side of Mount Ebal, across from Mount Gerizim. He sacrificed bulls and goats, thanking God for giving them victory over Jericho and Ai.

Mounts Ebal and Gerizim

Tomb of the Patriarchs, where Abraham is buried.

CAVES

Caves are very common in Bible lands. Elijah once hid in a cave in Mount Horeb. God spoke to him in a wind, in an earthquake, in a fire, and in a still, small voice. Abraham bought a cave near Hebron to bury his wife Sarah. Abraham, Isaac, and Jacob were all buried there, too.

MOUNT MORIAH

As a test, God once asked Abraham to sacrifice his own son, Isaac. God wanted to see if Abraham loved God more than anything else. Abraham traveled three days to Moriah, where he prepared an altar for the sacrifice. At the last moment, an angel stopped him. Many people think Moriah was the same hill in Jerusalem where Solomon later built the temple.

Then Joshua did something he had promised Moses he would do. He read from the Book of the Law, as the people stood on either side of the Ark of the Covenant, facing the priests. He read the blessings and the curses of the Law.

"You will be blessed in the city and in the country," he said. And half the people said "Amen." "Cursed is anyone who makes an idol," he said. And the other half said "Amen." This continued as he read all the laws that Moses had written down. Everyone was there, including the women and children.

Soon Joshua and the people conquered the mountains with God's help. The land was divided between the tribes. For many years, the Hebrews lived in the mountains. They were safe from the chariots of their enemies there. They would go to the Tabernacle at the village of Shiloh to worship God.

A Great Loss

◆ ◆ ◆

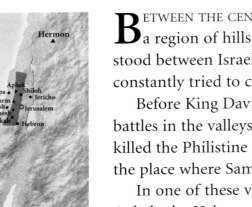

The Western Hills

IRON ENVY

When the Hebrews first settled the promised land, they had no blacksmiths and no iron. The Philistines did not want the Hebrews to make weapons. So the Hebrews had to take their plows and other farm tools down through the western hills to have them sharpened.

BETWEEN THE CENTRAL MOUNTAINS and the sea in Israel, there is a region of hills with excellent valleys for farming. These hills stood between Israel and the Philistines, a warlike people who constantly tried to conquer the Hebrews.

Before King David finally defeated them, there were frequent battles in the valleys between these hills. This is where David killed the Philistine giant Goliath with a slingshot. This is also the place where Samson lived and fought against the Philistines.

In one of these valleys, near Aphek, the Hebrews suffered a great loss. They were defeated in battle by the Philistines, who killed about 4,000 of them. They returned to their camp, thoroughly discouraged. "Why did the Lord allow us to lose?" they wondered.

Then they had an idea. They sent messengers to Shiloh and asked the two sons of the high priest Eli to bring the Ark of the Covenant. They thought the Ark would give them luck. Eli's sons brought the Ark without asking the Lord what they should do.

A carving of the Battle of Lachish

THE LACHISH LETTERS

When the Babylonians conquered Judah and destroyed Jerusalem, two walled cities in the western hills were the last to fall. These cities were Lachish and Azekah. Archaeologists have found letters written from Lachish at that time that tell about the final days of the kingdom. The Lachish letters even mention Azekah.

The Hebrews cheered as the Ark was brought into the camp. The Philistines heard them and were afraid. "Now we're in trouble," they said. But their officers encouraged them. "Be strong and fight like men," they said.

The next day, the battle began again. The Philistines fought hard, and the Hebrews fled before them. Eli's sons both died, along with 30,000 Hebrews. The Philistines captured the Ark and took it to the temple of their god Dagon.

That night, the idol fell over and broke to pieces on the ground. After that, the land was overrun with rats, and the people began to get large infected sores. Finally, after seven months, they decided to send the Ark back to the Hebrews. They put the Ark on a cart and hitched it up to two oxen. They put gifts on the cart, too.

TREE FREE

In Old Testament times, the western hills had many groves of sycamore fig trees. King David appointed a man to oversee the harvest of the figs. Eventually the trees were cut down and used for firewood. The name of one village there today means "mother of charcoal."

Without anyone to lead them, the oxen took the Ark up through one of the valleys in the hill country. The Lord led them to the village of Beth Shemesh, where the people rejoiced that the Ark had been returned. But they looked inside the Ark and 70 of them died.

So the Ark was moved to Kiriath Jearim, and it remained there for 20 years until David brought it to Jerusalem.

SON OF SORROW

When Eli's two sons were killed by the Philistines, one of their wives was about to have a baby. She died delivering her son, but before she died she named the baby Ichabod, which means "no glory." She said "The glory of the Lord has departed from Israel" because the Ark had been captured by the Philistines.

The Conversion of Cornelius

◆ ◆ ◆

Western Coastal Plain

THE GAZA STRIP

The Philistines built five great cities: Gaza, Ashkelon, Ekron, Ashdod, and Gath. Gaza was at the south end of their land, on the ancient coastal highway where the desert meets the wheat fields. Many Arabs live there today in an area called the Gaza Strip.

A BROAD, FLAT PLAIN extends along the coast south of Mount Carmel. An ancient road from Mesopotamia to Egypt passed through this plain. Many armies marched up and down this road, as the Egyptians, Assyrians, Persians, Babylonians, and Romans all tried to enlarge their empires.

The northern end of this plain, called the Plain of Sharon, was filled with thick oak forests and low-lying swamps. South of this were the fertile plains of Philistia, where wheat grew in abundance. This wheat was often stored in underground pits carved in stone. The Philistines built five walled cities there—with plenty of food to hold out against their attackers. Even King David never controlled this area.

But the Romans did conquer these cities, and they built an important seaport at Joppa. The Apostle Peter visited Joppa and raised a woman named Dorcas from the dead. After that, he stayed at the home of a tanner named Simon. While he was

Seaport of Joppa

there, he went up on the roof to pray, and he had a vision. A sheet was lowered from heaven three times. It was filled with animals Jews were not allowed to eat. Each time a voice commanded Peter to get up and eat, and each time he refused.

"I can't eat this food," Peter said. "It is unclean." "Don't call anything I have made unclean," God said. Then Peter woke up.

Roman aqueduct at Caesarea

A CITY WITH A SEWER

Shortly before Jesus was born, King Herod built a magnificent city and seaport at Caesarea. It contained a theater, a stadium, and public baths. Fresh water ran down from Mount Carmel along a stone bridge called an aqueduct. The city even had a sewer system that was flushed by ocean tides.

About the same time as Peter's dream, an angel came to Cornelius in Caesarea, about 30 miles away. Cornelius was a Roman officer who wanted to know and serve God. The angel told him to send for Peter in Joppa.

When Cornelius' men came and asked Peter to go to Caesarea, he gladly went. He went in and talked with Cornelius and his family. "Our law says we are not to even visit people who are not Jews. But the Lord has shown me that none of his creatures is unclean."

Cornelius told Peter about the angel who came and visited him. Then Peter told Cornelius about Jesus and how he had died for our sins. "I realize that God accepts people from every nation who fear him and do what is right," he said.

After that, Cornelius became a Christian, along with his entire family.

THE NAME GAME

The land where the Philistines lived was called Philistia and only included the coastal plains. In New Testament times, the Romans used the name Philistina for a Roman province that included most of Israel. Today, the name Palestine is often used for the entire Holy Land.

SAILORS AND SOLDIERS

The Philistines occupied the southern coastal plain about the same time as the Hebrews occupied the hill country. The Philistines were a seafaring people who had tried to conquer Egypt without success. They may have come from the island of Crete.

The King Is Dead

❖ ❖ ❖

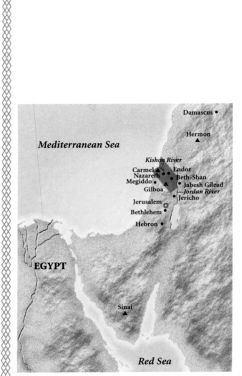

Valley of Jezreel

CHILDHOOD HOME

Jesus was raised in Nazareth along the rolling hills north of the Valley of Jezreel. As a boy, he probably played on the hilltops overlooking the valley. In towns along the valley, he healed ten lepers and a boy with seizures, and he raised a widow's son from the dead.

THERE IS A FERTILE VALLEY in northern Israel called the Valley of Jezreel. The Kishon River snakes through the valley, leaving rich soil along its banks when it floods during the winter. Deborah and Barak destroyed the army of Sisera in this valley when his chariots got stuck in the mud. And it was here, on Mount Carmel, that Elijah killed the 500 prophets of Baal after he called down fire from heaven.

A pass connects the valley to the Jordan River. The pass is guarded by the city of Beth-Shan, for which the valley is named. In the days of Saul, the Philistines came north along the coastal highway and down the valley, trying to circle Israel and destroy it.

Saul met them near the entrance to the pass, and the two armies camped on either side of the valley. Saul's army was on the south side, on Mount Gilboa. But the prophet Samuel had died, and Saul had no one to ask for advice.

So Saul disguised himself and went to a witch who lived at Endor. He asked her to

THE WITCH OF ENDOR

Saul disguised himself when he went to the witch of Endor because he had ordered that all witches be put to death. When Samuel actually appeared, the witch knew who Saul really was and she was afraid. Saul promised that he would not hurt her. The Law of Moses forbids the practice of witchcraft.

call on the spirit of Samuel. Both the witch and Saul were amazed when he actually appeared. "Why are you disturbing me?" Samuel asked. "Because the Philistines are fighting against me and the Lord has left me. What should I do?" Saul begged.

"There is nothing you can do," Samuel said. "The Lord has taken the kingdom from you. Tomorrow you and your sons will die." Then he disappeared, and Saul fell on the ground in fear.

The next day, the Philistines attacked Saul's army. The fighting grew fierce and Saul was wounded with arrows. He asked his armor bearer to kill him so the Philistines would not capture him and torture him, but the young man refused. So Saul fell on his sword and killed himself. His three sons died, too.

The Philistines found Saul's body and cut off his head. They hung his body on the city wall at Beth-Shan for all to see. Beth-Shan was at a crossroads where the Valley of Jezreel joined the Jordan River. But some Hebrew soldiers came at night and cut his body down and buried it under a tamarisk tree far away in the east across the Jordan River, at Jabesh Gilead. Then the people mourned for seven days. The first king of Israel was dead.

Beth-Shan

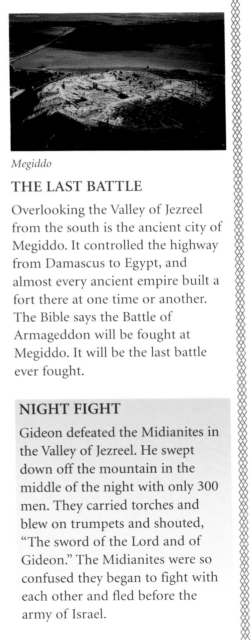

Megiddo

THE LAST BATTLE

Overlooking the Valley of Jezreel from the south is the ancient city of Megiddo. It controlled the highway from Damascus to Egypt, and almost every ancient empire built a fort there at one time or another. The Bible says the Battle of Armageddon will be fought at Megiddo. It will be the last battle ever fought.

NIGHT FIGHT

Gideon defeated the Midianites in the Valley of Jezreel. He swept down off the mountain in the middle of the night with only 300 men. They carried torches and blew on trumpets and shouted, "The sword of the Lord and of Gideon." The Midianites were so confused they began to fight with each other and fled before the army of Israel.

Safe at Sea

The Far North

GENTILE CITIES

Many of the people on the east side of the Sea of Galilee in Jesus' time were not Jews. There were ten Greek cities east and south of the lake. These were called the Decapolis (which means "ten cities" in Greek). In Jesus' time, there was also a new Roman city called Tiberias. At first, Jews refused to go there because it was built on top of a cemetery. Tiberias is still there today.

J ESUS SPENT much of his ministry around the Sea of Galilee, a large lake in northeast Israel. Each spring, the hills north and west of the deep blue lake burst forth with flowers and the chatter of sparrows.

These hills are filled with narrow valleys where farmers grew wheat along the canyon floors and tended vineyards and olive orchards on the steep slopes. It was a great place to hide for robbers and rebels and teachers the authorities did not like.

The lakeshore itself was a busy, bustling place. Boats crossed the lake from Bashan carrying grain for Rome. Soldiers marched along the highway beside bustling camel caravans carrying goods from Egypt and the east. Many travelers heard Jesus teach there, and they carried his message across the empire.

The major industry was fishing. Jesus called at least half of his disciples from the tough and independent Galilean fishermen. He often used the small boats of his fishermen friends to cross the lake. But one evening, he sent them ahead of

Hazor

SOMETHING'S BURNING

Joshua completely destroyed three cities when the children of Israel conquered the promised land. One of these was Hazor, which he burned down. It was the capital of Canaan and one of the largest cities of that time. Hazor was in Galilee, several miles north of the lake. The city was rebuilt and later fortified by kings Solomon and Ahab.

Cliffs by the Sea of Galilee

A CLIFF HANGER

High cliffs overlook the Sea of Galilee on the east. Jesus once cast demons out of a man below one of these cliffs. The demons entered a herd of pigs and ran into the water. The man was set free and he asked Jesus if he could follow him.

him to the other side. It had been a busy day, and he was tired and wanted to think and pray.

That evening, he saw his disciples straining at the oars of their small boat because the wind was against them. As the night grew darker, the wind blew even harder. Finally he went to them, walking on top of the water.

At first the disciples were terrified. They thought he was a ghost. "Don't be afraid," he said. Then they recognized him.

Peter stood and called to him, "Lord, if that is you, let me come to you on the water." "Come," Jesus said. So Peter climbed out of the boat and began to walk to Jesus. But then he became frightened as the waves continued to roar. He began to sink.

"Lord, save me!" he called. And Jesus reached out and caught his hand. "Oh Peter, you have so little faith," Jesus said. Together they walked to the boat, and when they climbed inside the wind stopped and immediately they were at the shore.

"You are certainly the Son of God," the disciples said. And Peter's faith began to grow. Later, after his resurrection, Jesus came to the shore of the Sea of Galilee again. He asked Peter to feed his sheep—his followers—and Peter became the first leader of the church.

THE SEA OF GALILEE

The Sea of Galilee was also called the Lake of Gennesaret and the Sea of Tiberias. It is about 13 miles long and 7 miles wide. The lake is 650 feet below sea level. Winds often whipped down the valleys to the west causing frequent, violent storms in the winter.

Questions & Answers

◆ ◆ ◆

Q: What's the lowest place on earth?

A: The lowest point on the face of the earth is the surface of the Dead Sea. It is about 1,300 feet below sea level. This large lake is surrounded by desert. The water has enormous amounts of salts and minerals, so much that fish can't live there. That is how it got its name.

Q: How did the Dead Sea get to be so dead?

A: The Jordan River runs into the Dead Sea, but there is nowhere for the water to run out. It's hot in that part of the world, so the water evaporates. But the minerals stay in the water and build up over time. It's the saltiest water in the world—and it's so dense you can't even sink!

Absalom's Tomb

Q: Who is buried in Absalom's tomb?

A: Not Absalom! The five-story structure cut out of the rock on the east side of Jerusalem is called Absalom's tomb, but David's son isn't buried there. The tomb was built about 1,000 years after Absalom died.

Q: Does it snow in Bible lands?

A: Very rarely, except in some high mountains. Snow is so rare that it is remembered the way we might remember a hurricane or tornado. One of David's warriors was remembered because he killed a lion "on the day of the snow"—two exciting things in one day!

Q: Where is Israel?

A: Israel is in Asia, what we call the Middle East. But many ancient civilizations thought of them-selves as being the center of the earth. Israel is called the navel of the earth.

Q: Did Jesus travel a lot?

A: Not really, he spent most of his time in Galilee. But two impor-tant highways came through there, so he had easy and frequent con-tact with lots of people without having to leave home. As an adult, he probably never went more than a hundred miles from home.

Q: Why did people go "up" to Jerusalem?

A: Jerusalem was built on a mountain, and pilgrims had to go up to get there. On the other hand, you had to go down to leave. The road to the east was steep, drop-ping 3,300 feet in just 15 miles. When the good Samaritan went down to Jericho, he followed this road.

Q: What did people do with their garbage?

A: Throw it in the street, mostly. Ancient cities didn't have garbage trucks, but people could clean up around their own homes. In Jerusalem, people often burned their garbage in the Hinnom Valley. The Hebrew word *ge'hinnom* is the basis of the New Testament word *gehenna*, which means hell.

292

Q: Is the Bible the only way we know what life was like back then?

A: No. Thousands of ancient documents detail daily life in Bible times. A library discovered in Nineveh had over 26,000 clay tablets. Thousands more were found at Ebla, Ugarit, and other cities excavated by archaeologists. These records not only help us understand what life was like, but often confirm names and places mentioned in the Bible.

Q: Did people live in caves?

A: Sometimes, but not in the sense that you see cartoons of cavemen with clubs crouched around a fire. Lot lived in a cave after Sodom was destroyed. Elijah hid in a cave. But caves were used mostly for burial or storage. One famous ancient city, Petra, was carved out of rock. One of the Indiana Jones movies was filmed there.

Q: What's the most famous rock in the world?

A: Probably a huge rock sitting right where the temple used to be. This rock is 58 feet long, 55 feet wide, and 5 or 6 feet high. Some people say this is the rock where Abraham offered Isaac, where Solomon built an altar, and where Muhammad ascended to heaven. There is a

Petra

magnificent Muslim mosque there now called the Dome of the Rock.

Q: Were there earthquakes in Bible lands?

A: The Bible tells about three earthquakes—one each during the time of Isaiah, Jesus, and Paul, but there may have been more. The Great Rift Valley runs north and south through the Holy Land all the way down into Africa. This valley is formed by two plates deep inside the earth that sometimes rub together and cause earthquakes.

Q: Where did Jesus die?

A: Jesus died at a place called Golgotha, which means skull. But no one is exactly sure where it is. Two different places in Jerusalem today are thought to be Golgotha. There are also two different places thought to be the location of Jesus' burial and resurrection.

Q: How big is heaven?

A: It's not clear where heaven is or how big it is. But the Apostle John had a vision of a city that came down from heaven, and it was huge. This "new Jerusalem" was a perfect cube measuring 1,500 miles on each side—the distance from New York City to Houston.

How the Bible Came to Be

❖   ❖   ❖   ❖

WHERE DID THE BIBLE come from? How was it written and copied and translated? These are important questions, questions that help us know if we can believe what it says. The answers involve many fascinating stories about people who were very careful to write down God's Word and share it with others—including you. As you understand where the Bible came from and how you got it, you will treasure it even more.

Language Lesson

◆　◆　◆

GOD USED WORDS to create the world. For example, he said "Let there be light," and there was light. Whom was God speaking to and what language did he use? No one knows. But the Bible says he made a man named Adam and talked with him right away. Adam talked, too, and he named the animals. God made a woman named Eve, and she talked with Adam and with God. She even talked to a snake!

Soon Adam and Eve had children—lots of children! And their children had lots of children. There were towns and cities and villages filled with people who had names for themselves and for everything around them. But the people were wicked and hated God. So he destroyed all of them in a flood, all except for a man named Noah and his family.

After the flood, God told Noah and his children to spread out and fill the earth. So the process started all over again. Noah's children had children. They learned to make bricks and mortar and build cities.

One of Noah's great-grandsons was a mighty warrior

THE NAME OF GOD

The first word used for God in the Bible is Elohim, which simply means "God." Later, other names were used, such as El Shaddia, which means "God Almighty." He had a personal name, too: Yahweh. It means "he is." When Moses asked God what his name was, God said "I am who I am."

IN THE BEGINNING

"In the beginning God created the heavens and the earth." That's how Genesis, the first book of the Bible, begins. But another book in the Bible, the Book of John, begins this way: "In the beginning was the Word." Then John says that God's Word became a man named Jesus Christ.

named Nimrod. But Nimrod did not want to obey God's command. He gathered the people together on a plain near Shinar, and they began to build a tower, the Tower of Babel.

The tower would reach the sky, and everyone would gather around it. "Then we won't be scattered across the earth," they said. They were proud, and they wanted to make a name for themselves. They would stick together and defy God.

The Bible says all of these people spoke the same language. So God knew how to solve the problem. He said: "Since they have the same language, they can work together and do just about anything they want. I will confuse their language so they will not be able to understand each other."

And that's just what he did. Suddenly, the men working on the tower could not understand each other. They were speaking different languages. The work stopped. The people were confused. They found others in the crowd who were speaking the same language they were. Then they wandered off together and did what God had asked. They settled in different parts of the world, each with different languages.

WORD POWER

The Bible teaches that we should be careful how we use words. For example, the Book of James says our tongue can be like poison and hurt people, or like a fountain and help them. Words can also tell us which way to go, like the helm of a ship or the bit in a horse's mouth.

DON'T BABBLE!

Today, the word babble means to talk without making any sense. The word comes from the Tower of Babel. The Hebrews said the word meant "confuse." But the people who later lived there called their land Babylon. They said the word meant "the gate of God."

Writing the Law

❖ ❖ ❖

CN Y RD THS BK?

The Hebrew alphabet had no punctuation—and no vowels. Not only that, the words ran together. If we did the same thing, the first verse of the Bible would look like this: NTH BGNNNGGDCRTDTHHVNN THRTH. Because there were no vowels, we aren't sure how some of the words sounded.

BACKWARD AND FORWARD

The Phoenicians wrote their letters in a straight line, from left to right and top to bottom, like we do now. The Greeks wrote to the end of the line and then started back from the other direction. The Hebrews wrote from right to left—starting on what we call the last page!

MOST ANCIENT PEOPLE developed a way to write. At first, they drew simple pictures of things they wanted to describe. A man might trade a bale of cloth for four oxen and scratch a simple picture of four oxen on a tablet of clay to record the deal.

Eventually, pictures represented actions, too, like walking or sleeping or shaving. They also represented ideas, like love or hunger. But there might be thousands of these pictures, one for every word. The Egyptians had a very elaborate picture alphabet called hieroglyphics. Most writing was used, however, for government and religion.

This is the writing Moses would have been taught when he was raised by Pharaoh's daughter. The Bible says he was educated "in all the ways of the

Egyptian hieroglyphics

Egyptians, and mighty in words and in deeds." But by his day, the symbols had started to stand for sounds instead of words. This made it easier to remember. Eventually, alphabets developed, with a letter for each sound.

When Moses led the Hebrews out of slavery in Egypt to the promised land, he wrote down what happened. He also wrote down the stories of their ancestors, from Adam to Joseph. And he wrote down the laws God gave him. Christians believe God helped him get the stories and laws exactly right.

God didn't take any chances with the Ten Commandments, however. He wrote them down himself. After the people left Egypt, they camped at Mount Sinai in the desert. One day there was thunder and lightning at the top of the mountain, and the earth trembled. The people were terrified.

God called Moses to the top of the mountain. For 40 days, he told Moses what to write in the Book of the Law. But just before Moses left, God wrote the Ten Commandments on two stone tablets with his finger. The Hebrews treasured these tablets and kept them in a golden box called the Ark of the Covenant.

A SACRED LIBRARY

There are 66 books in the Bible. These were written by at least 40 different authors over a period of 1,500 years. It took almost 1,000 years to collect the books in the Old Testament. The New Testament was written in a much shorter period of time, about 30 years.

Eventually, Moses wrote most of the first five books in the Bible. After the Hebrews conquered Canaan, Joshua read from these writings at Mount Ebal. The Hebrews were very careful when they copied these writings. By the time of Ezra the scribe, about 400 years before Jesus was born, they had been collected together with other writings to form the Old Testament we have today.

FIRST ALPHABET

The Phoenicians usually get credit for the first alphabet. They were famous seafaring traders. They had to keep records and send messages. So they developed an alphabet with just 22 letters to stand for all the sounds. Their alphabet became the basis of the Greek alphabet and later the Roman alphabet, which is the one we use today.

The Beginning of Books

◆ ◆ ◆

IN ANCIENT TIMES, people first wrote on clay tablets, scratching symbols and words with a sharp, thin stick called a stylus.

But the Egyptians invented the first paper, although it was not like paper today. It was called papyrus, named after a reed that grows along the Nile River. They cut the papyrus into long narrow strips and glued them together to make paper.

Papyrus was too brittle to be folded, so it was rolled onto a stick. The pieces of papyrus could be as long as 40 feet. These early "books" were called scrolls. Only the rich could afford scrolls made of papyrus. It had to come from Egypt—and the Egyptians charged a lot of money for the precious papyrus.

So people began to write on strips of animals skins, too. This was called parchment. It was also made into scrolls. People called scribes were trained to write on these scrolls using a pen made from a reed or feather and ink made from ashes.

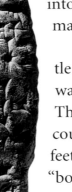
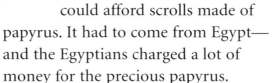

Cuneiform clay tablet

WHAT TO INCLUDE

Hebrew scholars decided which books to include in the Old Testament. They made this decision official at the Council of Jamnia in A.D. 90. Leaders of the early church decided which books to include in the New Testament at the Council of Carthage in A.D. 397.

Ink pot

WRITING IMPLEMENTS

People in biblical times usually had to write with a sharpened reed, or stylus, on clay. Their other choice was to make brush pens from reeds and use ink made from soot. They also wrote with ink and a pen or brush on broken pottery pieces, called ostraca. These were usually short notes— the pieces were just the right size!

One of King Josiah's scribes found an old scroll containing a copy of the Law. He read it to the king, who was very sorry the people had not obeyed God. He ordered all the idols to be destroyed. For hundreds of years, the scribes continued to make copies of the scrolls containing the Scripture, being very careful not to make any mistakes.

By New Testament times, papyrus was more common. Many Jews had a copy of at least part of the Law. There were scrolls in the synagogue, too. Jesus read from the prophet Isaiah in the synagogue at Nazareth.

The Apostle Paul was a rabbi, a well-educated man who knew much of the ancient Scriptures by heart. As he traveled from

place to place teaching about Jesus, he started many churches and made many friends.

He wrote several letters to different churches and people on scrolls. These eventually became part of the New Testament. Not long after that, a new way to make a book was invented.

By then better paper was available. It was cut and folded and sewn together to make a book much more like what we have today. This early book was called a codex. It was a big improvement. Scribes could write on both sides of the page, and it was easier to carry and to use.

Unrolled amulet scroll

OLDEST FRAGMENT

The earliest biblical texts ever found were short fragments in two silver good luck charms, or amulets. They come from the period when the temple was destroyed by the Babylonians in 587 B.C. The words are a blessing by Aaron from Numbers 6:24–26.

WHAT'S IN A NAME?

The word Bible comes from a Greek word *biblion*, which means "book." Eventually, the word came to mean just one book, the collection of 66 books we call the Bible. This name has been used for Scripture since about A.D. 400.

The First Bibles

THE OLD AND NEW Testaments were copied by hand until 500 years ago. The scribes who copied the early Bibles had a very important job. Fortunately, they took it very seriously.

For example, the scribes who made copies of the Old Testament were so careful they counted the number of words and letters in each section. When they made a new copy, they counted the words and letters in the new copy to make sure they had not copied anything wrong.

By New Testament times, most Jews spoke Greek more often than they did Hebrew. Greek was an important trade language. Anywhere you went, people could speak it. So by that time the Old Testament had been translated into Greek. This version of the Old Testament was called the Septuagint, and it was the Bible used by most early Christians. The writers of the New Testament often quoted from this version.

The New Testament itself was written soon after Jesus died. The gospels told the story of Jesus' life. The apostles wrote letters to the churches. These were collected and approved by church leaders about 300 years later.

Today, there are about 15,000 copies of all or part of the New Testament, some from as early as 50

COMPARED TO WHAT?

Scholars try to make sure our Bibles are as accurate as possible by comparing ancient scrolls or parchments with each other. There are more than 5,000 manuscripts of the New Testament, making it the most accurate of any ancient writings.

CHAPTER AND VERSE

The Bible was not written with chapters and verses like we have them now. In fact, both Greek and Hebrew were written without any breaks at all—not even between sentences. Jewish scribes added verses soon after the time of Christ. Chapters didn't come until 1,300 years later.

to 100 years after the original books were written. One of the oldest complete copies of the New Testament is called the Codex Sinaiticus from Mount Sinai. It was discovered in a church on Mount Sinai, the place where God gave Moses the Ten Commandments.

In 1844, a man named Tischendorf went there looking for ancient manuscripts. (A manuscript is a book or scroll written or copied by hand.) To his amazement, he found 43 old leather pages in the trash! The monks who lived there said they didn't know if there were any more or not.

So he went back 10 years later and 15 years later, searching for more of this precious copy of the New Testament. On his last trip, a monk showed him the whole thing, wrapped in a red cloth. Tischendorf tried to buy it, but they refused to sell it, so he started copying the entire manuscript by hand. But he was able to help the monks get someone elected as archbishop, and so they finally gave him the manuscript.

Codex Sinaiticus

A REAL TREASURE

The New Testament that Tischendorf found ended up at a church in Russia. In 1933, the Russian government needed money and sold it to a museum in England. They sold it for half a million dollars, the most ever paid for a book up to that time.

HOW MANY BOOKS?

The Jewish Old Testament and the Christian Old Testament include the same material, but the Jewish version has fewer books. That's because Christian printers divided up some of the longer books into two parts, such as I Kings and II Kings.

A Famous Bible

❖ ❖ ❖

FOR HUNDREDS OF YEARS, every copy of every book was made by hand. Scribes made copies and made copies of copies, a long, slow process.

By the middle ages, making Bibles and other important books became an art. Letters were carefully drawn, with fancy flourishes. Colors were added. Some letters were combined in new ways. Making books like this took even more time, and books became more expensive. Few people had any books at all.

But a man named Johannes Gutenberg changed all that. Gutenberg was a goldsmith who lived in Germany. Some small books were printed by carving pictures in a block of wood and stamping them on paper. This gave Gutenberg an idea. He borrowed a lot of money and went to work, trying to print letters using small metal blocks.

Gutenberg tried different combinations of metal, melting it and pouring it into molds. Eventually, he made over 300 different raised letters and symbols. He wanted to print books as beautiful as the ones made by hand.

BESTSELLER

More Bibles have been printed and sold than any other book in the history of the world, over 3 billion copies since 1815. Millions of copies of the Bible are also given away free by missionaries and other Christian groups.

A LABOR OF LOVE

To print three pages of his Bible, Gutenberg needed 46,000 pieces of type, each of which had to be made by hand. It took a whole day to set one page of type and an hour to print ten copies of the page. It took him two years to print 150 copies of his Bible.

Then he combined the letters to make words, and he put them in a wooden frame.

Finally he succeeded. Sometime between 1440 and 1450, he invented the printing press. He put ink on the letters and laid a piece of paper on top of that. Then he pressed the paper onto the ink using a wine press. He printed small books and a calendar. And then, probably in 1455 (we are not sure of the exact date), he printed the first real book ever—the famous Gutenberg Bible.

The Bible was the most important book at that time. In the next 25 years, Bibles were printed in Latin, German, Italian, Dutch, and Spanish. Soon, Bibles only cost one fifth of what they had cost before.

Modern printing press

Other books were printed, too. Gutenberg's invention changed the world. Books were available to everyone. Newspapers were now possible. More people could read or share their ideas with others.

Unfortunately, Gutenberg was not a very good businessman. He didn't pay back the money he borrowed. A man he borrowed money from sued him and took his printing press. Gutenberg died a poor man, even though he had changed the world.

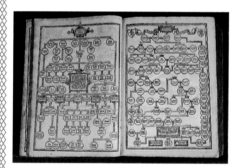

Gutenberg Bible

A WORK OF ART

Much like the beautiful manuscripts that came before it, Gutenberg's Bible was a work of art. It was almost 1,300 pages long, published in two large volumes that were bound by hand. An artist drew the first letter of each chapter in red.

PRINTING PICTURES

Some books were printed before Gutenberg invented the printing press. This was done by carving pictures in blocks of wood and stamping them on paper. This began in China and Japan, but soon spread to Europe. Most of the time, this process was used to print cards or illustrations. Books with a lot of words were copied by hand before Gutenberg.

Bibles for Everyone

◆ ◆ ◆

GUTENBERG INVENTED the printing press, and Bibles soon became more affordable and more available. But there was still a problem. Most Bibles were printed in Latin, and only the priests could read Latin. People did not have Bibles in their own languages.

Several men tried to solve this problem. One of them was a young German monk named Martin Luther. Luther could read Latin. But as he read and studied his Bible, he became convinced that everyone should be able to read the Bible, too. He wanted to translate the Bible into plain, everyday German.

He was already a famous scholar who had an argument with the Pope. So he disguised himself and went from village to village, listening to the common people talk. He took careful notes. Then he hid in a small room with just a table, a chair, a bed, and his lute. There he translated the New Testament into German in four months. It was first printed in 1522.

King James I

THE KING'S BIBLE

In 1604, King James the First appointed about 50 scholars to produce an English Bible. These men worked on this project seven years, comparing ancient manuscripts with earlier English translations. For 350 years, the King James Version has been the most popular English Bible.

A CATHOLIC BIBLE

About A.D. 400, the pope asked a man named Jerome to translate the Bible into Latin. Jerome checked his translation against manuscripts in the original languages. He even got Jewish rabbis to help him translate Hebrew. His Latin Bible, called the Vulgate, became the official version of the Catholic church throughout the Middle Ages.

The people loved Luther's Bible. Many paid as much as two months' wages for a copy. Over 100,000 copies were printed in just three years. Then Luther turned his attention to the Old Testament. This was harder work, and it took him 12 years with the help of some friends. They were very careful. Once it took three of them four weeks to translate three lines from the Book of Job.

Making Bibles everyone could understand was a great idea, and others tried to do the same thing in their language. The first man to print a Bible in English was William Tyndale. He received no encouragement from leaders of the church. They thought the Bible should only be available to ministers.

In 1525, Tyndale went to Germany and visited Luther. He settled there and begin to translate the New Testament into English. When it was finished, his Bible was printed and smuggled back into England, where the people bought them eagerly. But the church leaders still opposed the idea and ordered them to be burned.

In 1535, Tyndale was arrested and put in prison. He was later burned at the stake, but he had already done his great work. Many later translations would use large sections of his Bible. Soon the English Bible would be available to everyone.

KIDS INCLUDED

Church leaders did not want Tyndale to translate the Bible into English because they did not think ordinary people could understand it. Tyndale didn't agree. He told one church leader, "If God spares my life, in a few years I will cause that the boy who drives the plow will know more of the Scripture than you do!"

FIRST ENGLISH BIBLE

Tyndale's English Bible was the first one printed, but not the first one translated. About 150 years earlier, in 1382, John Wycliffe translated the Bible into English. About 200 copies were made by hand. Wycliffe sent preachers around the country to read the Bible to the people in their own language.

Bibles in Every Language

◆ ◆ ◆

MANY COUNTRIES in Europe had Bibles in their own language by A.D. 1750. But what about the rest of the people? William Carey cared about these people. He was a Baptist preacher in England whose congregation was so poor he had to make shoes to support his family. Carey hung a map of the world over his work-bench and prayed for the people who had never heard the good news. In the meantime, he studied Greek, Latin, and Hebrew, the languages that would help him translate the Bible.

In 1792, he took his family and sailed to India. They lost everything they owned in a boating accident, and he had to take a job in a factory. But while working with the people from India, he mastered their languages. In 1801, he published a Bible in Bengali, one language of India. For 30 years, he taught in Indian schools, using his salary to print more Bibles. He translated the whole Bible into 9 languages and the New Testament into 27 more. In just 30 years, Carey and his helpers made the Bible available to 300

A LONG TIME

Robert Morrison volunteered to go to China as a missionary when he was 19 years old. He went there in 1807 and was there for seven years before he made his first convert. In the meantime, he had translated the New Testament into Chinese.

million people, about one third of all the people in the world at that time.

Carey's work excited others. Bible societies were formed and translations continued. By 1900, Bibles in about 1,000 languages were available. In this century, many groups have continued to work at translating the Bible. The largest of these is Wycliffe Bible Translators. It started when Cameron Townsend went to Guatemala in 1918 to sell Spanish Bibles. He realized most people there did not speak Spanish. So, in 1934, he recruited two students to help him translate the Bible into the local languages.

Today, over 5,000 Wycliffe missionaries are at work around the world. Dawn Clark, for example, joined Wycliffe with her husband, Steve. They went to Papua New Guinea with their two children and spent 11 years helping to translate the New Testament in the Sio language. She and her husband both got sick with jungle fever, but they kept working. She would sit out under the trees, listening to the people talk and trying to understand how their language worked.

There was a great celebration when the work was done. One woman told Dawn, "I tried to understand the Bible before, but now I can read it myself. I finally understand."

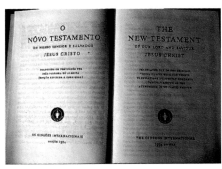

A BIG JOB

There are almost 7,000 languages in the world. Wycliffe Bible Translators say over 4,000 languages have no portion of the Scripture available. They have translated the New Testament into almost 450 new languages and are at work translating over 1,000 more. They want to translate the Bible into every language. Go to their website, www.wycliffe.org, to check their progress.

STREET TALK

When he translated the Bible into everyday German, Martin Luther said he had to listen to "the mother in her house, the children in the street, and the ordinary man in the marketplace." Modern translators try to follow this advice. One African tribe called its missionary "the white man with the book who torments us with questions."

A HARD JOB

Translating the Bible is not easy. Some concepts are difficult to get across. For example, how do you explain the desert to an Eskimo? Often a tribal language will only have a few hundred words to translate the thousands of words in the Bible. It takes modern translators many years to do the job. Then they often have to teach the people who speak that language to read.

The Jewish Bible

◆ ◆ ◆

THE JEWISH BIBLE is called the Tanakh. It includes the same books as the Christian Old Testament, but they are arranged in a different order.

The Jews divide the Tanakh into three parts; the Torah, the Prophets, and the Writings. The Torah is the first five books of the Bible, the ones many believe were written by Moses. These are the most important books, because they contain the Law.

The next section of the Tanakh is the Prophets. This includes the major books about the history of Israel, including Joshua, Judges, Samuel, Kings, and the writings of the prophets Isaiah, Jeremiah, Ezekiel, and Daniel. The shorter writings of 12 other prophets are included as one book.

The final section is the Writings. This includes stories, such as Ezra and Ruth, and books of poetry, including Psalms and Proverbs.

After the Jewish people were conquered by Babylon, they wanted to understand and follow the Law better. They organized synagogues where the people could learn the Scriptures. Their teachers, called rabbis, discussed the Law

TRADITION OF THE ELDERS

The teachers who tried to teach and obey the Mishnah in Jesus' time were called Pharisees. Jesus sometimes referred to the traditions of the elders. He was referring to the unwritten rules collected by scribes. Jesus often disagreed with the Pharisees about how these rules should be obeyed.

GOOD ADVICE

The Talmud has many wise sayings. One of these is, "If your wife is short, bend your head and take her advice." Another one says, "He who seeks a friend without faults will remain friendless."

THE ARK

Every synagogue has a special closet or box, called the ark, where the sacred scriptures are kept. These books or scrolls in the ark are considered so holy that only certain people could hold them. In Jesus' day, that man was called the hazzan. In the ancient village of Capernaum, where Jesus taught, the ark was on wheels! Archaeologists have even found a carved picture of it.

and how it could best be obeyed. They came up with many rules.

About 200 years after Jesus was born, a famous rabbi known as Judah the Prince collected and wrote down these rules. This collection is called the Mishnah. The Mishnah was not copied or published, however. It was memorized by repeating it over and over. The word "mishnah" means to repeat.

Later rabbis continued to discuss the Mishnah. They added more rules and stories, trying to make it clear what the Mishnah required people to do and why it required them to do it. After the destruction of the temple in A.D. 70, these comments became more important. Some of these comments were collected and written down in Jerusalem over the next 200 years.

Since their nation had been destroyed, the Jews spread out across the world. Between the fourth and sixth century after Christ, some rabbis in Babylon expanded on these discussions of the Law. The Mishnah was collected along with their comments and the comments collected in Jerusalem; this is called the Talmud.

The Talmud is almost as important to the Jews as the Torah. Both books help the Jews know and understand God's Law.

THE TANAKH

The Jews call their Bible the Tanakh because it is divided into three parts: the Torah (Law), Nemi'im (Prophets), and Kethubim (Writings). The first letters of these Hebrews words are T-N-K, which come together in the word Tanakh.

LOTS OF DISCUSSION

The Mishnah is divided into six parts. These cover farming, festivals, marriage and divorce, civil laws, sacrifices, and cleanliness. The Babylonian Talmud, which explains these rules, is almost 6,000 pages long—12 thick volumes.

The Christian Bible

❖   ❖   ❖

CHRISTIANS DIVIDE their Bible into two parts, the Old Testament and the New Testament.

The Old Testament tells the history of ancient Israel. Christians believe the Old Testament helps them understand what God is like and what he wants from his people. Christians usually divide the Old Testament into four parts: law, history, poetry, and prophets. Altogether there are 39 books in the Old Testament.

The Law includes the first five books of the Bible. These books tell about the creation of the world. They tell about Abraham and his descendants: Isaac, Jacob, and Joseph. They tell about Moses and how he led the children of Israel out of slavery in Egypt. These books also include the Ten Commandments and many rules about how to serve God and love others.

These are followed by 12 books of history. These tell about the judges of Israel, including Deborah and Samson, and about the kings, such as David and Solomon. The next five books include songs and poems and prayers. The rest of the books are the writings of 16 prophets who warned the people about their sins and promised a deliverer would come to save them.

ABCs

Several poems in the Bible are written like alphabet books. Each verse starts with a word that begins with one of the 22 letters of the Hebrew alphabet. Some examples are Psalms 25, 34, 37, 111, 112, 119, and 145. These are called acrostics.

Jeremiah

THE LONG AND THE SHORT OF IT

The longest book in the Bible is Jeremiah, although Psalms has the most chapters. The longest verse is Esther 8:9, about 85 words. The longest chapter is Psalm 119, with 176 verses. The shortest chapter is Psalm 117, just two verses long. The shortest verse is just two words: "Jesus wept" (John 11:35).

Christians believe this is Jesus. The New Testament tells of his life and teachings. It also includes instructions written by followers of Jesus about how they should live. There are 27 books in the New Testament.

The first four books are called the gospels, a word that means "good news." Four different men wrote down what Jesus said and did. They told about his miracles and wrote down his sermons. They told about how he died and came back from the dead.

The next book is the Acts of the Apostles. This tells about Jesus' followers right after he returned to heaven. These followers were filled with the Holy Spirit. They preached the gospel everywhere they went. Some of their letters make up the next 21 books. These letters encouraged early Christians and corrected them when they did wrong. They do the same things for Christians today.

The last book in the Bible is the Book of Revelation. It was written by the Apostle John. He saw heaven in a vision. He wrote about what he witnessed there and about the end of the world. Death and sin will be destroyed, and Christians will join Jesus in heaven.

WHERE IS GOD?

Two books in the Bible don't even mention God. These are the Song of Solomon, a long love poem, and the Book of Esther, the story of a queen who saved her people. Some rabbis found the name for God in Esther. It was in the first letter of four Hebrew words in a row.

WHEN DID IT HAPPEN?

Neither the Old Testament nor the New Testament are organized in the order they were written. In the New Testament, the first book written was either James or Paul's letter to the Galatians. They both appear near the end. The Gospel of John may have been one of the very last books written, although it appears near the beginning.

The Dead Sea Scrolls

❖ ❖ ❖

IN 1947, a young shepherd boy named Muhammad was searching for a lost goat in the rocky hills near the Dead Sea. He tossed a rock into a hole and heard the sound of something breaking.

Muhammad crawled into the hole, which turned out to be a cave. On the floor of the cave were several large jars containing leather scrolls wrapped in cloth. Muhammad and his friends sold eight scrolls to antique dealers in Jerusalem. These were bought by scholars, who began to study them. One young scholar took pictures of a scroll of the Book of Isaiah.

He sent them to an American archaeologist. Soon he got a letter back. It said: "Congratulations on the greatest manuscript discovery of modern times!"

The scrolls, called the Dead Sea Scrolls, turned out to be about 2,000 years old. Archaeologists and others searched nearby caves and found more scrolls or pieces of scrolls. Shepherds found more scrolls, too, and sold them to the archaeologists. They even broke some of them up in pieces so they could sell the pieces and make more money!

The most important find was the Isaiah scroll. It was about 24 feet long

JOINING UP

To join the community at Qumran, a man had to go through three years of instruction. During this time, he had to take many ritual baths and meditate on Scripture. He also had to sell all of his possessions and give his money to the group.

Qumran

and 10 inches high. Eventually, researchers found pieces of every book in the Old Testament except Esther. These scrolls were at least 1,000 years older than the oldest scrolls ever found before.

The scrolls had been copied by a group of scribes called the Essenes, about the same time Jesus lived. As the area around the caves was searched, archaeologists found an ancient community called Qumran. There was a room at Qumran just for copying Scriptures. The Essenes lived together, keeping very strict rules about food, bathing, and other things. One scroll was a book of rules for the Essenes. Another scroll—written on copper—was a list of buried treasures.

Dead Sea Scroll

Since their discovery, researchers have tried to put the pieces of the ancient scrolls together. The project is like an ancient jigsaw puzzle. The results are encouraging. The scrolls are almost exactly like the copies from 1,000 years later. This shows how careful the scribes were in making copies of the Scriptures.

The Bible has been carefully preserved for us to learn from and enjoy.

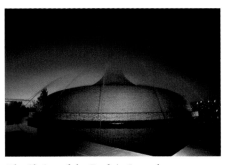
The Shrine of the Book in Jerusalem

WELL PROTECTED

In 1948, the government of Israel bought several of the Dead Sea Scrolls from scholars for about $250,000. The scrolls are now housed in a special climate-controlled, dome-shaped museum in Jerusalem, called the Shrine of the Book.

WHY HIDE?

The Essenes hid their scrolls in caves to protect them from the Romans. One of the scrolls, the War Scroll, tells about how the Essenes could defend themselves. The Romans attacked Qumran and burned it in A.D. 68. But the hidden scrolls survived.

WAS JESUS AN ESSENE?

John the Baptist may have been an Essene. He lived in the same area and had some of the same ideas. Some of the disciples may have been Essenes, too, at least before they followed Jesus. Jesus knew about the Essenes and talked about some of their ideas, but he had many ideas that were quite different.

Questions & Answers

❖ ❖ ❖

Q: What is an epistle?

A: Paul often wrote letters to churches he had visited or to people he had met. Thirteen of these letters are now books in the Bible. These are called epistles. Peter, James, John, and Jude wrote epistles, too. No one knows who wrote one of the epistles, the Book of Hebrews.

Q: Is the Bible complete?

A: Most Christians agree that the Bible includes everything God wanted to say. Obviously, he could have said more. In fact, the Apostle John said Jesus did so many wonderful things all the books ever written could not contain them.

Q: Are there any poems in the Bible?

A: Six books in the Bible are composed almost completely of poems. Hebrew poetry did not rhyme, however. It used a lot of repeating sounds (*pachad wapapchat wapach*) and a lot of exaggeration. Acrostics were popular also. This is when each line begins with the next letter in a word or in the alphabet.

Q: Does every book in the Bible talk about God?

A: Every book in the Bible helps us understand what God is like and what he wants. But two books— Esther and the Song of Solomon—never mention him by name. Jewish rabbis did find an acrostic of God's name in the middle of Esther.

The angel Raphael heals Tobit using the liver and gallbladder of a fish.

Q: Do numbers in the Bible have any special meaning?

A: Many people believe certain numbers in the Bible have special meanings. For example, three stands for the Trinity. Seven is for completion, since God rested on the seventh day of creation. There were 12 months in the year, 12 tribes of Israel, and 12 apostles. Many important things happened in 40 days or 40 years.

Q: What's the Bible all about?

A: The Bible has many books written by many people. But they all point to the same idea. The Old Testament stresses that there is one true God and that people fail to worship him and obey him as they should. In the New Testament, Jesus says he is God's Son and the only way people can come back to the Father.

Q: What is the Apocrypha?

A: The Apocrypha is a part of the Catholic Bible, but not the Protestant. It contains more material added to the books of Esther and Daniel. There are also books that are about the history of the Jews after they were exiled to Babylon. There are ten books in the Apocrypha, which has many amazing stories in it.

Q: Are there angels in the Apocrypha?

A: Yes! The angel Raphael healed a man named Tobit

using the liver and the gallbladder of a fish. The angel was sent by God to help Tobit—that's pretty amazing!

Q: Were there strong women in the Apocrypha?

A: Sure! Judith was a very beautiful Jewish widow. She helped save her city by cutting off the head of Holofernes, the attacking general. Without a leader, the attackers were defeated by the Jews, and the city was saved.

Judith saves her city by killing Holofernes, a general of the attacking army.

Q: Did Joseph really have a coat of many colors?

A: He may have, but the Bible doesn't actually say that. It was a special coat, but it may have just had sleeves, which were rare for coats at that time, or fancy buttons. The Bible doesn't say there were three wise men either. The best way to find out what the Bible says is to check it out yourself!

Q: Can I speak Hebrew?

A: Probably not. But you know a few Hebrew words. Hallelujah is Hebrew for "praise the Lord!" Amen means "so be it." Hosanna is the word the people used to welcome Jesus to Jerusalem. It means "save us."

Q: Can anybody else speak Hebrew?

A: Hebrew nearly died out by the end of the Old Testament, but Jewish rabbis have kept the language alive for over 2,000 years. About a hundred years ago, a Jewish teacher began to encourage all Jews to learn Hebrew again. Modern Hebrew is used in Israel today and is based on the Hebrew of the Bible.

Q: What did Jesus say about calling people names?

A: Jesus said anyone who called his brother *raca* might have to go before the judge. The word was an insult in Bible times, and it came from a word that means empty. It meant something like blockhead or airhead, but Jesus didn't think it was appropriate, especially when spoken in anger.

Q: Did the flood really happen?

A: The Bible is not the only book that tells the story of a great flood. Many ancient cultures had similar stories. The Babylonians had a story about a king who met an ancient hero who survived a flood by building a boat—just as Noah had. These other stories help prove the Bible is true.

Q: Does God have any other books?

A: The Bible refers to books God keeps in heaven. Both Daniel and Revelation speak of a day when these books will be opened and people will be judged. The most important of these books is the Book of Life, which records what we have done. Malachi talks about a "book of remembrance," and Psalms says there is a record of our tears.

Index

❖ ❖ ❖